Transnationalism Reversed

SUNY series, Praxis: Theory in Action
_____
Nancy A. Naples, editor

Transnationalism Reversed

Women Organizing against Gendered Violence in Bangladesh

Elora Halim Chowdhury

Published by State University of New York Press, Albany

For information, contact State University of New York Press, Albany, NY
www.sunypress.edu

Production by Kelli W. LeRoux
Marketing by Michael Campochiaro

Library of Congress Cataloging-in-Publication Data

Chowdhury, Elora Halim.
    Transnationalism reversed : women organizing against gendered violence
in Bangladesh / Elora Halim Chowdhury.
        p. cm. — (SUNY series, praxis)
    Includes bibliographical references and index.
    ISBN 978-1-4384-3752-1 (pbk. : alk. paper)
    ISBN 978-1-4384-3751-4 (hardcover : alk. paper)
    1. Women—Violence against—Bangladesh. 2. Feminism—Bangladesh.
3. Women—Bangladesh—Social conditions.   I. Title.

HV6250.4.W65C574 2011
362.88082'095492—dc22   2011004374

10 9 8 7 6 5 4 3 2 1

To Nasreen Apa,
for inspiration and imagination,

To my parents,
for love and encouragement

Contents

Acknowledgments

This book, like any other, is a product of years of collaboration. The writing of it has been a journey through many phases and geographies. This journey began in the Dhanmondi office of Naripokkho in Dhaka, Bangladesh in 1996, during a conversation with Nasreen Huq who inspired, challenged, and encouraged every idea and page of this book. My deepest regret is that she could not witness its fruition. The work and vision of Naripokkho is at the heart of this book, and I wholeheartedly thank each and every activist there who opened their doors, made me feel welcome, and gave so generously of their time over the years. I am especially indebted to Bina Akhter for her tenacity and her indomitable spirit. Her love of life, and commitment to feminism and justice has been the lifeblood of this book.

As a participant-observer, there was a phase when writing about the campaign against acid violence in Bangladesh was insurmountably difficult for me. I owe the deepest of gratitude and appreciation to Professor Cynthia Enloe at Clark University for nudging me ever so persistently over that hurdle, and for being such a brilliant and devoted teacher over the years. Also at Clark, very special thanks are due to Professors Barbara Thomas-Slayter and Parminder Bhachu for their sharp insights and strong support of this project; and to Gai Liewkeat, Michelle Rowley, Young Rae Oum, and Insook Kwon—my Clarkie peers—for their dazzling minds and enduring solidarity.

Research and writing of this book have been supported by grants from the University of Massachusetts Boston Dean's Office, and a Future of Minority Studies (FMS) Post-Doctoral Fellowship at Syracuse University. I am deeply grateful for the space and intellectual camaraderie extended by the Women's Studies Program there, which allowed me to focus undivided attention to this project. Professor Chandra Talpade Mohanty's generous mentorship at Syracuse was invaluable. My wonderful colleagues and students in the Women's Studies Department, and beyond at UMass Boston provided enduring support, and a vibrant intellectual home within which to grow and nurture this book. Professor Jean Humez provided feedback on earlier drafts, and was especially generous to read and comment on the final manuscript in its entirety. Riva Pearson, research assistant extraordinaire, cannot be thanked enough for her diligent and enthusiastic efforts in helping me complete this book. Her judicious editing, formatting, and referencing made those processes relatively painless. To the anonymous reviewers who offered critical feedback on this book, and previously published parts in the form of articles and book chapters, I am deeply grateful. Sincere thanks to my editor, Larin McLaughlin of SUNY Press for believing in this project, and for her enthusiastic support in the early stages of the publishing process. Profuse thanks to Andrew Kenyon, Kelli Williams-LeRoux, and Michael Campochiaro for guiding me through the later stages. Warm appreciation to Shafiqul Alam Kiron for providing the brilliant cover image featuring survivors of acid violence at an International Women's Day Rally in Dhaka, Bangladesh. To Kiran Asher and Aimee Sisco I owe special thanks for their astute suggestions on the cover design.

My writing and thinking took on new directions since the early days of the dissertation research. Along the way, many people have provided intellectual support, vision, and ideas. In particular, I would like to acknowledge Ping-Ann Addo, Srimati Basu, Connie Buchanan, Amy Den Ouden, Alka Kurian, Liz Philipose, and Elora Shehabuddin.

To my parents, Shamsun Nahar Chowdhury and late Professor Fazlul Halim Chowdhury, and my siblings, Sadeka, Zakia, and Enam, who provided unwavering support, I am so deeply indebted for all that they have taught me about love, compassion, and humanity. To Alok, my life partner, without whose steadfast support, deep understanding, and appreciation of my work this book could not have been completed, I owe heartfelt gratitude. Finally, joyful acknowledgment of Zain and Zahin, my two precious gifts, for showing me every day that life is beautiful.

An earlier version of chapter 1 appeared in 2005 as "Feminist Negotiations: Contesting Narratives of the Campaign Against Acid Violence in Bangladesh," in *Meridians: Feminism, Race, Transnationalism*, 6(1), 162–93. An earlier version of chapter 2 appeared in 2007 as "Negotiating State and NGO Politics in Bangladesh: Women Mobilize Against Acid Violence," in *Violence Against Women: An International and Interdisciplinary Journal*, 13(8), 857–73. Chapter 4 appeared in June 2010 as "Feminism and Its 'Other': Representing the 'New Woman' of Bangladesh," in *Gender, Place and Culture*, 17(3),

301–18. An earlier version of chapter 5 appeared in 2009 as "Transnationalism Reversed: Engaging Religion, Development and Women's Organizing in Bangladesh," in *Women's Studies International Forum*, 32(6), 414–23.

Prologue

The work on acid violence had the power to stir one's imagination...
we did the work because it moved us. It was the work of creativity and
imagination. In the beginning that is what mobilized us. We did not
have resources, or support, but we had the imagination.

—Nasreen Huq, Naripokkho activist,
and founder of the campaign against acid violence

In September 2000, I received a phone call from Bina Akhter inviting me to
an event honoring television journalist Connie Chung and her ABC *20/20*
team for the Amnesty International Media Spotlight Award. Chung's report
"Faces of Hope," which aired nationally in the United States in November
1999, had featured the experiences of two young Bangladeshi women, Bina
Akhter and Jharna Akhter (no relation to each other). The event honoring
Chung's work, along with that of Teri Whitcraft, the show's producer, was to
take place at the Yale Club in New York City and be hosted by Whitcraft's
mother. A number of Bina's friends had been invited, and I told Bina that
it would be my pleasure to attend. I had just moved to New York City that
summer and was looking forward to seeing my old friend and to witness
such a momentous occasion honoring her story. Bina and Jharna would be
flying in from Cincinnati, where they lived with their American host family.[1]

"Faces of Hope" had reported on a growing epidemic of acid attacks
against women in Bangladesh. Connie Chung and her journalistic team
told their American prime time viewers that the incidence of acid throwing
had become highly prevalent among lower socioeconomic groups, in both
Bangladesh's urban and rural areas. The ABC reporters noted that the perpetrators were mostly young men and adolescent boys, while the targets were
primarily females between twelve and twenty-five years of age. As we will

see, although this profile of targets and perpetrators was accurate in the late 1990s when ABC produced its report, in more recent years there has been a shift; today, women, children, and even men are being attacked by acid throwers of both genders, though women continue to comprise the primary targets. According to an UNICEF-Bangladesh report, the overwhelmingly female targets of acid violence are attacked for reasons ranging from rejection of sexual advances from men, refusal of marriage proposals, family or land disputes, vengeance, and unmet dowry demands (UNICEF, 2000).

The televised story had an angle expected to give it immediacy for its American viewers. In particular, the *20/20* report focused on the compelling story of a courageous young girl, Bina Akhter, whose strength and tenacity in the face of unspeakable horrors left the television audience stupefied. The story peripherally focused on Jharna Akhter, another young girl who had also been the victim of an acid attack. Connie Chung's visit to Bangladesh preceded by a few days Bina's and Jharna's "coming to America," sponsored by a U.S.-based organization called "Healing the Children." The organization had arranged for the Shriner's Hospital in Cincinnati to donate surgery for these two teenage acid violence survivors. The narrative of *20/20*'s "Faces of Hope" culminated in the momentous journey from Dhaka to Cincinnati leaving its intended American viewers with the promise that the girls, on their way to recovery, were being transported in good hands and extricated from the oppressive lives left behind in Bangladesh.

I arrived at the Yale Club promptly at 2:00 p.m. The plush interior and leather sofas were a stark contrast to the surroundings and circumstances in which Bina and I had last met. As I was signing the guest book, I heard Bina's voice exclaim with pleasure, "Elora *Khalamoni* [auntie], you are here!" I turned and saw Bina resplendent in a brown sari with a gold border. Her hair was tied in a loose ponytail, and a few carefully styled strands sheathed her injured eye. She rushed toward me with a warm embrace. It had been two years since I had seen her, and it took me a few minutes to register Bina, now seventeen, in her new role. Jharna, fourteen, soon followed, greeting me with a quieter warmth. She seemed content to be in the shadow of Bina, who busily introduced her guests to one another and offered us soft drinks and hors d'oeuvres being served by men in uniforms.

Bina had been a strong, vocal leader in the campaign against acid violence in Bangladesh, a campaign I had originally covered as a journalist and then studied as a researcher. When I had last seen Bina, then fifteen, in Dhaka in 1998, she was helping to create a network of female survivors of acid attacks, women's rights advocates, local journalists, doctors, lawyers, and even members of the Bangladeshi government. Following her medical treatment and residence in Cincinnati and the showing of *20/20*'s report, Bina, here in New York, held center stage in a gathering of western philanthropists, international journalists, and human rights actors.[2] Here, however, Bina appeared not as an organizer of an antiviolence campaign, but rather as the lone representative of it. Amid the Yale Club's plush decor, Bina skillfully represented a cause that had always been hers, but now from a different angle and for a different set of actors and audience. The hosts of the celebratory event presented Bina to the room of influential New Yorkers as the spokesperson of a campaign that had a complicated genealogy involving the efforts of manifold collaborations and institutions spanning the divides of time, geography, and ideology.

I searched the room for familiar faces. I recognized the former communications officer from UNICEF-Bangladesh and said hello. I learned that she was now in UNICEF's New York office. We had met briefly in Dhaka in 1998, while I was a consultant with UNICEF doing research in preparation for the establishment of what would become the Acid Survivors Foundation. Later, Bina introduced me to a number of the staff of international donor agencies who were her personal friends or had had some involvement with the work against acid violence in Bangladesh: the journalist who wrote a feature story on Bina for *Marie Claire* magazine; the undergraduate student who wrote a term paper on acid throwing; the "gender desk" officer of United Nations Development Program (UNDP); United States Agency for International Development (USAID) staffers; and even a few Bangladeshis with relationships to Bina and Jharna similar to mine.[3] Some of the guests at the New York ABC event had made Bina's and Jharna's acquaintance in the United States, once the *20/20* documentary had been aired and an avalanche of responses from sympathetic patrons had befallen the sponsors.

That afternoon at the Yale Club Connie Chung and Teri Whitcraft made impassioned statements about "discovering" the plight of Bangladeshi women, deciding to "do something about it," and "exposing" this despicable atrocity to the American public. Several other speeches were made during the course of the afternoon, including one by Bina who profusely thanked, first, ABC for bringing to the attention of the international audience such a crime against humanity; second, Healing the Children for sponsoring her and Jharna in their path to a "new life"; third, Shriner's Hospital for providing medical care; and, finally, the aid workers and the journalists for their humanitarian work. She assured her listeners that the combination of efforts of everyone in the room truly had changed her life.

That afternoon I left the Yale Club with mixed feelings. I was happy for Bina and Jharna, who had been sponsored by international agencies and voluntary organizations to undergo reconstructive surgery in a reputable burns hospital in the United States. I was happy that they would be able to pick up the shattered pieces of their lives, whereas many acid violence survivors in Bangladesh faced inadequate medical care and treatment. I was in awe of the strength demonstrated by these two teenage girls who left their families and everything familiar in search of restoring some semblance of "normalcy" to their physical and emotional well-beings. At the same time, looking back at that New York event afterward, I began to think of Bina as personifying what might be called the story of the "progress narrative," the transformation of a victim to a survivor and then to an activist. This progress narrative about acid violence survivors had been used both by women's rights activists in Bangladesh and the western sponsors who assisted in bringing Bina to the United States, although with disparate goals. Whereas the organizers in Bangladesh who mobilized the antiviolence campaign, which Bina joined, intended for victims to eventually shape its direction as activists, the sponsors in New York seemed to imply that Bina's transformation from victim to survivor to activist was solely enabled by their intervention, which extricated the young women from local oppression. I felt disappointed in the simple, self-congratulatory progress narrative crafted by the "benevolent" patrons—and to an extent by Bina herself—who had sponsored that day's event. These institutions were supporting Bina and Jharna's recoveries in a way that effectively erased other crucial elements of their struggle, including the anti-acid violence campaign mobilized in the mid-1990s, primarily by Naripokkho, a Bangladeshi women's advocacy group founded in 1983.[4] Without that piece, this became yet another story of western philanthropists "rescuing" passive and helpless third world women.

As this book will show, it was the efforts of local groups like Naripokkho that had created both the conceptual and organizational groundwork for placing acid violence against women and girls in Bangladesh into the global landscape of gendered human rights violation, and had mobilized attention to the issue for both national and international actors. Further, as the following chapters will show, it was the strategic interventions by Naripokkho's activist women that opened up the space to develop services for survivors of acid violence by local, national, regional, and international actors. While this activism should be acknowledged and even celebrated, I believe it is equally important to consider how the fruits of those efforts by a Bangladeshi women's group were co-opted by certain local and international institutions, resulting in a rewriting of the complex genealogy that had led to the public recognition of acid violence as an "issue." My concern is not just with the erasure of local activists' roles in global initiatives to fight gender violence but also with the dominant narratives of global feminism that enable only certain, partial stories to be told.

As I left the Yale Club that September afternoon, it did not seem to me to be a mere accident that this event was being held not at a Bangladeshi women's center in Dhaka, but rather at an elite U.S. university's exclusive club in midtown New York City. The choice of location for this celebration of two young Bangladeshi women's courage, the hosting of the celebration not by their own media or government but rather by a powerful western television corporation, and the choosing by a western-based independent human rights group, Amnesty, of a U.S.-based media corporation for a prize, combined to reproduce a colonial progress narrative by a resurrection of what feminist legal scholar Makau Mutua (2001) calls a triangularized metaphor in western human rights discourse that pits "savages" against both their "victims" and "saviors." According to Mutua, in the human rights story the savior is the human rights corpus itself, with the United Nations, western governments, international nongovernmental organizations (INGOSs), and western charities as the rescuers and redeemers of an unenlightened world. The savior promises freedom for the victims, who are primarily women and children, from the tyrannies of the (third world) state, tradition, and culture. Mutua posits that in reality the human rights institutions themselves serve as fronts to sustain a historic relation of inequality. The savior is ultimately "a set of culturally based norms and practices that inhere in liberal thought and philosophy" (p. 203). Together, the three dimensions of the triangular-ized metaphor maintain the human rights regime just as in its particularized rendition at the Yale Club event the victimized third world women were saved from localized oppression through western intervention.

The metaphor is infused into the doctrines of powerful first world-based institutions that profess to do humanitarian work in third world nations. Hence, Mutua's three-sided metaphoric narrative helps us understand the discourse of human rights as a space for the systematic creation of concepts, theories, and practices that reinscribe inequalities even after the dismantling of formal domination with the end of colonial rule. That is, human rights discourse, even as it claims to protect the rights of the oppressed, has simul-taneously served to naturalize the ongoing efforts to control the "savage" or the "underdeveloped" world by the west. Similarly, Liz Philipose (2008) interrogates the wide appeal of international law to human rights and feminist advocates for providing redress for gender violence, despite its colonial genealogy and indubitable role in the service of imperialist, racialized, and masculinist power. While Philipose does not deny the strategically valuable use of international human rights law by feminist advocates, she nevertheless urges a revisioning of its colonialist underpinnings and implications.

In this case, while it is true that ABC News, Healing the Children, Shriner's Hospital, and UNICEF all contributed immensely to enable Bina's and Jharna's medical treatment in the United States, there are critical "others" whose names and efforts went unmentioned that afternoon at the Yale Club. Similarly neglected was the fact that this trajectory was but one—and not necessarily the most desirable by all—possible option for gender violence survivors to follow. These invisible actors had enabled the better-known, better-financed, and better-connected institutions to make important interventions in supporting survivors of acid violence in Bangladesh. They may have had other goals that were subsumed by the global progress narrative of victim-survivor-activist, but without these other actors, whose visions may have disrupted the dominant narrative that unfolded at the Yale Club, Bina's story remains incomplete.

A March 30, 2000 ABC News clip describes the "Faces of Hope" program this way: "The report, which aired November 1, 1999, exposed a little-known crime in Bangladesh as every year hundreds of young women are permanently disfigured, blinded and/or killed when sulfuric acid is thrown in their faces by men" (ABC News, 1999). The producers and journalists of *20/20* certainly exposed the western audience to this particular "little known crime," but it is important to ask the question little known to whom? While it is true that the number of victims of any violence anywhere is never itself a guarantee that that violence and those victims' sufferings are "well known," it is important to note that by 2000, acid violence was certainly not "little known" in the context of Bangladesh. As the ABC report itself indicates, Bangladeshi activists had already documented hundreds of young women who were victims of acid violence yearly. Neither are the efforts by Bangladeshi groups, in particular women's advocacy groups, completely absent in supporting the victims and mobilizing medical, legal, state, and media professionals to actively take up this cause. The very fact that Bina and Jharna were chosen among the hundreds in Bangladesh was the result of years of careful negotiations among various invested parties.

It is analytically dangerous to imagine, then, that Bina and Jharna's stories began when ABC's camera crew turned their lenses toward them. Before getting deeper into Bina's and Jharna's stories subsequent to their being featured in "Faces of Hope," we have to ask, When did their stories really become an issue of public concern? Tracing Bina's and Jharna's stories back will allow us to document and explore the dynamics of the anti-acid violence work initiated in the mid-1990s by Naripokkho, a women's advocacy group founded in 1983 in Bangladesh. Complicating the narration of the acid campaign in this way will then enable us to launch a nuanced critique of global feminism that pays attention to women's struggles in multidimensional ways at the local, national, and transnational levels.[5]

In this book I present several contesting narratives of the anti-acid violence campaign in Bangladesh. It is my contention that the success of the campaign can be measured by the creation of an independent coordinating service-providing body called the Acid Survivors Foundation (ASF), founded and financed by the international donor agency UNICEF-Bangladesh. Ignoring the complexity of the genealogy of the anti-acid campaign, the dominant narrative presented by ASF, UNICEF, the international media, and even the Bangladeshi media, erases the agency of the Bangladeshi women activists whose groundwork made the work possible. This is symptomatic of global feminist discourse, operating through international human rights organizations, that too often essentializes rescuers and victims on either side of the North-South divide. Thus, this is at once a story of the development of the anti-acid campaign, the charting of distinct and evolving narratives of multiple actors' entrance in and engagement with the campaign, and a critique of the very frameworks that make stories like these intelligible to a global audience. It is an attempt to make the women activists' part in the campaign matter—not simply in an uncritically celebratory way, but in a manner that illuminates the challenges in doing transnational feminist organizing—and thus to shift the discourse of global feminism.

Introduction

This book aims to make visible the complicated transactions and uneasy alliances between women activists in Bangladesh and local and international development and human rights organizations. All of these groups participate, sometimes together and sometimes on their own, in the process of improving services for victims of gender violence and transforming structures of gender discrimination that enable and sanction women's oppression. I intend to detail the complex processes of transnational movement building while highlighting diverse forms of local activisms. At the same time I will make visible the intramovement dynamics that lead to conflicts of unequal power relations among differentially located women, what Gayatri Spivak (1999) has called the "intra-cultural differences" in transnational women's networks.

In this chapter, I will introduce some key debates surrounding transnationalism and women's organizing and illustrate the ways in which they help us understand the context, in the global South in general and in Bangladesh in particular, within which development and nongovernmental organization (NGO) initiatives around women's empowerment have been conceptualized. Locating women's transnational organizing in Bangladesh within these debates underscores the value of paying attention to multiple layers of power operating in transnational movements for gender justice.

At the heart of this book lies an investigation of women's organizing against gender violence in Bangladesh. By showcasing the exemplary work of one particular women's group, I discuss both the possibilities of transnational networking and its less discussed effects and consequences within local level organizing. I use Elizabeth Friedman's (1999) concept of "transnationalism reversed," to which I owe the title of this book, to focus the discussion of the consequences of transnationalism to a "local" women's campaign. Friedman argues, and I agree, that while the successes of feminist transnational organizing has received a great deal of attention from scholars of social movements, not enough has been said about some of its lesser known, and perhaps unintended consequences and challenges to "local" women's movements. By emphasizing intramovement, intraorganizational, intracampaign dynamics, I wish to expand the ongoing feminist analysis of the indeterminate ways that communities of women mobilize against gender inequality. Specifically, I am interested in how and whether transnational praxis of gender violence advocacy articulates with local feminist responses.

Critical Feminist Perspectives on NGOs, Development, and Nation-Building in Bangladesh

Bangladesh has been featured prominently in scholarly discussions of the growth and role of NGOs in the 1980s and 1990s. Not only is it home to some of the world's largest NGOs, but these organizations have played a vibrant role in social and political mobilization in the country. In addition to providing services like credit, health care, and education, the NGO community has also played a significant role in democratic nation-building, alongside the government. These multifaceted roles have been likened to those of a social movement, and NGOs, like social movements, have historically drawn participants from all walks of life and spanning all social classes, including the urban elite, leftist intelligentsia, rural elite, and the poor.

The rise of NGOs and their impact in the global South have not gone without criticism, however. Broadly, these critiques and debates can be categorized in three camps. The first recognizes the critical role of NGOs, especially in the context of weak states failing to protect and provide for their citizens. The second sees NGOs as agents of neoliberal development implementing new forms of imperialism that help maintain a chain of dependency linking transnational corporations, states, donors, and, at the lowest end, the "target population" of development initiatives. In this vein, scholars Lamia Karim (2004) and Dina Siddiqi (2006) both see NGOs as facilitating the global capitalist reach into the private lives of citizens, particularly the poor, who are brought into the chain as clients, rendering them vulnerable to forces of modernization, patriarchies, and cultural and economic globalization. A third and more nuanced critique, within which I wish to situate my own work, emphasizes the complex and often contradictory roles that NGOs play, and the multifaceted relations they foster with states, donors, and clients. I believe this third approach is more useful and even honest in illuminating the very difficult terrain of doing feminist work in a postcolonial context, given the multiple challenges of globalization, neoliberalism, and patriarchy.

It is true that NGOs have been and still are central to nation-building in Bangladesh, both as service providers and as vehicles for progressive organizing, often challenging government and corporate top-down approaches to development. It is also true that they are tied to colonialist discourses of development and donor-driven neocolonial "empowerment" projects for the poor in the third world. Such discourses perpetuate dependency on "aid," prioritize external agendas over locally based ones, and weaken and co-opt locally directed vision and capacity. Some scholars have characterized the post-1980s NGO boom as the "rise of a new managerialism" through which neoliberal governments, in collaboration with international development aid and policy strategists, have claimed to enhance efficiency by cutting public sector services, parceling them off to private sector companies, and deploying corporate management techniques (Townsend and Townsend, 2004). This type of development assistance, incorporated into NGO agendas, focuses more on making societies governable rather than meeting the needs of local populations. These strategies, suggest Townsend and Townsend, have made NGOs suspect as "guns for hire" in furthering corporate goals, enculturating a climate of gate keeping through monitoring and evaluation schemes that make NGO staffs more accountable to the donors than to their clients. However, a concurrently flourishing rhetoric of "partnership and participation" gives the illusion of equity in the industry and muddies the underlying hierarchical management structure. In this system, bigger NGOs often became the parent organization funding and managing smaller ones.

Rather than encouraging accountability toward clients, rigorous monitoring mechanisms tend to protect donors from public scrutiny. Staffs are trained to prioritize meeting the goals of the NGO, and to acquire technical skills like fluency in English language and drafting reports according to certain formats, rather than to adapt the organization's style to locally based needs. Academic research is commissioned through development organizations and presented in these preformatted styles that are absorbed by the NGOs to legitimize their own existence instead of producing knowledge accessible and useful for broader publics. These reports are rarely disseminated in the form of academic books and journal articles but are often shelved in the libraries of donor agencies to be presented and discussed in international conferences as country case studies. What is more, high-level NGO staffs are often criticized for drawing corporate salaries, driving expensive cars, working in air-conditioned offices, and taking frequent foreign trips, all of which add to the distance from the clients whose needs they are apparently serving.

It would be a mistake, however, either to characterize NGOs as a monolithic structure or to delink a critique of them from postcolonial development processes. Obioma Nnamaeka (2004) has discussed how colonialism has shaped particular forms of "underdevelopment" and imprinted certain legacies and distinctive frameworks in which social movements and civil society organizations are likely to grow in postcolonial contexts. Racist, classist, and patriarchal theories of development and empowerment tend to recast issues of freedom, rights, and justice in the global South into normative economistic and technical language, and NGOs can be seen as sharing in such colonial legacies. Although NGOs in Bangladesh operate within an asymmetrical terrain of power, where any space to organize autonomously is seriously compromised by their dependency on multiple global forces, individuals who work in them come with heterogeneous backgrounds and motivations. Even as these individuals work for organizations that arguably perpetuate neocolonial attitudes and policies, some are able to push for creative transformations, however limited, within them. Further, the vibrant NGO sector in Bangladesh draws individuals from a wide range of backgrounds, identities, and skills. For instance, the NGO sector, aside from providing much-needed services for the poor, has also created a class of middle-ranking jobs. Women in particular, influenced as they may be by the modernist ideals of empowering and uplifting the poor, have found in NGOs desirable alternative avenues for employment.

Women's organizations, which have simultaneously benefited from and transformed the proliferating NGO sector in Bangladesh, have faced critiques similar to the ones stated above in relation to NGOs in general. While not all women's organizations are NGOs, and women mobilize against gender oppression and injustice in infinite number of ways and venues, in this book, I am interested in emphasizing the globalization and "NGOization" of social movements and the particular consequences to women's transnational organizing in Bangladesh. Even those organizations, which are not NGOs, and have worked to protect and further women's rights both before and after the "NGO boom in feminism," function within a landscape in which their activities are inextricably entangled within the NGO culture of women's development.[1] Rather than assuming that women's organizing is simply affected and impacted by NGOization, however, I seek to highlight how women actively shape the dynamic terrain of transnationalism.

While I will further elaborate on this point in chapter 5, here, however, I want to draw attention to how the national women's movement in Bangladesh, while implicated within the NGOization of social movements, and thus the national and global neoliberalisms that characterize this process, nevertheless still performs crucial movement activity within that context.

Sohela Nazneen and Maheen Sultan (2009) have argued that women's organizations are unevenly impacted by the NGOization process in Bangladesh, in that some national-level organizations—including Naripokkho—are more successful in maintaining autonomy and a feminist agenda, unlike smaller ones that are more susceptible to be eclipsed by neoliberalism. While this is an important distinction, it is nevertheless true that women's transnational organizing is inextricably woven into the processes of NGOization. At the same time, here, I want to draw attention to the unequal relations between the urban, elite women who run the NGOs, and the clients, women from rural and poor backgrounds, which have been the topic of much scholarly discussion.[2] Likewise, when national urban elite groups participate in transnational feminist networks, power relations between them and their Northern counterparts are vastly unequal. Although women's NGOs are doing significant work, it is nonetheless important to recognize that Northern and middle-class feminist ideology and practices can limit democratic feminist organizing on multiple scales.

Feminists in Bangladesh largely work within the constraints of what Lamia Karim (2004) has called the "NGO paradigm," with its links to the government, donors, and INGOs. These linkages shape the kinds of conversations that can emerge in public and inhibit rigorous critiques of western and elite development ideology and practices. Further, they hinder grassroots feminist organizing and limit the scale of independent social development work done outside of NGOs. The NGO linkages to international institutions do open up possibilities for new kinds of alliances, but they simultaneously curtail the flourishing of perhaps more organic and radical ones. Scholarly critiques of local NGOs, therefore, must be cognizant of this structural dependence and the fact that powerful international NGOs most often are not affected by criticism; whereas, smaller local organizations can be hurt by them. Accountability in this chain of dependent organizations tends to run vertically upward, but not the other way around.

This kind of dependence represented by the relationship between local and international organizations hinders solidarity among differentially positioned women in the dependency chain. Yet just as women's NGOs themselves are part of a transnational dependency chain, they do offer a venue for feminist organizing that is also transnational. It is worth investigating whether the dynamics within and between NGOs will consolidate and/or weaken the power of the global, national, and local elite. As will become clear in upcoming chapters, resistance to such global power structures can take manifold and unexpected shape and form, spanning demands on the state, community-based and/or NGO organizing, social movements, cross-border alliances, and everyday survival strategies. An important question this book will engage with is How will feminists be able to manipulate the potentially resistant space of the NGO, given that their political strategies within NGOs are limited by NGO dependency on the very "global feminist" structures local feminists are trying to resist?

Transnational Feminist Frameworks

My work builds on a substantial legacy of feminist scholarship on cross-cultural dynamics of women's movements. The 1990s in particular marked the ascendance of transnational feminist activism by riding on the momentum of two decades of United Nations conferences for women. Feminists specifically targeted international policy arenas and intergovernmental organizations to mobilize concerns about gender in national and local contexts. Networking and advocacy on a global scale enabled locally based activists to mobilize strong transnational collaborations in order to pressure the recalcitrant state policy apparatus to engender important policy changes both nationally and globally. Sonia Alvarez (2000) defines this kind of transnationalization of women's organizing as "local movement actors' deployment of discursive frames and organizational and political practices that are inspired, (re)affirmed, or reinforced, though not necessarily caused, by their engagement with other actors beyond national borders. This happens through a wide range of transnational contacts, discussion, transactions, and networks, both virtual and 'real'" (p. 32). Thus, local and transnational forces shaping women's movement dynamics are seen by Alvarez as mutually constitutive and inextricably intertwined analytically. For example, the U.N. summits and NGO participation engendered conversations about gender violence and women's human rights constructed through transnational negotiations.

However, Jacqui Alexander (2005) cautions against a relativist reading of the transnational, which can obscure the power of Northern constituencies over their Southern counterparts, and points to how national and transnational processes might be mutually constitutive but are nevertheless imbricated in asymmetrical power relations (p. 183). It is this understanding of transnationalization, coupled with Chandra Mohanty's (2003), in which she emphasizes the interconnectedness of women's struggles, histories, and experiences across communities in cross-border organizing, that I find most useful for my work.

It is important to note here that analytically this transnational feminist analysis is in contradistinction to *global feminism*, which emphasizes a unidirectional North-to-South flow of ideas, resources, and mobilization. A *transnational feminist* praxis, as I use the term, refers to women's organizing that recognizes, in theory and in practice, the multilayered power relations shaping women's struggles in North-South as well as South-South contexts. Again, this is decidedly different from usages of the term *global feminism*, which tends to flatten the diversity of women's agency and positionality in presenting a universalized western model of women's liberation based on individuality and modernity (Grewal and Kaplan 1994). Rather, Jacqui Alexander and Chandra Mohanty (1997), urge an analysis that intertwines "the global and the local" and choose the term *transnational* as a corrective to the notion of "global sisterhood," which they find as resurrecting the "center/periphery" or "first-world/Third-World model" of feminist organizing (p. xviii). The term *transnational*, although mindful of continued significance of national boundaries, is also different from the term *international*, which tends to prioritize discrete national borders.

In their recent anthology, *Critical Transnational Feminist Praxis*, Amanda Swarr and Richa Nagar (2010) consult what are now considered two canonical transnational feminist texts of the 1990s, *Scattered Hegemonies: Postmodernity and Transnational Feminist Practices* by Inderpal Grewal and Caren Kaplan, and *Feminist Genealogies, Colonial Legacies, Democratic Futures* by Jacqui Alexander and Chandra Talpade Mohanty, as they strive for their own conceptualization of the term. At the risk of capturing briefly an extensive discussion on the points of convergence and divergence between these texts, and to avoid rehashing the same debates eloquently unfolded by Swarr and Nagar, suffice it to say here that key to the first text (assert Swarr and Nagar) is an attempt to decenter feminism from its essentializing Northern tendency toward more heterogenous formations. Central to the second is an approach to feminism that is more relational, comparative, and historical. While acknowledging the importance of both, Swarr and Nagar appear to be drawn to Alexander and Mohanty's allegiance to cross-border feminist praxis, collaboration, and activism, which "move[s] through and beyond the global/local dichotomy" (p. 10). Further, it is these authors' resolute reminder of accountability to feminist communities in struggle that most animates my own vision of transnational feminist praxis. Like Swarr and Nagar, I too intend to blur the distinctions between theory/method, individually/ collaboratively produced knowledge, and academia/activism with a commitment to "combine struggles for sociopolitical justice with feminist research methodologies, thereby extending the meanings and scope of transnational feminist theory and practice" (p. 13).

The discussion of "local" women's organizing in my work emphasizes the variety of ways in which communities of women mobilize against diverse forms of oppression against a background of the intramovement, intraorganizational, and intracampaign dynamics across borders. Using a transnational feminist analysis thus enables me to mount a critique that is contingent and multifaceted and that strives toward shifting the discourse of global feminism away from its universalistic tendency.

While the transnationalization of women's organizing has certainly produced desirable results of many kinds, particularly in policy advocacy, scholars have also pointed to less celebratory ramifications, which as mentioned earlier, Elizabeth Friedman (1999) calls "transnationalism reversed"—a concept to which this book owes its title. This lesser discussed "flip side" of the globalization of women's movements has engendered disparate and differentiated consequences for movement dynamics and practices. Even as they enable crucial cross-border collaborations, intramovement tensions also generate contradictory consequences within such collaborations. For instance, new kinds of divisions and hierarchical relationships have emerged within feminist organizations at the same time that these have tended to experience growth. Hence, it is necessary to expand our theoretical understanding of transnational organizing and illuminate the inter- as well as intramovement tensions, in an attempt to imagine more equitable and just feminist alliances across borders of nation, class, and race.

In this book I map the trajectory of the Bangladeshi women's campaign against acid violence in the mid-1990s and beyond. The transnational organizing of Naripokkho, a Dhaka-based women's advocacy organization, led to the successful creation of a donor-funded umbrella organization for providing comprehensive care to survivors of acid attacks. However, the creation of this organization led to several effects unintended by the campaign: Naripokkho's own diminished engagement with the campaign, the co-optation of the women activists' survivor-centered strategies by the newly created institution, the gradual consolidation of a neoliberal agenda by the newly established Acid Survivors Foundation programs, the estrangement of key activists from the campaign, and the (re)affirmation of a progress narrative within which the stories of survivors were told by various actors. This book highlights the complexities, contradictions, and paradoxes of diverse women's organizing that are often left out of homogenizing representations of women's movements and transnational alliances.

A Note on Theory and Method

In the tradition of Nagar and Swarr's articulation of transnational feminist praxis, this volume is invested in a politics that combines struggles for social justice with feminist epistemology in the interest of expanding conversations about cross-border solidarity and collaboration. These writers state unequivocally that all academic production is necessarily collaborative, even if the author's voice is privileged, and often celebrated, as the sole narrator. Even though academic knowledge is essentially created and informed by multiple engagements with communities—students, colleagues, peers, research collaborators, activist circles—the institution of academia recognizes the "solo feminist," thereby furthering the academic/activist, theory/method, individual/collaborative divides (Pratt et al., 2010, p. 84).

Using transnational feminism as the grounding for its intellectual and political endeavor, this book adheres to a lens and set of practices that pay attention to various overlapping systems of power such as capitalist development, globalization, imperialism, and patriarchy. It also looks at the ways in which these systems rearrange colonial and neocolonial power relations in different locations, and how these processes engender and are influenced by complex and contradictory modes of subjectivities and agency. A transnational analysis emphasizes reflexive action and critique while consciously illuminating their temporal and spatial constitutions (Swarr and Nagar, 2010, pp. 3–5). Further, moving away from easy imaginings of collaboration and solidarity characterizing much of 1990s "global feminism," this volume emphasizes the contradictory and shifting ways in which collaborations take shape, often emerging only out of conflict and negotiations. As this research shows, transnational feminism cannot be assumed a priori but is always contingent, shaped by its specific historical and institutional realities.

In this study, I rely heavily on the ethnographic method of participant observation, used here in conjunction with a second valuable method, narrative interpretation. To that end, in addition to participant observation, I have employed other written sources such as archives; news reports; pamphlets; statistical data collected by the state, national NGOs, and international agencies; audiovisual materials; e-mail correspondences; life narratives; and secondary literature generated by scholars. Like Anthropologist Akhil Gupta (1998), I firmly believe that "the claims made in an ethnography and the presentation of the ethnographer's knowledge—are shaped not only by the kind of data collected but also the manner in which those data were obtained" (p. 29). Like him, I am concerned with "how the [researcher] is positioned within the text, questions of polyvocality, the representation of respondents' voices, problems of translation, the 'staging' of dialogic encounters, concerns about authorship, the use of photographs and audiovisual techniques, and the [researcher's] responsibility" to both their respondents and to the research community as a whole (p. 29). While I cannot elaborate on each issue here, in the following chapters I will address some of my key methodological choices. I hope that in keeping with the tradition of a feminist ethnography in terms of the representation of research findings within the text and the choices I make in the analysis, I can encourage active and ongoing reinterpretation from the readers, including those who are the subjects of the research. Moreover, I would like to employ Gupta's idea of resisting "analytic closure," and thereby to make the text "vulnerable" to reinterpretation, reanalysis, and rethinking, attributes he lists as the essential qualities of a sound ethnography (p. 30).

Gender violence in general, and acid attacks against women in particular, has a longer genealogy in Bangladesh and in the surrounding region than I am able to impart here. It is my purpose to trace the work of women activists in Bangladesh specifically in the mid-1990s and later. I focus on these years in part because of the strategic negotiations of that time period that were carried out by feminists in Bangladesh with key institutions transnationally, in order to create a public discourse on acid violence, and thus to develop a socially recognized campaign by and for Bangladeshi women. At the same time, my choice is shaped by my own involvement with the campaign in three roles over the years: that of a journalist, a U.N. consultant, and an independent researcher, respectively. My analysis is based on interactive reflections on the multiphased and multisited trajectory of the campaign, with the aim to broaden the discussion of gender violence to a global human rights arena. The roles I occupied allowed me an "insider's" perspective of the day-to-day workings of a women's advocacy group, as well as other key actors such as international NGOs and state institutions. It is important to note, however, that gathering information through these intimate relationships was a potentially risky endeavor because traditional ethnographic research calls for the researcher to maintain some level of an "outsider" status to preserve analytic integrity. The paradox whereby a feminist researcher simultaneously is an insider/outsider in the process of gathering information and crafting a research project, arguably in collaboration with the research subjects is, I believe, a valuable contribution to the feminist ethnographic approach. On the one hand, it might be considered risky to rely on the subjective reflections of interlocutors with whom I have a long-term association as an ally. However, one may also argue that all knowledge is subjective and collaborative despite academic and institutional structures that claim otherwise. On the other hand, giving primacy to the multiple and disparate voices, strategies, experiences, and narratives of the antiviolence campaign woven together to be read as one of the many contesting stories posed in this study complicates our understanding of diverse women's activism. Akhil Gupta posits that juxtaposing multiple discourses, and not attempting to provide a unified and coherent narrative out of disagreements and contestations are actually commensurable with the argument made in a text that strives to enhance understanding of a postcolonial moment.

Jayati Lal's (1996) discussion of the "insider/outsider" dynamic and dilemma in feminist ethnographic research is enormously helpful. Instead of taking either position as a given, she argues that these identities are actively constructed and given meaning in the practice of research. For instance, I may be an insider to Bangladesh but my "return home" after years of graduate school training in North America also makes me an outsider who has to negotiate a renewed sense of belonging in a location that is now unfamiliar. Lal, who is an Indian national, writes about her own experience of doing fieldwork in Delhi as a PhD student from a North American university: "More important than a sameness that might be assumed in my possible identity as an insider are the power differentials and class inequities that divide those insiders and the divisions between the researched and researcher that are created by the very act of observation" (p. 193).

In the long course of my research, each instance of my engagement with activists and staff at Naripokkho, survivors of acid violence, and the various actors in the campaign like state representatives, U.N. officials, journalists, international human rights advocates, and so on was constituted through a different set of power relations and presumptions on all sides, based on gender, nationality, class, age, and educational and professional status. For instance, at the event honoring ABC producers at the Yale Club, I was at once an insider to Bina's circle of friends from Bangladesh, and therefore a witness to the trajectory of her arrival in the United States, and at the same time an outsider to her newer circle of American patrons, to whom I was a "native informant" from which to seek affirmation for their progress narrative. I am also reminded here of the numerous occasions in the mid- to late 1990s when Bina and other survivors of acid violence working and volunteering for the Naripokkho campaign led me to the homes of young women survivors, many of whom lived outside of Dhaka city in rural Bangladesh, and to the Burns Unit at the Dhaka Medical College Hospital (DMCH), for research purposes. In these very different settings, my upper-middle-class, urban background, less than perfect Bangla, and status as U.N. consultant or PhD candidate in elite western institutions, undoubtedly demarcated the boundaries of the participation and collaboration.

One particular encounter with the director of a major NGO providing affordable health care to the poor, drove home this point. Early in my involvement with Naripokkho, when I was working as a journalist for a national English-language daily newspaper, I was invited to the home of this man, who was collaborating closely with Naripokkho organizers, to discuss putting together a project proposal for donor agencies to fund a burn unit at the NGO he directed. Because of time constraints, as I had to leave Bangladesh to start my PhD program in the United States, I was unable to collaborate on this project. A year later, when I again visited the same director, this time in his office, to solicit some information in my role as a development consultant for UNICEF, he refused to have a conversation with me and asked that I leave his office on the grounds that his relationship to the donor agency I was representing was conflicted. He spoke to me, with palpable contempt, of my own allegiance to this donor agency and the material benefits of my position there—in stark contrast to my previous position in a local newspaper. Where I was once considered an "insider" to the campaign, because I had been recruited to write for it, here I was considered someone who had "defected" for material gain. What complicates this picture even more is that it was on the recommendation of Naripokkho activists that UNICEF had hired me as the consultant on the acid violence project—because the feminist group preferred an "insider" from the campaign for this work. Such encounters seem to suggest that the insider/outsider dichotomy in research is less about fixed identities and more about critical and reflective positionings.

With regard to another complicated insider/outsider moment, I am reminded of the number of times I sat patiently at government representatives' offices—always in air-conditioned waiting rooms as opposed to the stuffy corridors with other visitors, no doubt because of my class status. At the same time, my age and gender did not provide me with the stamp of importance required to be seen immediately by these government officers. Additionally, I was always expected to answer questions like "What is your father's name," and "What does your father do?" by way of social screening before any information would be imparted to me.

Another revealing research moment was the day I arrived at the Naripokkho office to meet Bina on our way to DMCH in a rickshaw as opposed to a car, my usual mode of transportation. (The driver was sick and had taken the day off.) As Bina climbed onto the rickshaw with me, she said with genuine concern, "Elora *khalamoni*, you should be careful doing this work. I am sure people are watching you" ("*shabdhan e cholo, shob lok jon dekche*"). This remark clearly alluded to my class status and the fact that norms of middle-class femininity required that I not be "seen" so publicly—in a rickshaw without the protection of the car—associated with a campaign perceived to be risky for young women. The grand gestures of hospitality that followed every visit I made with survivors and their families made me internally cringe with embarrassment—whether offering me the best chair in the room, ordering tea and snacks from the hospital cafeteria, or laying out a multicourse meal on the dining table and sending to the corner store for Coca-Cola and Fanta (to appease my ostensibly "foreign" taste). I was reminded time and again of the inevitably unequal and even exploitative relationship between researcher and the subjects of research.

There is a fine line in ethnographic research, particularly by researchers from the North in research settings in the South, between academic feminist knowledge production and academic feminist colonization. I take my cue from Jayati Lal, who refers to Michelle Fine's urging feminist researchers to persistently " 'examine the hyphen at which Self-Other join in the politics of everyday life,' and to work against inscribing the Other" (quoted in Lal, 1996, p. 200). Moreover, the mediated relations circumscribing research processes, and the productive engagements resultant in the hyphens are fraught with questions of accountability and responsibility.

Swarr and Nagar (2010) rearticulate questions regarding accountability posed by Peake and de Souza, asking, "What do women in the South—placed in different points in organizational hierarchies—stand to gain and lose from transnational feminist exchanges? And how much of themselves are northern-based feminist academics willing to put on the line, given that they work in institutions that reward obedience and status quo, and that widely discourage the convergence of action and research?" (p. 212). In order to better articulate my own relationship to these questions, it is important to note my engagement with the anti–acid violence campaign in its various stages and consequently the shifting communities to whom I am accountable.

When I first began writing about this topic in the mid-1990s, it was in my role as a journalist-cum-ally of the Naripokkho campaign. The audience was the general public as well as the specific communities that the activists wanted to mobilize. The purpose was to raise awareness, and the process was transparent in the sense that each piece was reviewed by Naripokkho activists before publication. These pieces were circulated by the organization in various registers in which they organized nationally and globally. Second, as a research consultant for UNICEF, the next phase of writing and research involved producing and packaging knowledge in a format comprehensible to funders, which often involved the translation of activists' and survivors' experiences and ground realities into the global logic of development and humanitarian interventions seeking tangible results. In my current role, as a feminist researcher located in the northern academy, I am cognizant of institutional expectations around producing knowledge that will benefit my ascendance in the academy (tangibles like book, recognition, tenure, and promotion), as well as of my desire to produce knowledge that is meaning-ful for the various communities—collaborators in struggle who informed the research (outcomes here are less quantifiable).

All of these relations—both within and outside of the academy—are of course fraught. For instance, in my first year on the tenure track I was told by a senior colleague in the department that engaging in collaborative research and coauthored manuscripts would be risky for my tenure because the academy preferred single-authored projects. On the other hand, in sharing drafts of the manuscript with Naripokkho activists prior to publication, I have been cautioned about revealing too much or too little, waiting for the right moment to minimize risk and to maximize impact, misrepresenting internal organizational dynamics, and taking my analysis too far, thus bordering on a betrayal of the very community that this work is meant to advocate for. My shifting insider/outsider positions have been called into question repeatedly as I have navigated the tricky waters of transnational praxis. As Geraldine Pratt et al. (2010) show, it might become necessary at certain points of col-laborations not to collapse the roles of the academic and the activist and to maintain a strategic distance (pp. 65–71). I say this not to take analytic license to position myself as the "solo feminist" author, but to simply point out that there are instances in collaborative research when our (feminist academics) analysis might be at odds with that of our (activist) collaborators. It is only through rigorous and persistent reflexive engagements in those paradoxical moments—and emphasizing the juxtaposition of narratives that Gupta argues is key to texts striving to represent the postcolonial condition—that we can tease out the contradictions inherent in transnational praxis.

As the following chapters will show, multiple community collaborators compel multiple and tiered allegiances and accountability. For example, as the campaign evolved and expanded, its many constituencies did not always exist in harmonious relationships with one another, and their agendas were not compatible. As a researcher, it becomes necessary to carefully track my shifting locations and relationships as they unfolded with respect to each constituency over time. In this regard, I realize that critiquing large and powerful international donor organizations and western-based media networks is less risky and sometimes more necessary than critiquing smaller NGOs and community-based organizations, and individual movement actors. After all, the communities we engage in research with are not homogenous, and they do not necessarily have singular interests. I have found that narrative analysis is valuable in addressing this question of critiquing actors in movements with which one is allied, because it enables emphasizing the multiple agendas and questions of the diverse constituencies of this project, as well as illuminating the competing ways subjects actively shape their "presentations to suit their own agendas of how they wish to be represented" (Lal, 1996, p. 204). Rather than canceling out, prioritizing, or even suppressing competing agendas, narrative analysis enables the weaving of a more nuanced and even politicized telling.

Narrative analysis allows us to question the perceived ineluctable distinction between factual reporting and storytelling by suggesting that facts, like fiction, emerge when researchers and writers interpret and give meaning to them in particular ways. Facts do not exist prior to this meaning-making process involving both the witness and the interpreter of the act. Rather, as Leslie Rebecca Bloom (1995) points out, meaning is constructed in the style of storytelling. This approach is informed by the idea, espoused by Jonathan Potter, Margaret Wetherell, Ros Gill, and Derek Edwards in their article "Discourse: Noun, Verb or Social Practice?" that meanings are created through discourse and not simply reflected by them (Potter et al., 1990). However, people are influenced by dominant narrative themes that allow them to arrange meanings in contextual and perhaps familiar ways. These observations lead researchers to the valuable knowledge that stories are socially constructed and can appear to change along with voices of narrators. Discursive and narrative analyses give me the opportunity to self-consciously construct meanings through my use of narrative lenses, choices of actors, and the selection of when a story begins. In this book, by examining competing narratives of the anti–acid violence campaign (including my own), I make meaning of how these stories are created and re-created over time and with what consequences.

Moreover, feminist narrative analysis makes available to women structures for writing about their multifaceted experiences against the grain of dominant masculinist narratives. Careful reading of women's voices help us examine their roles, choices, and sufferings in a way such that they are able to assume power rather than be further marginalized. Teresa de Lauretis (1987), using Carolyn Heilbrun's argument, suggests that when women are deprived of narrative frames that allow for complex self-representations, they are deprived of power. By presenting contesting narratives to weave a more complex view of transnational organizing, I want to make visible the agency of diverse women activists in the struggle for representation and subjectivity.

Feminist narrative analysis, by refusing analytic closure, encourages interpreters to constantly reexamine their own conclusions and recognize the instability of authorship. Kathleen Barry (1990) refers to this intersubjectivity in research as an opportunity for researchers to "become interactively involved with the subject through interpretation of meanings" (pp. 77–78). Feminist ethnography in turn takes as its central investigative unit the interactive relationship between the feminist researcher and her respondent as active agents in the process of meaning making, blurring the distinction between theory and method. For this reason, a combination of narrative interpretation and feminist ethnography is fitting as the chosen approach to interweaving theory and method in the act of self-reflexive storytelling. Taking my cue from feminist ethnographer Ruth Behar (1993), I add a cautionary note here as the author of this study: my voice as an interpreter/reader is ultimately privileged, and producing texts out of life stories runs the risk of "colonization of the act of storytelling" by turning each story into a "disposable commodity of information" (pp. 12–13). Here, Shari Stone-Mediatore's (2003) assertion is valuable: narrative analysis opens up the possibility of considering the text not as "objective truth" but rather as "ways of seeing" (p. 38).

Feminist postcolonial theory as a genre is helpful as it explains the myriad influences shaping the subject of one's research and the implications of the investigator's location in the pursuit of and production of knowledge. It has explicated and complicated the symbiotic relationship between the (researcher) self and the (researched) other. The perceived contradictory locations of the "home" and the "field," as well as the legacy of colonialism that implicitly shapes this relationship is marked by the researcher being situated in "the West" and the researched "elsewhere," complicating further the politics of representation in this study (Visweswaran, 1994). My position as an insider/outsider encompasses my roles as journalist, development consultant, activist, and independent researcher spanning Bangladesh and the United States. I hope this work will have meaning for all of the communities from which my understanding has benefited. I also want to point out that in studying transnational feminist organizing, I have followed some participants and interlocutors in multiple sites in Bangladesh and the United States. Hence, the location of the subjects of research has also been mobile, adding more layers to the spatial and temporal contingencies in a transnational analysis.

One area of postcolonial feminist scholarship and ethnography in particular that is tremendously important for this work has been the explicit theorizing of feminists' relationships to "women," or ways in which women of the global North are discursively constructed as feminists (read: liberated, free, independent) in relation to women from the South (read: oppressed, bound by culture, dependent) (John, 1996). While considerable scholarship exists about the power dynamics between white colonizers and native women, less attention has been directed to the colonial framework shaping women's relationships to one another within national and local spaces, particularly as they manifest through the script of global feminism. Hence, this study extends that conversation to also include the power differentials in such relationships within feminist and women's networks in disparate spatialities.

There is of course a long colonial history, discussed both within and outside feminist scholarship, of representations of third world women's victimization by *their* own patriarchal cultural and religious institutions—and the consequent justified rescue missions and military interventions enacted by forces of the global North (Mohanty, 1991; Mani, 1990; Narayan, 1997; Lazreg, 1994; Trinh, 1989). Feminists have argued that these depictions have acquired a renewed vigor in the post–September 11, 2001 climate of reductionist understandings of women's oppression in the Muslim world (Abu-Lughod, 2002; Razack, 2008). Clearly, these depictions do not tell the whole story, particularly of the forces and policies that originate in the North and maintain the subordinate status of women in these so-called zones of oppression. Moreover, the racialized gender dimension of the rescue narrative—famously described by Gayatri Spivak (1994) as "White men are saving brown women from brown men"—is supported by abundant visual and textual representations in the mainstream media sensationalizing the plight of third world women. This logic becomes ingrained in the psyches of consumers of mainstream media to such a degree that representations like these need no contextualization or explanatory narrative (p. 92). Shahnaz Khan (2008), speaking of Afghan women, likens such images, particularly of the "veiled Muslim woman," to creatures confined in a "public zoo, providing voyeuristic spectacle and affirming splendors and freedoms of a singular Western culture and the misery and oppressive nature of the equally singular Third World/ Muslim culture" (pp. 161–62).

Concomitant to the production of the oppressed third world/Muslim woman is the ubiquitous image of the racialized premodern, aggressive, yet feminized, third world/Muslim man. Sherene Razack (2008) argues that the deployment of allegorical figures of the "dangerous Muslim man," "imperiled Muslim woman," and "civilized European" are the cornerstone of neo-imperial construction of the third world/Muslim Other, in contrast to the "civilized" white nations. Not just a story, these representations serve to provide and legitimize the governing logic and relation of empire (p. 5). The machinery of colonial discourse can achieve these racialized and gendered effects simply through the use of such images and terms like *traditional*, *Muslim*, and *cultural practice*. One of the questions I am interested in exploring in this book is how such transnational productions of gender, and gender violence in particular, do or do not correspond with "local" feminist conceptualizations. In this particular historical moment, feminists must pay attention to the global representations of the Muslim world—of which Bangladesh is a part—and the dominant stories they tend to support or subvert.

The national women's movement in Bangladesh, for historical reasons I elaborate on in chapter 5 of this book, maintains a resolutely secularist position. That is, religion by most advocates of social justice is viewed as a private matter. At the same time, the activists I worked with did not see any contradiction between their faith in Islam and their political struggles for women's emancipation. In my research I rarely encountered activists who would use religion as an explanatory framework for acid violence. If and when the question of religion and violence was broached, activists stated or implied that an authentic understanding of Islam would clarify that gender violence was strictly condemned. However, activists did attribute increased violence against women in part to the "gradual infiltration of fundamentalist and/or reactionary Islam," which they saw as an external threat to the nation. Using religion as an instrument for mobilizing the antiviolence campaign, however, was not commonplace.

In contrast, in the west gender violence in Bangladesh—the third-largest Muslim majority nation—is invariably packaged through an Islamic/culturalist framework (as we will see in the discussion of "Faces of Hope" in chapter 3). The latter, I argue, serves the larger imperial project of empire from which certain variants of feminism make the rescue of Muslim women their own sustaining mission. That is, this same colonial and neo-imperial logic is inherent in global feminism as well as in humanitarian interventions. In attempting to complicate our understanding of feminist struggles, subjectivities, and agency in multiple sites, this work is located in the conjuncture of all of these above-mentioned genres: feminist ethnography, critical ethnography, narrative analysis, feminist postcolonial studies, critical development, and transnational feminist studies.

Chapter Overviews

This book comprises a cluster of five essays tied together by the common thread of women's transnational organizing around gender violence. Together, these pieces aim to contribute to new theoretical understandings of the historically asymmetrical planes constituting uneven relations of power within women's movements. Chapter 1, "Feminist Negotiations: Contesting Narratives of the Campaign Against Acid Violence in Bangladesh," traces and analyzes the complex trajectory of the anti–acid violence campaign in Bangladesh. I demystify the claim that men's acid throwing against women and girls is an "aberrant cultural practice," showing that this phenomenon needs to be understood within broader systems of gender inequality and intersecting forces of globalization and socioeconomic shifts in the region.

The chapter traces the development of the antiviolence campaign by feminists, beginning with the efforts of the women's advocacy group called Naripokkho to turn incidents of acid throwing against women and girls in Bangladesh into a concerted public campaign, by mobilizing key players at the national and international levels and making strategic alliances with them. I show that the expansion of the campaign over time as a result of the diversification of actors involved at both the national and international levels has not only generated institutional support to survivors of acid attacks but has also had some unintended consequences. The new services, albeit having greater reach, espouse an individualistic neoliberal strategy without adequate attention to systemic change. This is a story of the challenges of women's organizing and its negotiations with transnational politics and subsequent successes and failures.

Chapter 2, "Local Realities of Acid Violence in Bangladesh," showcases the story of Nurun Nahar, a survivor of acid violence in Bangladesh, and to lesser degree Bina Akhter, in order to demonstrate that despite protective measures, state, medical, and legal institutions continually fail to respond adequately to violence against women and deny women rights to state protection, which are supposedly guaranteed by law. The failure of state institutions to ensure appropriate care has been somewhat mitigated, I argue, by NGOs, particularly women's groups, which are nevertheless heavily constrained due to the volume of demand, scarcity of resources, and a funding culture inhibiting horizontal collaborations among women's groups. This chapter emphasizes the local contexts within which women activists operate, including patriarchal and intransigent social and cultural systems. Additionally, it reflects on how women's NGOs have created alternative strategies and visions for victimized women's recovery and empowerment in the absence of a strong state and within dominant cultural, economic, and political structures.

Chapter 3, "From Dhaka to Cincinnati: Charting Transnational Narratives of Trauma, Victimization, and Survival," spells out the implications for women's movements of the growing trend toward transnational forms of organizing. By juxtaposing multiple narratives of the anti–acid violence campaign by international actors, survivors, and local women activists, I aim to weave together a more complex understanding of transnational feminist praxis and women's subjectivities. The chapter highlights the story of Bina Akhter, who has been called alternatively the "star of the acid campaign" and "self-serving" by Naripokkho activists, and an "angel of mercy" in the U.S.-based ABC television network's "Faces of Hope" report. Through the use of Bina's story, I urge a move beyond dualistic framings of women's experiences of violence that position them as "good victims" or "bad victims." I challenge the terms "victims" or "survivors," arguing for a more liberatory epistemology that allows for dynamism, fluidity, and most importantly narrative agency. I also discuss the fallout that occurred in the anti–acid violence movement when some of the survivors chose to remain in the United States, violating the terms of the contract that allowed them to enter the country for reconstructive surgery. I argue that this controversy must be understood not only as an instance of intramovement differences among individuals, but also as a demonstration of the global structural inequality that shapes the trajectories of such movements.

Chapter 4, "Feminism and Its Other: Representing the 'New Woman' of Bangladesh," explores the use of entertainment-education media by women activists as a mobilizing tool. Analyzing the 2006 telefilm, *Ayna (The Mirror)*, which takes up the topic of acid violence, I look at the contemporary production and representation of the "New Woman" in Bangladesh in the context of globalization and development and in contrast to an earlier context of anticolonialist and nationalist struggles. Deploying film as a vehicle for education-entertainment, the director of *Ayna* provokes an important conversation about human rights advocacy, transnational feminist alliances, women's subjectivities, victimization, and agency. At the same time, a textual reading of the film, in conjunction with ethnographic study of women's activism in Bangladesh, allows for a juxtaposition of the neoliberal underpinning of the film's representations of development and women's empowerment with the lived experiences of women participating in and/or benefiting from such "humanitarian interventions."

Finally, chapter 5, "Transnational Challenges: Engaging Religion, Development, and Women's Organizing in Bangladesh," broadens the discussion of transnational feminist praxis beyond the Naripokkho campaign and locates women's activism in Bangladesh within the intersecting forces of rising religious extremism, state politics, and global capitalist development. This chapter explores the question of whether and how the transnational production of violence against women in a "Muslim nation" articulates with "local" feminist responses. In particular, I point out, the national women's movement in Bangladesh, historically aligned and intertwined with the secular nationalist struggle for liberation, followed by the state- and donor-driven neoliberal development agenda, has positioned itself in opposition to Islamist politics. This nationalist-secularist stance, in opposition to an Islamist one, however, has not adequately addressed the intersections of gender and religion in the nationalist and civil society politics in a transnational age. Invoking the secular-nationalist struggle and its cross-class alliances as the impetus for democratic nation building in the current political climate, where Islamist politics are perceived as a unilateral threat, I argue, can be limiting in vision and reach.

The landscape of Bangladeshi politics has shifted such that divisions among the nationalists, feminists, secularists, and Islamists are no longer clear-cut, if they ever were. For example, violence against women is frequently attributed by local and global media and secular and feminist NGOs to a "backlash against modernity" by Islamist groups. Deeper analysis reveals the political, social, and economic forces leading to gendered violence and encourages a more nuanced analysis of the proliferation and diversification of Islamist politics in the region and the exigencies shaping feminist politics.

This introspective and self-reflexive examination of the power relations among and within women's groups encourages feminists to strive for a broader praxis that challenges colonialist narratives of women's empowerment in the global South. By shedding light on the complexity of local women's organizing and their negotiations with transnational politics, I show the multiple layers and linkages involved in feminist struggles. In so doing, I want to challenge the assumptions made in universalizing discourses of women's oppression and activism, and highlight the unexpected and even unlikely alliances and trajectories that transnational feminist projects may engender.

Chapter One

Feminist Negotiations

Contesting Narratives of the Campaign against Acid Violence in Bangladesh

The campaign against acid violence in Bangladesh in the 1990s developed across three broad phases. Initially, in the first phase, the campaign arose through national and international publicity generated by Bangladeshi activists of Naripokkho, a Dhaka-based feminist advocacy organization. The spread and growth of the campaign in the second phase marked significant victories and produced divergent and competing investments in the campaign. The third phase culminated in the campaign's co-optation by international development aid-driven intervention. By addressing the tensions between competing visions of social transformation and women's empowerment articulated by local women activists, on the one hand, and international donor agencies, on the other hand, this chapter examines the consequences of international aid and NGOs in rearticulating the relationship between women, gendered violence, and the state.[1] It studies the growth and development of a contemporary campaign around gendered violence by historicizing the discourse of acid violence and interventions challenging it. In so doing, I shed light on the multiple interests, agendas, and constraints governing the response to violence against women in the global South. The chapter provides an opportunity to analyze and explore these complicated transactions between victims, feminist organizers, the state, and international donor organizations.

Incidents of acid attacks against both men and women have a long history in Bangladesh, its surrounding region, and other parts of the world. However, the use of acid attacks against women as a form of gendered violence, specifically in recent decades, needs to be understood in the larger context of socioeconomic, political, and cultural transitions in Bangladesh. Following the War for Independence in 1971, which left the country socially and economically devastated, Bangladesh has witnessed a decline in agriculture-based economy, a growth of landlessness, an increase in landless laborers, and amplified unemployment. Naila Kabeer (2000) has pointed to the intrusion of market relations into the employment of labor, setting in motion the gradual dissolution of older forms of family organization and the erosion of traditional systems of support among landless peasants. The intensified competition in the rural economy has produced a diversification of livelihoods as well as migration to urban areas. Combined effects of population growth and declining farm size set in motion a shift from an older agricultural peasant economy to a more monetized one. Not all social groups, however, were affected equally. Wealthy farmers and the rural elite were able to invest in accordance with new opportunities while the urban educated and the middle-class sections had access to secure employment. These changing socioeconomic dynamics have affected the rural and urban poor (women in particular) and have been met with governmental and non-governmental aid interventions.

Like many developing nations, Bangladesh opened up to economic liberalization programs with the support of the World Bank and the IMF in the early 1980s, leading to the promotion of export-oriented manufacturing. Together with the impetus generated by the United Nations Decade of Women and Development (1975–85) these new initiatives aimed to integrate women into some of their projects. Over the last two decades, an increasing number of women from poor and lower-middle-class backgrounds, have participated in "income-generating" activities of the development sector as well as sought employment in garment factories in metropolitan areas (Kabeer, 2000, p. 60). These factories rely predominantly on female labor because it is cheapened and seemingly easier to control.[2] A vast majority of the women in these factories come from rural areas, but a significant proportion also come from urban areas, many of whom were previously employed as domestic workers. While there has been economic gain involved, the increased physical mobility entailed by these new activities has also adversely affected women's and their family's honor and status. In other words, the liberatory aspects made possible by the new socioeconomic developments were negotiated within patriarchal bargains.[3]

There were inevitable gendered implications for the changes in economy and society following the War of Independence.[4] Norms of female seclusion permeated the shift to a cash economy, making women's participation in the labor market a site of contestation. The transition from subsistence to a monetized economy accounts for a key change in gender relations: namely, the replacement of marriage payments to the bride and her family with the "demand dowry" that favored the groom and his family (Rozario, 1998, p. 269). The rise of dowries contributed to the fragility of marriage relations with increases in divorce, frequent remarriage, abandonment, and separation. Within the context of asymmetrical gender relations and changing socio-economic dynamics, the growing practice of dowry only intensified women's economic devaluation, whereby girls were viewed as liabilities and boys as assets. According to Naila Kabeer (2000), these various changes indicated the deterioration of both women's status as women and the "patriarchal contract" (men's obligations toward women).

Evidence suggests that the diversification of women's livelihoods met with responses such as the active mobilization of powerful interest groups (family, local communities and networks, religious functionaries, and the state machinery) in defense of their privileged position in the social order (Kabeer, 2000, p. 60). Nonetheless, market forces, the advent of export-oriented manufacturing such as the garments industry, and the emergence of the NGO movements working toward the empowerment of women on the grassroots level, contributed to a visible and sizable female labor force. This led to a significant shift from long-established norms of female seclusion in Bangladesh. Known as the "silent revolution," in the changing social landscape of Bangladesh, it was not unusual to see rural women bicycling to work or large numbers of young and "unaccompanied" women on the streets of Dhaka on their way to and from work (Amir, n.d.). While, on the one hand, women experienced greater integration into the economy, on the other hand, their participation and mobility disrupted existing social and political structures. Women's increasing participation in the labor force in some cases compromised the terms of the obligations men had toward women in their families. It was commonly perceived that women were taking away jobs from men and thus the natural role of primary breadwinner. Religious groups in particular, joining forces with elite male social structures, denounced the women by organizing public forums and even circulating audio recordings vilifying women who were transgressing social norms (Kabeer, 2000, p. 83).

Feminist researchers have posited that hostile attitudes and reactions toward women's emerging visibility and participation in new roles, particularly in the context of increasing socioeconomic disempowerment of men, often manifests in male-initiated abuses against women, including physical violence, and degradation of women. Anthropologist Dina Siddiqi (1991) has noted that the so-called "invasion" by women into previously male-dominated public spheres may have broken the norms of female seclusion but has at the same time redefined those norms to take on new significance in the context of globalization and wage labor. Strict disciplinary measures and surveillance continue to govern female behavior both in and outside of work spaces. This emergent new order in Bangladesh has been accompanied by systematic violence against women as exemplified by the steady increase in fatwas, rapes, acid attacks, murders, battery, and trafficking (Ain O Salish Kendro, 2001).[5] While reported incidents of acid attacks have only ranged from 150 to 450 cases per year, other forms of reported violence, with the exception of fatwas, have been consistently higher in number (Ain O Salish Kendro, 2003). According to the yearly reports by Ain O Salish Kendro, recent decades have seen an escalation of not only acid attacks but also in gendered violence against women across the board (Ain O Salish Kendro, 2001). In such a context, acid throwing against women and girls has to be seen within the larger trend of women's oppression.

Reportedly, acid victims have been until recently predominantly women and girls. The reasons for attacks have been overwhelmingly cited as marital, family, and land disputes, refusal to pay dowry, or the rejection of romantic advances and marriage proposals (Islam, 2004). At the same time, the rise of auto mechanic, leather, and garment industries has facilitated the widespread and unregulated availability of sulfuric and nitric acid, and has made acid throwing an easy and "expedient" form of violence.[6] A bottle of sulfuric acid currently can be bought for Tk 15 (approximately U.S.$0.25). The ease and frequency with which acid violence is committed reaffirm societal views that women are property, and their appearance an asset toward securing marriage. A study conducted by Women for Women, a Dhaka-based feminist research group, revealed that acid victims are often characterized as women who are "wayward and disobedient" ("*udhyoto meye*") by their community (Akhter & Nahar, 2003). Another study on the rising feminization of labor in Bangladesh showed that women workers were increasingly victims of three-dimensional violence: (1) in the workspace, (2) on the way to work, and (3) in the domestic space (Halim & Haq, 2004). In summary, changing forces of globalization and attendant gendered social order contributed to a climate leading to the precipitation of gendered violence in the national context of Bangladesh.

Organizing against Acid Violence

Naripokkho developed their anti–acid violence campaign between the years of 1995 and 2003.[7] It was also during these years that strategic negotiations were carried out by Naripokkho activists with key institutions in order to create a public discourse on acid violence against women in Bangladesh, with the purpose of developing a "socially recognized campaign" (N. Huq, personal communication, April 11, 2003). Its founders and members see Naripokkho as collectively working for the advancement of women's rights and entitlements, while also building broad-based resistance against violence, discrimination, and injustice. Their activities have included advocacy campaigns, research, discussions, workshops, seminars, training programs, national-level conferences, cultural events, and lobbying on issues of gender justice. Mobilizing against acid violence in particular was part of the organization's broader mandate of resisting gender violence.

Scholars of transnational organizing efforts have drawn attention to the complex and contradictory relationships within networks that involve actors as divergent as local women's groups, international donor agencies, and the state. Many of these transnational networks, while constituting an asymmetrical terrain of transnational solidarity and differences, may be held together by a perceived shared commitment. At the same time, however, participants are often sharply at odds over fundamental issues of agenda and strategy (Nelson, 2002; Riker, 2002). While international aid helps to institutionalize women's political struggles, the flipside of this institutionalization is that feminists must frame their struggles in terms of developmentalist aid frameworks in order to receive the funding. These frameworks often generate schisms and unintended effects on the movement dynamics, such as a deradicalization of movement agendas, as described in the works of Amitra Basu (2000), Amy Lind and Jessica Share (2003), and James Ferguson (1994).

This was clearly true in the case of Naripokkho. The envelopment of Naripokkho's anti-acid campaign by donor-driven interventions transformed its radical vision of structural change and women's communal empowerment into a neoliberal one of incremental change and individual transformation. The latter vision did not adequately recognize the distinction between policies and programs that addressed the practical needs of individual women survivors of violence and those who sought to transform women's positions within a structurally unequal set of social relations (Kabeer, 1994).

In order to fully illuminate the complex dynamics of the acid campaign, I organize my observations into three stages: from 1995 to 1998, when members and staff of Naripokkho began systematically devising a social campaign to transform incidences of acid attacks into a public issue; from 1998 to 1999, when Naripokkho's success led to a diversification and proliferation of actors engaged with the campaign, thereby expanding and changing its scope; and from 1999 to 2003, when the Acid Survivors Foundation gradually took over the role of the consolidated service providing agency to assist acid violence survivors. The third stage concurrently witnessed the gradual dissolution of Naripokkho's involvement with the campaign, as well as the articulation of a strategy for providing services to acid victims that is centered on Women in Development (WID). This strategy stressed income-generation and skills training as the means to empower socially marginalized women, thereby integrating them into the productive machinery of the state (Bhavnani, Foran, & Kurian, 2003). However, this was in contrast to Naripokkho's initial strategy of pursuing women's empowerment through awareness raising, emphasis on promoting women's individual and collective rights, as well as broader societal change. Tracing these shifting strategies tells us that within the climate of neoliberal development aid intervention, women victims are often integrated into productive schemes that ultimately do not challenge wider hierarchical structures in either Bangladeshi society or international development regimes.

Naripokkho members originally generated attention and funding to inquire into the severity and growing proliferation of acid attacks by focusing on the issue as part and parcel of a broader campaign challenging violence against women. The organization made the visibility of the survivors a key element of the campaign. However, a growing intervention of international donors in the 1990s, facilitated by a global shift from feminist collective organizing to the discursive weight of human rights discourses, led to a concomitant supplanting of the indigenous movement by transnational agendas. Transnationalization and availability of more resources, among other things, led to the medicalization of the campaign arguably compromising its social dimensions.[8] Transnational networks established a model of providing short-term services like reconstructive surgeries to survivors, over and rather than investing a greater amount of time and energy in empowering survivors of violence, as the Naripokkho activists had initially done. (In the early days of Naripokkho organizing, survivors of acid violence were often trained to be activists and organizers themselves.)

Finally, during the third stage of the anti-acid campaign, the Acid Survivors Foundation, established through the funding and support of the Canadian International Development Agency (CIDA) and the United Nations Children's Fund, UNICEF-Bangladesh, began to focus on the reintegration of survivors into society by returning them to a "condition as near as possible" to one prior to the attacks (Acid Survivor's Foundation, "Introduction").

This strategy reflected a neoliberal model of economic empowerment for the survivors that avoided questioning the social order by which gendered violence continued to be sanctioned. Nonetheless, ASF, backed by multilateral and bilateral donors as well as a strong civil society constituency, did exert pressure on the national government, lobbying for the development and implementation of effective medicolegal provisions for survivors of acid violence, and therefore ASF's impact has been a mixed one.

Naripokkho Launches Anti–Acid Violence Campaign

Naripokkho, literally meaning "pro-women," is a membership-based women's advocacy organization founded in 1983 (Naripokkho, 2002). The organization, which includes women with a wide variety of skills and expertise, is supported by its membership through their voluntary contributions of professional time and funds. Most of Naripokkho's membership includes women with professional occupations, but the organization also has a number of paid staff to run its day-to-day operations. The use of members' professional time and skills enables Naripokkho to take on earning activities such as research consultancies and gender analysis training, as well as grant-funded projects.

In 1995, when Naripokkho activists embarked on their work on acid violence, no systematic study or records provided comprehensive documentation of incidents of acid throwing on women and girls in Bangladesh. Bristi Chowdhury, then an intern at Naripokkho, commented that, "Acid violence was not yet a buzzword [in the mid-1990s]" (B. Chowdhury, personal communication, March 7, 2003). No serious or systematic attention had been drawn to the issue, and no discourse had been created to put acid violence in the landscape of the national and international gendered human rights violations.

Naripokkho's involvement began when one of its members, Nasreen Huq (who eventually became the coordinator of the acid campaign), came across two male relatives of acid survivor Nurun Nahar in the office of a daily newspaper. Nahar was a teenage girl who had had acid thrown at her by Jashim Sikdar, a rejected suitor, and his associates. (Her story is told more fully in chapter 2.) At the time, Nahar's male relatives were trying to persuade reporters of the newspaper to do a story on the incident. Failing to do so, they approached Nasreen Huq, who happened to be present at the newspaper office with some business of her own and whom they correctly assumed to be an activist who would be sympathetic to their plight. This accidental 1995 meeting stirred Huq and other Naripokkho activists' interest in doing work in this area, given the organization's long-standing broader focus on gender violence.

Bristi Chowdhury has described the initial phase of campaign building as consisting of researching and collecting data from various newspapers, libraries, medical facilities, and police stations to create a "violence logbook"; meeting with and providing support to victims of acid attacks and their families; and developing a network of allies with local and foreign journalists, activists, philanthropists, medical and legal professionals, and international donors who could potentially assist in the creation of a public discourse on acid violence (B. Chowdhury, personal communication, March 7, 2003). The emergent loose network mobilized itself around the goal of launching an international campaign that would simultaneously reinforce the voices of local women activists and affect national policy development priorities.

Nasreen Huq, the coordinator of the acid campaign, explained how she and her coworkers mapped acid attacks as a distinctive form of a larger, "global feminist"–conceptualized issue of Violence Against Women (N. Huq, personal communication, October 10, 1996). Feminist scholar Chandra Mohanty (2003) has written about the globalization of women's movements worldwide in the 1990s, as a result of transnational organizing following a series of U.N. conferences on women culminating in the Fourth World Conference on Women Beijing in 1995. This shifted the direction of global feminism to a rights-based approach otherwise known as the main-streaming of the feminist movement, which placed issues of violence against women successfully onto the world stage (Mohanty, 2003, p. 249). Naripokkho framed their own organizational work on violence against women in Bangladesh within the mandate of an international platform, hoping to leverage this issue onto the international women's rights stage and thereby to affect policy changes on the national front. Huq said in an early interview with me, "The focus on acid burns is part of an overall campaign on Violence Against Women, which draws on the government's mandate to address specific forms of violence articulated in the 1995 UN Beijing Conference on Women and the Program of Action of the International Conference on Population and Development (ICPD) in 1994" (N. Huq, personal communication, October 10, 1996). In retrospect, Huq's comment shows the mutually constitutive nature of local and transnational organizing, and the ways in which campaign directions often comply with policy imperatives.

As a result of the efforts of the Naripokkho activists in the mid-1990s, however, there also emerged a network of young girls and women who had endured acid violence. In April 1997, amid the escalating phenomenon of acid throwing in Bangladesh, Naripokkho activists organized a three-day workshop with a group of teenage survivors of acid violence. The purpose of this workshop was to present in a public forum the phenomenon of acid throwing as a form of gendered violence. The workshop aimed to point out the gaps in the needed services provided by institutions such as the medico-legal establishments, to mobilize key local, national, and international actors to take action, and to promote solidarity and visibility of the survivors whose economic and social lives had been affected as a result of the acid attacks. Naripokkho's approach was motivated by the belief that the experiences of the survivors should be central to the shaping of the campaign and its objectives and that the survivors should act as the leaders of the campaign.

The workshop was a collaborative effort as the activists of Naripokkho tapped into various resources, including their social and professional connections. The successful expansion of the acid campaign certainly hinged on Naripokkho's extensive network and strategic grounding within the national and international women's movements. For example, Save the Children, UK, offered the use of their formal conference room free of cost for the workshop sessions. Similarly, the Women's Voluntary Association donated their guesthouse to host the girls and their families at a nominal cost. Since many of the girls arrived in Dhaka days ahead of the workshop, Naripokkho staff volunteered to put them up in their own homes. UNICEF provided transportation over the three days. The U.N. Women's Association hosted a presentation and donated funds for the workshop.

Prior to the workshop, Naripokkho members contacted the Law and Home Ministries and set up meetings. A member of Naripokkho, who was a gender adviser to the Danish International Development Agency (DANIDA) and at the time was collaborating with the Bangladeshi government on a project called the Multi-sectoral Project on Violence Against Women, emphasized the importance of integration of the campaign into this larger project. Negotiations with the director of Gonoshastho Kendro (GK), an influential national NGO providing affordable health care to the poor, led to a fruitful alliance in envisioning the development of a new Burns Center. (At the time the only existing medical facility especially for acid burn survivors was located at the state-sponsored Dhaka Medical College Hospital and had a mere eight-bed capacity.[9])

The workshop featured sessions where organizers, and participants and their families, developed stronger relationships with one another, through group activities, which often took very emotional turns. For most of the

survivors it was their first time being in a room with other survivors and
sharing the experience of confronting the private trauma of disfigurement
in a collective setting. Bristi Chowdhury wrote in her 1997 report *Burning
Passions: A Study of Acid Violence in Bangladesh*:

> [The "Meet Naripokkho" session] was, quite possibly, the most
> emotionally exhausting session. Many members of Naripokkho
> came to welcome the girls. When I arrived, uncharacteristically
> late, Bina was saying to a member, who was feeling understand-
> ably shocked and sad, "you're feeling bad? Then look at me."
> (*Apnar kharap lagche? Ta hole amar dike takan.*) She said this in
> her distinctive jovial manner. . . . A few minutes later Bina was
> in floods of tears. She had gone up to Nasreen and asked, "Am
> I as horrific looking as the other girls?" (*Ami ki oder moto bisri?*)
> and then broken down. Nasreen calmed her down and she [Bina]
> sat down. (Chowdhury, 1997, p. 15)

Separate sessions were held with family members, particularly the
mothers of the young women, who had been the primary caregivers in the
long recovery process following the acid attacks. Mothers, grandmothers,
and younger siblings of victims were often directly injured themselves by
acid attacks because they tended to sleep on one bed, and attacks frequently
occurred in the home. Adult males and fathers in the family were also
affected because they were primarily responsible for providing financial
resources for the medical treatment and legal follow up. Family members
often spent weeks, even months at a time away from home at the hospital
caring for the young women. They tended to their daughters and sisters by
changing bed sheets, dressing their wounds, cleaning, cooking, and feeding
them. It was therefore obviously important to include family members in
the workshop.

The emotionally charged family sessions encouraged and strengthened
solidarity among women, a critical feature of the emergent Naripokkho
campaign. Bristi Chowdhury continued in her report:

> [W]hen all the harrowing stories were being told, no amount
> of logical thought could stop the tears. When I cried Rina [a
> survivor] held my hand tightly the way I had held hers when
> she had cried in DMCH [where the survivors recuperated in
> the Burns Unit and Naripokkho staff regularly visited them] and

Bina [another survivor] cradled my head like I had cradled hers. Even now I don't know if I was right to cry, maybe I should have remained strong so that they could feel that they could lean on me. . . . this was an important, if emotionally draining session. (Chowdhury, 1997, p. 15)

During the workshop, acid survivors and their family members were encouraged to map out their own future plans, visions of social justice, and recommendations for adequate services for victims of violence. The sessions also reflected an attempt on the organization's part to create an imaginative space for the girls, through such activities as painting and storytelling in order to express their feelings and develop friendships. In a session titled "Let Us Imagine" ("*Esho shopno dekhi*"), each young woman described what she wished for if she had the opportunity to do anything she liked. This is how some of them responded:

Ruma: "To look like I did before"

Selina: "To be able to see again"

Sonya: "To study, to go back to school"

Monira: "To raise my son properly"

Taslima: "To swim in the river"

Rina: "To be a film star, to dance, to sing"

Amina: "To go around as before"

Bina: "To meet up with all the other acid burnt women in this country and hold a huge rally on International Women's Day"

Nargis: "To be able to go back to work." (Naripokkho Workshop, April 24–27, 1997)

Naripokkho member Safia Azim pointed out in an interview with me shortly after this workshop that in the "Esho Shopno Dekhi" session, none of the girls had asked for revenge. Azim opined, "This means they are not mentally scarred or bitter because of their attack. All of us [survivors and Naripokkho staff] are encouraged by the workshop, it has brought us hope. It has given us strength" (S. Azim, personal communication, April 27, 1997).

Naripokkho activists provided a supportive space for the young survivors to develop the confidence to confront the consequent isolation and ostracism following acid attacks and to feel comfortable in being in public spaces. Bristi Chowdhury described one particular event designed to do just that:

> [S]urvivors, mothers and Naripokkho staff and volunteers from the "Theater Center" (a theater group who often help us out in Naripokkho functions) went to Shongshad Bhaban, the Parliament Building. Shongshod Bhaban is a place for boys to ogle girls and girls to more subtly ogle boys, it is a place for married couples to go openly and for unmarried couples to go covertly, but essentially it is a place for couples. Many people told us that we must either be mad or inhumanely insensitive to take a group of girls whose outside appearance was, to say the least, shocking, to this place and what is more on a Friday when the place is literally swarming. (Chowdhury, 1997, p. 16)

Naripokkho activists believed in reclaiming the public space and social lives of the young girls that the gendered abuse had so methodically denied. Chowdhury continued,

> We got out of the microbuses slightly apprehensive, but Nasreen [the campaign coordinator] covered her own apprehension by taking control of the situation and telling us to hold hands so that we were in one long line, then we sang, even those like me, who are tone deaf, sang. We started with "We shall over-come/*Amra korbo joy*" and went on to many more. We took over *Shongshod* that day! We were all standing on the steps singing and of course a large crowd of male oglers had gathered to watch the freak show (or at least that's what we thought), when one young man pushed his way to the front and asked if we would let him sing us a song, we were all doubtful about this thinking that perhaps he would make fun of them or something of the sort, but he proved us to be a bunch of paranoid cynics. He sang beautifully. All he wanted to do was have fun with us not at us; maybe he even wanted to show his solidarity with us. We had been worried that everyone would treat the girls as freaks and for a while the oglers did treat them as freaks but after a while they stopped having fun at our expense and began to have fun with us. (Chowdhury, 1997, p. 16)

Nasreen Huq emphasized that the Naripokkho workshop brought together a group of girls who as a result of the acid attacks had been deprived of living their adolescence. Thus, the session at the Parliament House was intended to reclaim not only the public spaces and social lives of young women but also their lost youth (N. Huq, personal communication, April 11, 2003). Chowdhury's report showcased these youthful activities. She said, "[A]t one point we were playing a game where you have to chase a person around in a circle and if you catch them before they get back to their place in the circle they are out, the audience were cheering us as in '*ey taratari, dhorlo dhorlo*,' (hey quick, quick she's going to catch you) and so on. It was fantastic; these guys [the public] were with *us*" (Chowdhury, 1997, p. 16).

In separate interviews, survivors and workshop participants Bina Akhter and Nargise Akhtar described their simultaneous feelings of trepidation and joy in confronting a public space with allies (B. Akhter and N. Akhtar, personal communications, April 27, 1997). The activists and survivors of Naripokkho together challenged what they had come to recognize as enforced isolation. As a result, the visibility of the survivors became a key strategy in the efforts to make public the anti–acid violence campaign (Del Franco, 1999). Safia Azim, a member of Naripokkho who was also a psychologist, said in an interview after the workshop that the work Naripokkho and the survivors did together encouraged many of the survivors to stop covering their faces in public (S. Azim, personal communication, April 27, 1997). Yet the response was not always positive. Surprisingly, the then-minister of Women's Affairs commented at one of the workshop activities to which he was invited, " 'These girls would have been better off dead' (*Ey meyera to jibito mrito, er cheye mara gele bhalo chilo)*" (Chowdhury, 1997, p. 17).

The sessions, designed to encourage the survivors to talk about their futures, apparently gave them a sense of community and prepared them to collectively make a statement to state representatives, journalists, doctors, lawyers, and police officers in a public forum called "Face to Face with Acid Survivors." One by one the young women stood up, some partially veiled, others without covering, some steadied by family members, others on their own, some with tears streaming down their cheeks, others with trembling voices, to recount their stories. The girls spoke at length about the long process of recovery and the ensuing hardships that the attacks had brought on both themselves and their families. They mentioned the inadequate ser-vices in the country's one burn unit in the Dhaka Medical College Hospital; the financial strain on their families when they pursued medical and legal redress; their own inability to continue with their education or meaningful employment, both due to a lack of finances and the loss of physical ability to see and to hear as a result of the acid attack; and the trauma and isolation that that they experienced. Moreover, the girls talked about the corrupt and ineffective judicial system, which, in spite of claiming to offer services, in reality systematically discriminated against the victims.

The April 1997 workshop was a significant turning point for the acid campaign. For the first time Bangladeshi civil servants and the international donor community came *face to face* with young Bangladeshi women who had endured acid attacks. Naripokkho activists' efforts had broken through an existing wall of official denial and trivialization of this phenomenon. At the end of the session, the same minister of Women's Affairs who had declared the survivors "better off dead" said, "I am so terribly ashamed. I ask myself, should I even be working for this country? This . . . [is] . . . our collective failure as a nation" (Naripokkho Workshop, April 24–27, 1997).[10] The breakthroughs achieved by Naripokkho's workshop launched acid violence against women in Bangladesh as an issue that needed instant and systematic attention from the state, the media, donors, and the medicolegal establishments. One concrete outcome of the conference was that state institutions granted Naripokkho funds for all workshop-related costs as well as medical and legal services to the young women participants. Clearly, this gesture by the state should not be belittled, given the grave financial situation facing the families of the young women. However, it is important to note that the larger question of systemic responses to structural violence was not as easily confronted. For instance, in a follow-up session at the home minister's office, a police officer from Lalbagh Thana was present with the First Information Report from Bina's case. This is a very important document filed by the victim and her family and is often tampered with by the police themselves, who may be bribed or threatened by the perpetrator and their protectors. The following conversation unfolded:

> The man [police officer] started with Bina's case. He said, "The main perpetrator was Pappu." Bina shook her head and said, "The main perpetrator was Dano." The police officer replied, "No, it says here in the FIR that the main perpetrator was Pappu." Bina replied, "I think I know who threw acid at me." The police officer responded, "You are wrong, here it says Pappu." At this point the Home Minister interrupted, "She was there, she knows who attacked her. For some reason a different man's name was recorded. I think this means that all the statements should be

taken down again, today." Later, over lunch a couple of police officers including a woman officer came to retake each girl's statement. (Chowdhury, 1997, p. 18)

What this exchange reveals is that the real perpetrator Dano and his associates had been successful in colluding with the police through bribe, intimidation, or political influence in erasing their names from the crime scene reports altogether. Drawing attention of state officials to such multilayered barriers that victims and activists must overcome was an important achievement of the workshop.

The conference also attracted the attention of the international community in Dhaka. Initially, major donors like UNICEF were not forthcoming with support for the workshop. In fact, Naripokkho activists had had several meetings with UNICEF staff to convince them that acid attacks were a "girl child" issue, an area of concern adopted by the Platform of Action at the U.N. Beijing Conference and subsequently by UNICEF. For that reason, they argued, it was relevant to UNICEF's activity areas in Bangladesh. The organization agreed to provide transportation during the workshop as a result of these meetings.

The workshop included a trip to UNICEF headquarters in Dhaka and a meeting with their staff. Bristi Chowdhury said in an interview:

For the girls UNICEF was a whole new world, full of plush furniture and *bideshis* (foreigners). We went up to the sixth floor where the meeting room is, the girls were very impressed by the view. The meeting started with a short introduction to UNICEF staff including the Country Director who lightened the mood by making jokes at the expense of the "silly *bideshis* who can't speak Bangla." We went around the room introducing ourselves, and each survivor told her story again over mango juice and biscuits. The girls presented the Country Director with a poster they had made. In return, each girl was presented with a t-shirt featuring a Meena doll—a character from educational videos sponsored by UNICEF—and an UNICEF information packet. Once the serious stuff was over, they took us in to a screening room to show us a couple of videos. . . . The second was a video with a song written and sung by John Denver called, "I want to Live." It had many stills of children from all over the world doing different

things like working, swimming, fishing, playing, etc. This video
brought tears to my eyes. A week or so later when Nasreen and
I met with UNICEF again, the Country Director admitted to us
that after we left, the staff there had all cried. (B. Chowdhury,
personal communication, March 7, 2003)

The face-to-face sessions with survivors and different actors like UNI-
CEF, organized by Naripokkho, stirred the local and international organizations into action. Schaffer and Smith (2004) have written about the effective
power and uses of narratives in mobilizing campaigns for human rights.
They have argued that stories of oppression invite ethical responses from
listeners and can in turn be deployed in both positive and negative ways to
support or obstruct the advancement of human rights (Schaffer and Smith,
2004, p. 5). Showcasing the stories of the girls certainly invoked reactions
from state and aid organizations, even as it also repeatedly objectified them
as victims and spectacles.

Concrete themes emerged from the workshop based on the particular
profile of the participants, all of whom were adolescents and young women.
One of them was a deeper understanding of women's gendered vulnerability
as an underlying cause of violence. The two leading explanations for why
the women had been attacked were revenge for unrequited love and hostility
over unmet dowry demands. The immediate needs that the survivors identified were medical, legal, and social, including opportunities for education
and employment.

On the medical front, there was simply a gross lack of proper and
affordable care for patients of severe burns. The families suffered massive
financial hardship in the process of accessing treatment. Bristi Chowdhury
pointed to the negligence of the DMCH staff in the early years of the
campaign, particularly toward poor patients. "Those days DMCH did not
trust us [Naripokkho]. We had to seek the Director's permission in order to
make the weekly visits. [The primary doctor in the burns unit] who is now
considered a hero at the time was inept at reconstructive surgery. He took
skin from Bina's thigh and put it on her forehead without using anesthesia
to operate. He didn't care because Bina was not a private patient, she didn't
have money. He reconstructed Rina's mouth in such a way that it stretched
permanently from cheek to cheek in a grotesque smile" (B. Chowdhury,
personal communication, March 7, 2003).

In the area of legal services, the workshop participants reported that
the perpetrators roamed around freely in their neighborhoods following the

attack, often with the protection of powerful political figures. In fact, many of the young men who were perpetrators were themselves known locally as *mastaans*, or local crime lords, with political connections, and most residents including the police were afraid of them.[11] If arrested, the family members and associates of these men would threaten and intimidate the victim and her family. They would bribe the police into withdrawing charges or fabricating evidence. At the workshop, when the ministers asked the participants about their specific "demands," Rina said, "When you look at my face, what kind of punishment do you think the people who did this to me deserve? What I would like is for no other girl to suffer the same trauma as me. I don't want another girl's life to be ruined like mine. I want a justice system that won't allow these thugs to walk around freely, nor get out on bail" (Naripokkho Workshop, April 24–27, 1997).

Socially, the participants expressed the importance of networking with other victims of acid violence, and to that end forming a nationwide committee that would convene regularly. They also pointed out that the attention generated by the workshop should be maintained through regular media coverage and ongoing events like public rallies and meetings. Continued organizing would enable the betterment of existing services, particularly in the medical field. Bina in particular vocalized these needs in a statement to the ministers at the workshop, "I would like to march in a rally protesting acid violence in next year's International Women's Day. I would like to work toward establishing a committee on acid violence, and urge journalists to talk to us and write about us so that the public is made aware and educated." Bina had told me in an interview after the workshop that she became very depressed when she went out because people would tease her. "People are scared of us, they scream and run away when they see our faces. Sometimes I feel as though it is not worth living now that God has given me this ugly face. I feel so hideous. When I meet other girls with burnt faces, I realize that I'm not the only one" (B. Akhter, personal communication, April 27, 1997).

Education and employment were also an issue of concern for the women. At the workshop, Bina said to the state representatives, "We would like to have jobs, to earn money, to go to school, to develop professional skills. Do you know that Nargis [a fourteen-year-old participant who used to work in a garment factory in Dhaka] was fired from her job after the attack? Many women having lost their eyesight now cannot work, they need to be trained to do certain kinds of work. There are no safe premises like hostels where we can stay with our families during the long medical treatment in Dhaka" (Naripokkho Workshop, April 24–27, 1997). Because the attacks had left many of them partially or fully blind, it was difficult to go back to school or find jobs suited to their situations. Opportunities were mostly concentrated in the cities, but there were no adequate housing options, such as women's hostels.

Following the workshop some the immediate needs of the victims were improved. Bristi Chowdhury recalled, "Money started to come in. A member of the royal family of Jordan sent a large sum upon reading an article in *Marie Claire* magazine. We wanted the international awareness. A plastic surgeon from India was invited to Gonoshastho by its director to develop a national project to train local medical staff in caring for burns patients. Simultaneously there were offers from medical professionals in Spain and Italy. The work took on a life of its own" (B. Chowdhury, personal communication, March 7, 2003).

At the same time, strengthened by the supportive feminist space of Naripokkho and the growing network, the young survivors began to participate more fully in the campaign and pursue other interests. For example, survivor Nurun Nahar enrolled in a technical college in Dhaka and moved into a women's hostel in the city. Bina Akhter began an internship in Naripokkho. Chowdhury elaborated on her new role in the organization, "The workshop generated much interest and support from national and international groups. Bina Akhter, the most vocal and articulate in the group of survivors from the workshop was an obvious choice to carry on the research and the networking. She proved to be brilliant at this work. Within a few months she had contacted over forty survivors around the country. She wrote to every single person we heard about through the newspapers or the hospitals. She connected with journalists, heads of organizations, philanthropists, even gave interviews in papers and on TV" (B. Chowdhury, personal communication, March 7, 2003). Thus the workshop and the supportive environment at Naripokkho was in part responsible for boosting the self-confidence of some survivors to take on more public activities.

Naripokkho's campaign strategy involved organizing the survivors of acid violence to be its leaders. This motivated Naripokkho's decision to hire Bina Akhter and Nurun Nahar and to continue developing a nationwide network with other survivors by visiting them at DMCH and in their homes as well as encouraging them to speak in public. Huq said in an interview, "We wanted to maintain the energy generated at the workshop and build on it. There had to be continuity because we knew there would be others. Bina Akhter was critically involved in handling the press, in developing a network, etcetera. In her we saw a whole spectrum unfold of victim to survivor to activist. Right in front of us. This is what we had dreamed of" (N. Huq, personal communication, April 11, 2003). Bina Akhter, in fact went on to become one of the most prominent leaders of the acid campaign. She was nominated by UNICEF to participate in the 1998 Amnesty International Young Leaders Forum in New York.

The workshop also allowed survivors to share experiences with one another as a collective, thus enabling recognition of those experiences as political and transformative (de Lauretis, 1986, p. 9). Such a visibility is particularly important in the case of acid violence because it challenges the motivation behind the crime, which is to force women into isolation and to end their social lives (Del Franco, 1999). Naripokkho was a catalyzing force in the process of building a critical consciousness among the survivors, which then encouraged many of them to become part of the campaign and even take on leadership roles. Naripokkho's intervention, then, set in motion the subsequent entrance of key actors into the continuing development and diversification of the campaign. These early interventions by Naripokkho were clearly continuous with the organization's participation in a larger movement against women's oppression.

The UNICEF Intervention

The second stage of Naripokkho's anti-acid campaign, lasting from 1997 to 1999, was marked by the diversification and gradual internationalization of the campaign. During this time, I was a member of a consulting team that was hired by UNICEF to conduct background research on existing services for the survivors as part of the broader objective of setting up the Acid Survivors Foundation. The 1997 acid workshop, in addition to mobilizing NGOs, the government, the media, and medical and legal professionals, had also stirred the interest of the international donor agency, UNICEF-Bangladesh, as discussed above. Over a series of strategic meetings after the workshop, Naripokkho activists had convinced UNICEF staff to recognize the relevance of the campaign to their own institutional agenda. When a host of reports by CNN, BBC, *Marie Claire, Ms.,* Oprah, and others made the realities of acid violence internationally known, offers of assistance streamed in from different parts of the world.[12] The global interest brought the executive director of UNICEF to personally visit from New York, to meet with acid violence survivors, and to urge the Dhaka office to get involved.

At the same time, the British High Commission set up an "inquiry" headed by a British expatriate writer, John Morrison, who was residing in

Bangladesh and who was married to a staff member of the Department for International Development (DFID). Morrison established the "Inquiry" desk at the Canadian International Development Agency premises in Dhaka, and he later became the first executive director of the Acid Survivors Foundation, which was founded and financed together by UNICEF and CIDA. ASF was developed with the purpose of coordinating medical, legal, and rehabilitative services for acid violence survivors.

Feminist scholar Deborah Stienstra (2000) has discussed women's transnational organizing in relation to the U.N. conferences between 1992 and 1996.[13] She has argued that women's movements have taken their strength from the organizing done locally and nationally and translated it into transnational networks in order to establish their position in the global discourse of women's rights affirmed by the U.N. conferences. Using a metaphor of dance, she effectively points out that just as dancers respond to changes in sound and music, women's movements respond to changes in the global political economy, the state, international financial institutions, and other forces at work in the world order. "The dance continues as the music changes, and the dancers contribute to how the music changes" (Stienstra, 2000, p. 211). The dance metaphor serves to explicate the negotiations in international as well as intranational women's organizing, and the complexities of and compromises that shape women's movements agendas. In this instance it is also an effective metaphor to explain Naripokkho's ongoing efforts to engage UNICEF staff to ascertain the donor agency's investment in the campaign against acid violence.

The backdrop for these negotiations was the U.N. General Assembly's 1979 adoption of the U.N. Convention for Women's Declaration on the Elimination of All Forms of Violence Against Women, which came into force as a treaty in 1981. Then, following the 1995 Beijing Conference on the status of women worldwide, the U.N. mandated the Commission on the Status of Women to integrate a follow-up process. All U.N. bodies were charged with establishing policy and taking action toward assuring equality and equity for women globally (Falvo, 1997, p. 1). UNICEF thus was committed to implementation of the Beijing Platform for Action (the comprehensive action plan outlining critical areas of concern for advancement of women to the year 2000 and beyond). The U.N. convention and platform of action served as the conceptual framework for designing and implementing programs that focused on UNICEF's priority areas, namely, education of girls; health of girls, adolescents, and women; and children's and women's rights (Falvo, 1997). As a result of Naripokkho's efforts and external pressures, UNICEF came on board as a partner in the acid campaign. This relationship, however, led to a considerable disconnect with the women's advocacy group in setting priorities and agenda.

For example, UNICEF supported bringing in from the United States a team of experts specializing in eye movement desensitization reprocessing (EMDR), which at the time was an experimental psychotherapy designed to treat victims of natural disasters, conflict, and war.[14] I interviewed one of the EMDR experts, a psychotherapist from Texas, who explained, "EMDR has been used in Bosnia, South America, Central America, Europe and Africa. Vietnam War veterans in the U.S. have also had EMDR treatment. You have to (a) believe that it works and (b) watch the healing to believe that it works. You have to localize EMDR, and that is why local professionals are important. And, (c) like clay, you have to adapt it so it is Bangali. EMDR has been used all over the world. We have to make it culturally appropriate. Human brain is same everywhere, physiologically we are the same" (Anonymous a, personal communication, June 25, 1998).[15] Another member of the EMDR team, a PhD psychologist commented, "EMDR works faster than conventional psychotherapy and takes the client through the process of healing faster" (Anonymous b, personal communication, June 25, 1998). While I am not qualified to comment on the effectiveness of such treatments for survivors of acid violence, I would like to point out that the decision to involve EMDR specialists was made without discussion with partners in Naripokkho or the survivors themselves.

Though they were actively seeking medical solutions, UNICEF was less focused on engaging in the structural causes of gender violence. Naripokkho had focused on altering the secrecy and shame associated with gender violence by hosting events to bring the survivors out in public. UNICEF, on the other hand, channeled substantial resources into providing psychotherapy to survivors individually. A medical doctor among the UNICEF staff said to me in an interview: "EMDR will help restore confidence in the victims so that they can function in society. You see, they will not be accepted in society. It is not our job here however to change society, we do not care what society thinks or whether they accept the women or not. Society has a long way to go, and we don't have that kind of time. We need to focus on the victims" (Anonymous c, personal communication, June 25, 1998). Subsequently, my conversations with the country director of UNICEF revealed a similar philosophy. She too spoke about meeting the needs of survivors in terms of enabling medical care. Like the physician, she commented that UNICEF could not solve or change local legal systems or change social values (Anonymous d, personal communication, June 25, 1998). What they could do was to provide resources for women to avail themselves of medical treatment, even if it required survivors to go abroad for it.

While therapy might appear to readers from western or northern cultural locations to be an obvious necessity for victims of trauma, an understanding of the Bangladeshi context is required to assess the problems of bringing in EMDR for acid attack survivors. In Bangladesh, counseling is practiced in rather different settings. Safia Azim, a professor of psychology in Dhaka University and member of Naripokkho, told me her view that alternate forms of "therapy" in Bangladesh would be more appropriate given that there was no existing "culture of therapy" similar to western countries. Survivors of violence often go to NGOs like Ain O Salish Kendro [a legal aid clinic] and Naripokkho for counseling instead. The activities of the acid workshop are particularly exemplary of a more informal counseling on an ongoing basis. In such a context, psychologists are involved differently than in a western context. Rather than putting local professionals through costly training in EMDR, and an even more expensive initiative to bring foreign professionals to conduct the training in Bangladesh, a better course of action, according to Azim, would have been to bring in trained counselors to teach at Dhaka University and thereby train and build capacity locally (S. Azim, personal communication, June 15, 1998).

Several survivors, including Bina Akhter and Nurun Nahar, were subjects of EMDR in 1998, but the extent to which it helped them has been questioned by both themselves and Naripokkho staff. During and prior to the treatment both girls had been working in Naripokkho in a supportive environment. They had been attending school and, in Nahar's case, living independently in a women's hostel in the city. Although it is possible to feel short-term elation immediately following EMDR treatment, said Safia Azim, these feelings are not sustained. Both Nahar and Bina admitted to recurring nightmares and depression in the weeks following EMDR (B. Akhter and N. Nahar, personal communications, July 1998). "I am suspicious of this notion of a 'miracle vaccine.' I think that's a myth," commented Professor Azim (S. Azim, personal communication, June 15, 1998). In his article, "Science," Claude Alvares (1997) claims that the relationship between modern science and development is "congenital." Science, he says, is desirable because it makes development possible and thus one reinforces the other in a circular fashion of, "I scratch your back, and you scratch mine" (Alvares, 1997, p. 222). He gives the example of the replacement of neem sticks by a universal commodity such as toothpaste, or *gur* (molasses) by white sugar. This replacement of local traditions with commodities serves to integrate local economies into a capitalist global one, at the same time setting into motion western-style modernization. As Azim's comments imply, in the context of EMDR, western products, whether necessary or not, are seen to treat "underdevelopment" in the form of miracle vaccines at the same time that global capitalism extends its markets. Similarly, by disregarding local context and need for culturally appropriate forms of counseling, UNICEF was initiating a costly intervention through EMDR that would neither reach wide swaths of people in Bangladesh, nor was it grounded on thoughtful research and discussion with their development counterparts on the ground. Scholar-activist Mallika Dutt (1998) has written about how the fruits of global feminist and human rights platforms have often professionalized social movements but have failed in making any real impact at the level of cultural change. The socially transformative campaign envisioned by Naripokkho was gradually being superseded by one geared toward helping individuals themselves to transcend their own situations. UNICEF staffers' recommendation to include the necessity of EMDR for acid violence survivors without fully understanding the different context in which counseling occurred in Bangladesh, indicate the international organization's limitation in inspiring meaningful social transformation.

International agencies like UNICEF suffer from bureaucratic limitations as well as unexamined eurocentrism. For example, the reason that EMDR featured so prominently in the UNICEF response to acid attacks is because this work to mobilize resources for acid violence survivors was undertaken by its Health Sector. Had it been assigned to the Rights Cluster it may have been better suited to assist in developing a broader and more social vision.

Another limitation was UNICEF's framing of the acid work within the Beijing Platform's mandate on protecting the rights of the "girl child," which initiated a separate category for girls from women, based however, on western understandings of childhood versus adulthood. I do not mean to undermine the importance of the recognition of the category, "girl child" in the Beijing Platform as it reflected the excellent work done by the participants in analyzing the gendered relations of social inequalities, and certainly opened up avenues for focused social mobilization, and attention to the gendered process of development and human rights policy implementation. Nonetheless, such a category also carried certain assumptions and values, which did not always recognize context specific realities with regard to women and girls.

In a paper investigating the relationship of gender violence to the rights of the girl child, an area of concern identified in the 1995 Beijing Platform of Action commissioned by UNICEF, Cathy Falvo writes:

> [B]ased on UNICEF definitions of the women and of the girl-child, the well-being of women and of girl children overlap. A child is anyone eighteen years of age or younger—yet a girl becomes a woman when she is married (in places this maybe as young as 10 or 12) or when she becomes pregnant (officially the reproductive age of females starts at 15 but in actuality often starts earlier). . . . Thus any discussion of VAW [Violence Against Women] must include the girl-child within the meaning of woman. (Falvo, 1997, p. 1)

UNICEF's entry into the area of gender violence was through a limited focus on the "girl-child," a factor that may have influenced Naripokkho to focus on adolescents and young women in their workshop. They knew to shape the campaign to the current donor priorities, which happened to be the "girl-child," following the recent U.N. conference and its mandates being implemented in Bangladesh. Falvo's paper goes on to say:

> The aspects of VAW in which UNICEF actually becomes involved should be based on a number of considerations: what is the relevance to the health of children, what is the magnitude of the problem both worldwide and in a given locale, what ways is the issue already being addressed whether by UNICEF or other organizations, and whether or not UNICEF staff in an area have the ability or interest to address the issue along with all the other work they are doing. (Falvo, 1997, p. 3)

Thus, the kinds of services the UNICEF office in Dhaka was most invested in reflected the larger international organization's own agenda, as distinct from that of the local activists. UNICEF's interest was to enter the discussion on gender violence through a health perspective and to focus primary attention on the girl child. This point is best demonstrated through an e-mail exchange between two members of the UNICEF staff, discussing a request for support by the Obstetrical and Gynecological Society of Bangladesh (OGSB), during the time of my consultancy. The e-mail exchanges I share below copied me, and were forwarded to me respectively by UNICEF staff to assist in my research on the topic. The OGSB was interested in conducting a study on violence cases at DMCH, and to train staff there on appropriate care for victims of violence. The e-mail exchange is as follows:

> I think this is fantastic in the sense that they have themselves initiated to work on violence against women and they are definitely in charge of the process! From UNICEF they want (except from funding) a focal point on violence who can attend meetings together with them, give advice, provide material on violence and suggest resource persons for seminars, training etc. . . . I see this as another opportunity for UNICEF to address violence using the health system as the entry point. (Anonymous e, e-mail communication, August 6, 1998)

The enthusiasm emanating from the e-mail is both about linking gender violence to health, and the initiating of the work by "local" agents (referred to as "they"). The response to the e-mail from another senior official at UNICEF read:

> Good initiative. Please make sure that we provide THE VERY BEST IDEAS about BEST PRACTICES, PEOPLE AND PRODUCTS, from the world at large. Please use the resources such as unifem, global women's organizations, our own hqs [headquarter's] gender group, INTERNET, etc. I am concerned that we are going around in a very, very small little circle, missing the enormous amount of experience already available. Of course I do agree that we need to have it be a Bangladeshi process as well— BUT NOT ONE THAT IGNORES WORLD EXPERIENCE. That is precisely what UNICEF CAN ADD. (Anonymous f, e-mail communication, August 6, 1998, emphasis in the original)

This exchange occurred roughly around the same time that Naripokkho and UNICEF were going through negotiations to develop a joint response to acid violence. The timing helps us understand UNICEF's approach to gender violence, not only through the lens of health but also as distinguished from "local" initiatives. UNICEF sought to position itself in the role of a global provider of ideas, practices, and products. Similarly, in its response to acid attacks, UNICEF decided that EMDR (a global/western response) was the best "solution" to a "local" problem. It was as the repository of "expert" knowledge that they could provide aid to Bangladeshi victims of violence. In both their response to acid attacks and the discussion on the appropriate response to the OGSB request, the conceptual separation of the local and global actors into distinct and hierarchical realms of "recipient" and "provider," is presumptuous if not downright arrogant.

The anti–acid violence campaign had to be packaged conceptually in the specific areas of violence under consideration globally per the Beijing Platform, which included domestic violence, sexual violence, trafficking in sex and domestic workers, and female genital mutilation. This also partially explains Naripokkho's narrow focus on cases of sexual and domestic violence without broader attention to other kinds of disputes and conflicts, which were equally responsible for large numbers of attacks in Bangladesh at the time. All of the workshop participants had been attacked as a result of unrequited love, and unmet dowry demands, emphasizing the extent to which local organizing like that of Naripokkho can be shaped by international humanitarian aid priorities.

UNICEF's strategy was not only limited by its endorsement of EMDR as a "quick fix" solution to deal with victims of violence, and by responding only to the funding priorities of the moment (for instance, working within the category of the girl child), but this limitation spilled into other areas of campaign building as well. For instance, midway through the consultancy, the consulting team was instructed to set aside research on existing services (or lack thereof), and instead focus on interviewing 500 survivors of acid violence around the country to develop a database of information on their needs. Those interviews would then lay the groundwork for program development. No doubt this was a worthy proposal, but the practicality of developing a network of 500 far-flung survivors within a month was highly unrealistic given the time and resource-bound parameters of the consultancy. Moreover, such groundwork, albeit on a smaller scale, already existed due to the early research conducted by Naripokkho activists. If successfully done, building on Naripokkho's initial research would have been beneficial for overall organizing around gender violence, because presumably more stories of the kind collected by the activists would have made clear the systemic connections between acid attacks and other forms of gender violence and, therefore, facilitated a broader approach to confront it.

Honor Ford-Smith (1997) has written about the tendency of aid agencies in developing countries to fund short-term projects that will produce quick and measurable results. Starting with the questions, "Measurable by whom?" and, "By whose standards?" she comments: "Essentially, agencies wanted to know that their funding criteria had been met. The people who were presumably being served had little input in evaluating the achievements of the project; they had even less say in establishing the criteria for evaluation" (Ford-Smith, 1997, 232). Finding 500 acid-burned girls and providing them with rehabilitative care would have satisfied the funder's criteria of offering measurable solutions quickly. However, it contradicted the earlier survivor-centered strategy developed by Naripokkho, which focused on the individual and collective empowerment of survivors as leaders in their own struggle in the acid campaign. The activists had envisioned a society, where women would have access to services and resources, the ability to make informed decisions, and the power to self-determine their own economic and *social* choices. The programs designed by the activists sought to make this vision a reality.

In the initial stages of organizing, senior Naripokkho members had been reluctant to launch an anti-acid campaign precisely because of the lack of an existing discourse through which to frame the issue. In the spectrum of the types of violence committed against women in Bangladesh, such as rape, abduction, murder, and dowry killings, the numbers of acid attacks were at the time, as they still are, comparatively low. This fact worked both for and against mobilizing attention to the campaign. The workshop, by focusing on the vulnerability of the young women and showcasing their trauma, and choosing to emphasize those cases of acid attacks related to rejection of love and sexual advances, certainly made use of familiar narratives of "third world horrors" to garner support. At the same time, by delinking acid violence from broader questions of gender inequality and connecting systematically with other organizations mobilizing against gender violence, Naripokkho lost the opportunity to develop a more broad-based movement against women's oppression. This point was made to me in 2003, by the executive director of a leading human rights legal aid organization in Bangladesh. When I explained my reason for visiting their organization's library, she said somewhat cynically, "Oh, your research is on acid attacks! Yes, that is the current hot topic in the donor circles." Ironically, it was the organizing done by Naripokkho—also an influential women's organization in Bangladesh—that had set in motion the framing and consequent chain of events in this ever-changing campaign.

The second stage of the acid campaign thus emerged through the appearance of UNICEF among the diversifying set of actors. A combination of Naripokkho's successful efforts in conceptualizing acid violence as a national and international gendered violence issue, along with the U.N. headquarter's decision to act on what by the late 1990s had begun to be perceived by an international audience to be a violation of women's human rights, had set in motion the creation of the Acid Survivors Foundation in Bangladesh. Naripokkho strategically and successfully mobilized international actors including UNICEF to bring the acid campaign onto the scene of an international discourse on gendered violence. However, the choices that the new and often more influential international actors made were at times contradictory to those that would have been made if the local women's groups had been participants in decision making, as well as ill-conceived to meet the reality on the ground. This is particularly clearly exemplified by the decision to invest in EMDR for survivors, a decision that was neither made collectively with local partners nor shaped with a farsighted strategy. Moreover, the proliferation of actors also resulted in Naripokkho's own diminished role in shaping the dominant narrative of the campaign, which until then had made central the experiences of the survivors of violence. The alliance with a strong and powerful organization like UNICEF broadened the scope of the campaign and opened up access to resources previously unavailable, but at the same time it led to the loss of Naripokkho's critical vision for moving the campaign forward to deal with broader social justice issues.

The Consolidation of ASF

On March 8, 2003, International Women's Day, the Acid Survivors Foundation organized a rally at the Dhaka Press Club that brought together 200 survivors from around the country, along with representatives of the state, civil society, and donor community. It was a remarkable gathering, and was covered by Bangladesh Television and print media. The organizers of this event constituted a new landscape in the anti–acid violence campaign. By the spring of 2003, the leadership of the anti–acid violence campaign had shifted squarely to ASF.

The transitioning of the campaign activities to ASF was not seamless. Some scholars of social movements have theorized that campaigns are often catalyzed when sufficient financial means to organize and propagandize have been secured. However, in her cautionary study of women organizing in contemporary Russia, Valerie Sperling (1999) has noted that although aid from foreign sources can provide crucial support for social movement organizing in developing countries, at the same time it can exacerbate divisiveness within and between national and local groups, as well as unduly influence the priorities and agenda of those groups (Sperling, 1999, p. 220). In the case of the institutionalization of the anti–acid violence campaign in Bangladesh into the ASF, financial resources came primarily from western donors such as UNICEF and CIDA, but neither without strings attached nor without serious ramifications for the shape of the campaign.

In 1999, on its creation, ASF became the coordinating organization providing services for acid attack survivors. In spite of the contradictory outcome I will discuss below, I emphasize that the establishment of an umbrella organization such as ASF by UNICEF must be commended. Over the years, it has made important headway in the campaign, and from the beginning the organization was conscientious about incorporating local organizers into its leadership. With the exception of the donors, an Italian NGO and the British High Commission, the remaining eight members of the Board of Trustees at the time of its founding were then prominent Bangladeshi nationals and NGO representatives. One of its most noteworthy achievements was to lobby with the government to pass new and more stringent laws, namely, the Acid Crime Prevention Law 2002, and the Acid Control Law 2002, to enable the prosecution of perpetrators of acid violence and more effectively to criminalize the sale of corrosive substances without a license. ASF has also appeared to have adopted (or co-opted, some might say) Naripokkho's strategy of placing survivors and their experiences in the center of their programs—although its critics say this value appears more in the organization's rhetoric than its actual practice.

When ASF was first founded it primarily provided medical and rehabilitative services. It opened a thirty-five-bed nursing center and shelter home, Thikana House, as well as a surgical center, Jibon Tara, named after a woman who had died as a result of an acid attack. Over the years it has also developed legal, research, and most recently prevention units. The five units work together in assisting survivors along the recovery process. John Morrison, the first executive director of ASF, said at its founding in 1999 that effort must be made to make acid survivors into "productive and effective citizens of the country" ("All They Need," 1999).

The process of appointing John Morrison as ASF's first executive director was curious. The following e-mail message, forwarded to me by a UNICEF staff member, described Morrison's position in Bangladesh:

John Morrison is a British academic who is an accompanying DFID spouse. Because of the interest in Britain and the rest of Europe raised by a recent BBC TV item, the Embassy was contacted and he is the unofficial focal point for a couple of initiatives:

- An offer by the British Rotary Club to contribute ten thousand pounds for the burns unit
- An offer by a British plastic surgeon with contacts in Bdesh to visit and work here with national surgeons
- A very generous offer by a team of Spanish plastic surgeons to treat some 30 acid victims. Obviously, the airfares, living expenses and other expenses will have to be met by others—the surgery is free
- John is interested in linking up with any other initiatives but is more interested in getting something done than attending many meetings. (Anonymous g, e-mail communication, June 23, 1998)

Another UNICEF staff member wrote, "I found Mr. Morrison an extremely dedicated person whose 'vision' is to set up a foundation NGO for quality treatment of the acid survivors. The CIDA office has offered him a full time consultancy post here in Dhaka and is also willing to provide technical and financial assistance. I suggest that we introduce him to our group and see how best we could work together" (Anonymous h, e-mail communication, July 23, 1998). This exchange suggests that Morrison was not chosen to direct ASF primarily because he had the credentials to do so (knowledge of local context, gender violence, familiarity and relationships with key institutions, etc.). Rather, his appointment was the result of his interest in "getting something done." (We might ask, among the many players involved, including local organizations, who wasn't interested in the same?) Additionally, he happened to be a British national with strong international connections. These attributes might have seemed to make him eminently suitable to the funders for such a high-profile position, it appears, while none of the local organizers who had contributed to the development of the anti–acid violence campaign are mentioned in the e-mail as having been considered. The dates of these e-mail exchanges also allude to the fact that discussions to appoint Morrison as the executive director of the then-planned Acid Survivors Foundation were underway as early as June, when our research consultancy to determine its various parameters did not end until August; and, that these discussions were internal to UNICEF but not with the local NGO activists.

Morrison's appointment as ASF's first executive director begs for a postcolonial feminist analysis pointing to the co-optation of a campaign originally mobilized by women, by the neocolonial agents of humanitarian aid; once again we are reminded of the script of "White men are saving brown women from brown men" (Spivak, 1994, p. 92). Additionally, it is a moment that reveals what Gayatri Spivak also calls "the crucial instrumentality of woman as symbolic object of exchange" (Landry and Maclean, 1996, p. 227) within patriarchal transactions. Ironically, in the name of solidarity with "native women," the U.N. agency, in its neocolonial administrator role, passes the baton to the white male "expert."

The ASF came to fruition in a context where many NGOs were vying for attention and resources from international aid organizations, particularly in the area of gender-based oppression. In a conversation with UNICEF team members in 1998, I was told that the proposal to establish the foundation would be submitted to fifteen donor agencies nationally and internationally and that it would be a "big budget" initiative administered by private sector organizations and NGOs. The involvement of the government of Bangladesh was to be limited because of their apparent "corruptibility," bureaucracy, and intransigence. It is understandable that UNICEF would have frustrations regarding the state's instability. Nearly all of the state representatives who had been so thoughtfully approached by Naripokkho for the 1997 workshop, and who had made numerous promises to assist in the campaign, were no longer in positions to do so, because of the election of a new party to power. Yet, organizations like the U.N. and other foreign donors could hardly bypass the state completely in forming a major initiative such as the ASF, in the interest of the new organization's own sustainability and transparency. It is ironic that the so-called corruption of the state was such a big concern for this donor community when their own process for appointing the first executive director had been, to all appearances, less than open.

In another instance, I encountered this issue of donors not held to similar standards of accountability as their patrons. In the course of my research in 1998, I discovered that the British Rotary Club had donated medical instruments worth 10,000 pounds to Bangladesh in order to treat acid burned patients, not all of which were actually suitable for this kind of treatment. Western institutions perhaps unwittingly end up using the aid recipient countries as dumping ground for excess materials that may or may not be suitable for the specific cause they are supporting. Further, I found that some of this equipment was subsequently being sold to burn patients by a private organization, whereas the intent of the donation was to provide, not profit from, these materials.

By delinking the ASF from the government and mass-based movements of gender justice, the international donor organizations behind ASF risked depoliticizing the anti-acid campaign and even creating friction and competition among organizations working on gender oppression. A prime example of this was the tension between the director of a leading NGO providing affordable health care to the poor, and UNICEF. This director was an active member of the anti-acid campaign, who had approached various donors for assistance to develop a national plan to treat all burns—not just acid burns. His initiative would have involved building more facilities to house patients and to develop the capacity of medical professionals locally for all kinds of burns, including those occurring accidentally because of the increasing use of kerosene operated stoves in Bangladesh. Women were the primary victims of such burns, which actually occurred in higher numbers than acid burns. But his proposal did not meet with much interest from the donors, possibly because it did not have the same kind of resonance as a facility dedicated to acid burns, a "third world horror" carried out by brutish patriarchal men against *their* women.[16]

ASF's primary objective as stated in 2002 was: "To provide on-going assistance in the treatment, rehabilitation and reintegration into society of survivors of acid violence by identifying and improving existing services and to also work to prevent further acid throwing attacks." In the same document their mission is described as: "To aid the recovery of acid violence survivors to a condition as near as possible to that of their premature [previous] situation by providing treatment, rehabilitation, counseling and other support during their reintegration into society and afterwards. Simultaneously the Foundation will work to prevent further acid violence in Bangladesh" (Acid Survivors Foundation Website, 2002). To facilitate in the "reintegration" of survivors into society by returning them to a "condition as near as possible to that of their premature situation" seems a gross injustice in representing the process a survivor experiences post–acid attack. Rarely is a "return" possible even in the most insignificant of ways. This idea of reintegration of a survivor into the very society that sanctions acid violence is more damaging than supportive.

Through ASF's rehabilitation unit survivors are routinely "reintegrated" into society through training for clerical and service positions, or through being set up with micro–business ventures. This model of "rehabilitation" as Veronica Schild (2002) points out in a critique of development policies pursued by international agencies in the global South, assume "women need to be helped to develop their potential so that they can solve their problems themselves" (p. 185). These neoliberal development initiatives operate with the assumption that "helping" women is best achieved through integrating them into the "productive machinery of the state." It is not clear however, whether women's insertion in the productive machinery of the state as active economic agents translates into their meaningful participation in society.

Veronica Schild (2002), drawing on a term used by Marguerite Berger, chief of the Women and Development Unit at the Inter-American Bank, calls the women who are the subjects of such development ventures "reluctant entrepreneurs." She points out that many women participate in the income-generating and skills-training economic development programs out of a lack of alternatives they would genuinely prefer. These reluctant entrepreneurs, however, are reconfigured by the development agencies as "empowered clients," individuals viewed as capable of enhancing their own lives merely through making judicious, responsible choices. Schild characterizes this shift in development discourse as exemplary of new ways by which international elites govern subordinate populations. Similarly, in the case of social programs for acid survivors, one needs to ask whether the survivors' reintegration into society translates into meaningful participation and whether they are choosing to enter such positions given a lack in the range of possibilities.

Time and again during my research I was told by survivors and their family members that they felt there were no meaningful options for them. Bristi Chowdhury's (1997) research on the first years of the anti-acid campaign noted that most survivors wanted to continue their education or find meaningful employment, both of which were often dauntingly difficult because of the social stigma and public rejection of women victims. In the absence of programs that envision structural change, the survivors at best can be viewed as reluctant entrepreneurs as they are placed in service sector jobs or forced to remain at home without education or work prospects. Some young women were even married off to the same men who had attacked them in arrangements brokered between the two families, whereby the victim's family would withdraw the charges for a trial if the attacker would marry her. For families, such a solution might bring relief from the fear that their daughter would remain unmarried forever because of her disfigured face.

Nicoletta Del Franco (1999) observed that the main activities of ASF in its first years were giving financial and medical help to some survivors through a network that involved UNICEF, NGOs, and hospitals. Although she characterized the role of ASF in 1999 somewhat ironically as a "savior giving new hope and life" to survivors, she also acknowledged that this approach continues to stigmatize acid survivors as "victims deprived forever of their main roles as mothers and wives" (Del Franco, 1999, p. 16).

Thus, ASF provided services to integrate survivors into development programs without disrupting gender inequities or confronting systemic and institutional gender discriminatory practices and values contributing to gendered abuse. Critical explorations of the implications of a gender justice agenda as propagated by such models of social provisioning clearly show the very narrow range of possibilities for translating women's needs and demands into social action. As Veronica Schild has said, "Indeed, in the present context, this rights-based agenda, as implemented in practice, seems to be more a tool for a hierarchical and exclusionary project of social integration which is functional to the 'modernization' restructuring project more generally, than it is a means for enabling the meaningful citizenship of the majority of poor women" (Schild, 2002, p. 198). "Meaningful citizenship" can only emerge from development programs that ensure survivors economic and social access to services and resources and power to determine their own choices while simultaneously questioning those hierarchical structures and institutions that allow gendered abuse.

In more recent years, ASF has undergone some changes in its approach, which now involves survivors in shaping programs geared to serve them. In part, this change can be attributed to the recruitment in the first decade of the new century of several key staff of Naripokkho who had been involved in the Naripokkho-led anti–acid violence campaign in the mid-1990s. ASF's Referral, Legal, and Medical Unit coordinators are now former Naripokkho staff, who are well aware of gendered social hierarchies. According to Nasreen Huq, who has served as a board member for ASF, the presence of Naripokkho members in ASF provides continuity and has made a difference in shaping and influencing its agenda (N. Huq, personal communication, April 11, 2003).

Ultimately, though, ASF's vision has to be contextualized within larger debates on welfarist and neoliberal development visions in women's empowerment. Meghna Guhathakurta (1994) characterizes the development discourse on women in Bangladesh as primarily concerned with economic growth or welfare schemes and enacting "peaceful" change. This discourse excludes conflict, struggle, and resistance. Rather, it targets in a piecemeal manner a specific group of women, thus isolating and depoliticizing the issue at hand. In this way, acid survivors are pathologized as victims in need of rehabilitation and reintegration into society. Calling this strategy welfarist, says Nicoletta Del Franco (1999), it lacks a long-term vision because it does not recognize the need for change of the social system. At the same time, we recognize neoliberal tendencies in ASF's initiatives as it strives to "empower" individual survivors by channeling them into service activities without an attendant deeper focus on social transformation. Admittedly, the recent changes in ASF's staffing and practices have shown the beginnings of a more rigorous and systemic approach as exemplified by its lobbying with the government for appropriate legal redress. Nonetheless, many of its practices remain limited, continuing to track young women into "productive" citizenship programs.

Subverting the Development Discourse

One should not underestimate the importance of the services provided by an umbrella organization like the Acid Survivors Foundation. The creation of such a coordinated body of services reflects the achievement of the evolving campaign against acid violence in Bangladesh. Naripokkho activists acted as part of a larger women's movement in Bangladesh, and thus the conceptualization and organization of the acid campaign was enabled within a movement ideology. Yet ASF, on the other hand, did not emerge directly from a larger movement, but rather was only facilitated by it. It is limited in its vision by its structural location as a local NGO funded by international development organizations that subscribe to a mission that replicates a neocolonial vision of women's empowerment.

James Ferguson (1994) has said that mainstream development discourse falsely presumes international agencies, the state, or both to be the deliverers of benevolent and empowering interventions to the oppressed classes. Alternatively, he characterizes international development agencies and the state as "guardians of local and global hegemony" (Ferguson, 1994, p. 284). Their interventions, he posits, often facilitate the suppression of radical and grassroots forms of action initiated by those identified as requiring the intervention. In the early days of ASF, in particular, while grassroots forms of activism may not have been directly suppressed, events leading to its formation certainly points to the supplanting of local visions by those mandated as more important by international organizations.

External donors are seldom well positioned to be movement instigators, and thus the position and activities of ASF were, in its initial stages, incompatible with those of movement activists. ASF staffers' efforts, however, have generated multiple and contradictory discourses and narratives. Because ASF's birth was catalyzed by the groundwork laid by the activists of Naripokkho, many of whom are currently in leadership positions within ASF, they have made not insignificant contributions to the organization's evolving strategies and success stories. Some of the noteworthy developments within ASF include collaborating with influential national NGOs such as Bangladesh Rural Action Committee (BRAC) to disseminate educational materials on gendered violence and to monitor progress of survivors nationwide; conducting research in various districts on existing legal aid services; lobbying the government on behalf of drafting and passage of new laws against the unregulated sale of acid, as well as its violent use; advocating for government action to set up a National Acid Council and Special Tribunal overseeing speedy investigation of cases and speedy trial processing; and providing improved medical care and reconstructive surgery to survivors.

One of the more creative programs being developed by ASF's Prevention Unit includes community-based focus groups to raise awareness on the grassroots level across the nation. Two particularly innovative strategies have involved training survivors to lead the focus groups, and to enact dramatic performances of their own stories. These traveling theater productions have challenged societal perceptions of "acid victims" and encouraged women's articulation of their own stories. This harkens back to the original 1997 workshop, which featured both theater and participation of women in public spaces. Following one such performance in 2003, a group of youth in the community had spontaneously painted a mural expressing resistance to acid throwing (M. Huq, personal communication, April 14, 2003). Such grassroots efforts have the potential to mobilize participation across diverse social groups. Although commendable, such innovative organizing efforts remain sporadic and marginal to the Foundation's mainstream activities, due to lack of sustained funding and focus. More problematically, although ASF presents its strategy as survivor centered, there is no indication of any survivor's actual participation in decision-making processes. The organization remains rooted in a development approach, which is both welfarist and neoliberal as it views survivors as recipients of services who are in need of rehabilitation and reintegration into society in order to be made "productive citizens." Although the Foundation currently states that one of their objectives is, "[To] bring about long term change in attitudes and values that sanction and contribute to violent activities, particularly against women," their actual policies, spanning predominantly the medical and legal arenas with little emphasis on the social, do not adequately reflect such a vision (Acid Survivor's Foundation, "Introduction").

Admittedly, the newly developed Prevention Unit promises to do so but is constrained by project-based short-term funding options. For instance, training young women for service positions in the name of "rehabilitation and reintegration" does not amount to changing societal values and attitudes toward women as victims. This is a means to channel the socially marginalized and the "deviant," in this case poor young women who are perceived as "damaged and disfigured," into the productive machinery of the state. Chandra Mohanty urges the making visible of gender and power in such processes of global restructuring for naming the particular raced and classed communities of women as they are framed as, in this case, "productive citizens," and thereby routinely channeled into service industries (Mohanty, 2003, pp. 246–48). Kriemild Saunders (2002) has characterized this process, whereby the victimized woman figure in the South becomes incorporated into a progress narrative, as one that rationalizes the planned management and liberation of women in the South by the international development apparatus.

Having major donors like UNICEF and CIDA certainly makes ASF resource-secure, but ASF does not replicate Naripokkho's guiding vision and long-term strategies to empower women on their own terms while systematically challenging the socially sanctioned crime of acid throwing. As ASF took over coordinating services for acid violence victims, the grassroots and local feminist vision of Naripokkho was largely lost. Thus, the story of ASF's development on the base created originally by Naripokkho has implications for understanding local women's groups' relation to transnational feminist politics.

Conclusion

Indubitably, there is a need to expand our theoretical understanding both of local women's organizing and of the contexts in which they operate. In the case of Bangladesh, a complicated national and transnational web, involving a diverse set of actors, redefined acid violence against women as a gendered crime and helped create medical and legal responses to benefit its survivors. Although transnational funding was crucial to the campaign's organizational growth, international donors also brought with them welfarist rehabilitation programs and imposed imported and experimental therapy programs of dubious benefit to survivors.

In her discussion of the campaign, Bristi Chowdhury has pointed out that promoting dependency on international aid agencies, given the abdication of the state in providing adequate social services, was a key failure of the campaign (B. Chowdhury, personal communication, March 7, 2003). After all, western funding is impermanent, and a domestic funding base will ultimately be necessary if local women's organizing efforts are to attain sustainability. Nonetheless, through the creation of ASF, Naripokkho was able to use the international and national organizations to write a new chapter in transnational feminist organizing.

The self-validating progress narrative of ASF does not allow for women to be seen as complex subjects in agency and in struggle. Under the rhetoric of service for victimized women, ASF's programs promise that rehabilitation will promote social reintegration and economic independence for acid survivors, and clerical jobs will be conducive to their becoming "productive citizens," enhancing the society as a whole. However, this welfarist rhetoric fails to consider the incongruities of such programs with the lived experiences of women receiving them. Rather than promoting real empowerment, however, ASF's programs freeze recipients within discourses of victimization.

While one cannot undermine the assistance Promila Shabdakor acquired from ASF in getting her life together after the acid attack, simple narratives such as "I did not want to live. ASF inspired me to look at my child and family. Please all of you pray for me to sustain" does not show the array of roles and activities that constitute Promila Shabdakor (Acid Survivor's Foundation, 2003). Similar representations are plentiful in ASF's website. When phrased in these terms, acid survivors are constructed as super-beings who are inherently capable of overcoming the entire weight of their "rehabilitation" pending their ASF disbursement. It places much of the responsibility on the individual level rather than structural level. It reinscribes the survivors as poor and socially marginalized women in need of help from an organization such as the ASF, who in turn, is validated for its benevolence. This narrative creates a divide between "false overstated images of victimized and empowered womanhood, which negate each other" (Mohanty 2003, p. 248). In the discourse of ASF, acid survivors remain in a secondary space. Perhaps the future of the campaign lies in the rejuvenation of its initial broader movement-based agenda, which would require building and strengthening careful alliances with diverse social groups not the least of which are local grassroots communities with a vision to transform women's meaningful participation as full citizens in social, political, and economic aspects of society.

Chapter Two

Local Realities of
Acid Violence in Bangladesh

I first met Nurun Nahar in April 1997, at the Naripokkho Office in Dhan-mondi, Dhaka. I was there to interview survivors of acid attacks for a cover story to appear in the *Star Weekend Magazine*, the weekly publication of the English-language daily newspaper the *Daily Star*, for which I was a writer. Naripokkho had just hosted the three-day workshop (discussed in chapter 1), which publicized the growing phenomenon of acid violence against women and girls in Bangladesh, and had invited important state and non–state actors to listen to the stories of a group of adolescent girls. These girls, all teenagers and survivors of acid attacks, narrated their stories at a gathering of state representatives, doctors, lawyers, journalists, and international aid workers. Naripokkho activists believed and hoped that this remarkable event would catalyze a movement to systematically address the needs of survivors of acid violence as well as redress the structures of oppression sanctioning gendered violence in Bangladesh.

It was my work as a journalist that first introduced me to Nurun Nahar as well as to activists of Naripokkho. Since then, I have been variably involved with this campaign in a number of capacities. As the campaign developed and grew so did my relationships with the women centrally located within it. The previous chapter mapped the multiple and evolving narratives of the anti-acid campaign from the perspectives of Naripokkho, UNICEF, and the Acid Survivors Foundation. It provided a window into the various steps, difficulties, and complexities in the process of transnational organizing. This chapter provides a more detailed picture of the realities of acid violence in the domestic context of Bangladesh, as well as the critical interventions under-taken by state, NGO, and the women's movement. Here I offer an analysis of the challenges facing these multiple players to provide more insight into why they made the decisions they did. I feature Nurun Nahar's story, which she narrated to me over several interviews spanning multiple years. Her story offers a glimpse into the realities surrounding survivors as well as responses to acid violence in Bangladesh.

In 1995, when Nurun Nahar was a student of Class X (secondary school, equivalent of "tenth grade") in Bogra Union Madhyomik Biddaloy, a young college student named Jasim Sikdar professed his love for her. When Nahar refused his proposals, he began harassing her on the way to school. In the middle of the night on July 27, 1995, Sikdar and a group of his friends broke into Nahar's house while she slept beside her mother and younger sister. Sikdar and some of his friends dragged Nurun Nahar out of bed while others held her family members at gunpoint. Sikdar drew a bottle of acid from his pocket and poured it on Nahar's face. She fought back and in the process some of the acid fell on her hands and on those of her captors. After Sikdar and his friends ran away, her family and some neighbors tried to clean Nahar's wounds with Dettol antiseptic liquid, not realizing that the corrosive substance eating away her skin and flesh was sulfuric acid. Some neighbors went to get the village doctor, who refused to visit her in person out of fear of the perpetrators but advised her family to wash her wounds with water, give her some pain medicine, and take her to the nearest town for medical treatment.

The next morning, Nahar's family made the trip by boat and bus to the nearest hospital in Barisal. By the time they reached the hospital in the afternoon, Nahar had lost consciousness. She remained in this hospital for three days before being transferred to a hospital in Dhaka, the capital city, ten hours away. There she remained in the Orthopedic (Pongu) Hospital for eight months and underwent a series of operations.

Three days after the attack, Nurun Nahar's mother filed a police report in their village. The police would not accept the case without a doctor's certificate, which took another three days to acquire. By this time, the perpetrators had absconded. Meanwhile, Nahar's family had contacted both Naripokkho and the media to intervene in the case. It was this particular case, and meeting with Nahar and her family, Nasreen Huq later told me, that catalyzed into action Naripokkho's campaign against acid violence. Because of the subsequent publicity, the police responded and threatened to oust Jasim Sikdar's family from the village and seize his associates' property unless they handed themselves in. Several months later, Sikdar and his associates surrendered to the police, although their relatives continued to threaten Nurun Nahar's family to drop charges against them. A year after the case was filed, two men, including Sikdar, received death sentences, and three of the men were given life-terms in prison.[1] The convicted men have since appealed the sentences in the High Court. Legislation implemented by the Women and Child Repression Control Act of 1995, even prior to the anti-acid campaign's advocacy, already set the death penalty as the maximum penalty for acid attackers. This legislation enabled Nahar's lawyers to ask for the maximum sentence. As we have seen in chapter 1, ASF's lobbying led to the creation of further laws to criminalize the sale of acid. All of these legislations, however, seems to have little effect in the absence of broader social and economic opportunities for women's empowerment.

When Nurun Nahar returned home, she was uncomfortable with the attention from the people in the village. Yet she returned to school and passed her Secondary School Certificate Examinations, after which she moved to Dhaka and enrolled in college. She rented a room in a women's hostel, and worked part-time in Naripokkho alongside Bina Akhter to develop a national network of acid survivors. During this time, as the acid campaign gained momentum, Nahar underwent eye movement desensitization and reprocessing, the then-experimental therapeutic treatment for posttraumatic stress disorder that was sponsored by UNICEF-Bangladesh and provided by a team of experts from the United States (discussed at greater length in chapter 1). Then, in 1999, Nahar was part of a group of young women, sponsored by the Spanish government, who went to Spain for reconstructive surgeries. Since her return, Nahar has worked for a number of NGOs in Dhaka. At present she is involved in promoting acid prevention work with an international NGO, ActionAid in Bangladesh.

Nahar's story illuminates the gaps in services such as the medical and legal establishments, which obstructed and delayed the survivors from receiving adequate care. The health care services and professionals at the *thana* level (smaller local units) were not properly trained in caring for acid burns.[2] Although Nahar's family could well afford health care in their own district, the doctor did not know how to help her. In fact, he refused to see her at her home because he was afraid that he would end up a target of the offenders. Inadequate infrastructure led to delaying her arrival to the city and on arrival she had to wait days before admission into the hospital. During the eight months she spent at the Orthopedic (Pongu) Hospital, her mother and aunt alternated staying with her. The length and cost of care drained her family's finances, but because her case received high publicity as a result of Naripokkho's advocacy efforts, Nahar's family was able to secure some state and private funds. Other acid violence survivors in similar situations have not always had this same access to funding.

Legal services also provided obstacles to swift and efficient help for
Nahar. It took three days for her family to be able to file a court case
since the police would not accept a case before Nahar's family was able to
provide a doctor's certificate. This allowed the main culprit, Jasim Sikdar,
ample time to flee, which he did—to India. In fact, Nahar's family believed
that the perpetrators' families bribed the police not to accept the case. The
group of men who attacked Nahar already had a reputation in their village
as *mastaan* who regularly terrorized the public. They obviously wielded influence because the night of the attack they had a gun, which suggests ties to
powerful members of the community who maintain gangs. Clearly, these men
believed that they would get away with the crime because of their political
influence in the village. Nahar's family was persistently threatened by the
offenders' families in the months ensuing, to the extent that her mother had
to sleep in their neighbor's house and Nahar's younger sister left the village
altogether. Moreover, once the perpetrators were sentenced (the police ultimately had to cooperate because of the high profile of the case as a result
of Naripokkho's intervention), they immediately appealed to the High Court
to overturn the ruling. This bought them and their families more time to
plot threats against Nahar's family.

Nahar's story also shows how little her family or community knew
about dealing with acid burns. The immediate hours after the attack at her
home were filled with confusion. It was not commonly known prior to the
campaign against acid violence that pouring water—rather than the Dettol
used by the family to wash Nahar's wounds—would have diminished the
acid-inflicted damage. Only later did women's organizations begin to disseminate such information to the public.

Similarly, her story shows that at the time of Nahar's attack, public
perceptions of the women who were attacked were that they were somehow
deserving of violence, and these ideas led to the further victimization of
the survivors. For instance a young woman at the hospital who was sharing
Nahar's room maligned Nahar's character to her face and held her responsible
for provoking the attack. Moreover, when Nahar returned to her community
after the long months of treatment in Dhaka, she was made to feel like an
outcast. It was the connection she had made with Naripokkho activists and
the nurturing environment they offered her that enabled Nahar to make the
decision to leave her village, Baufol, and move to Dhaka in order to further
her education, find a job, and work with other survivors of violence.

Although a concerted effort to address acid attacks by civil society, the
state, and international donor community is still in progress in Bangladesh,

systematic and institutional discrimination against women continues to make it difficult both to protect victims of acid violence adequately and to make available the kinds of support these women need. This discrimination can be seen at all levels of assistance sought by the survivors

For example, even on the level of legal and medical responses, problems remain. In cases of criminal violence, specialized rules of evidence collection are required by the justice system. Women must file a First Information Report (FIR) at the police station, receive the appropriate medicolegal authorization from a police magistrate, and then go to a state hospital for a medical exam. On many occasions, doctors have refused to examine a woman who has been assaulted without an order from the police station or a magistrate (Azim, 2001). Yet timing is critical for the collection of medical evidence. The medical institution, perhaps unwittingly, colludes with the perpetrators in delaying the procedure and thus allowing them more time to abscond. We certainly saw this happening in Nahar's case, when the police would not accept a case for three days unless a medical report could be submitted. It was also clear when both the local hospital could not treat her, and the local doctor refused to come, fearing the consequences.

The FIR is the first written account of the events and the circumstances of the alleged crime. Both the prosecution and the defense view it as a valuable legal document. Only after the FIR is issued is a woman authorized to undergo a medicolegal exam from a state hospital. Women are expected to take the medicolegal authorization to a state physician, have all injuries documented, and return the form to the police to be kept as evidence until the court date. Moreover, women must find their own transportation to a state clinic or hospital. This is particularly problematic for women living in rural areas because the nearest government clinic could be far away, and many women do not have the means or capacity to travel (Azim, 2001). In this context, producing a viable medical report seems difficult if not impossible.

The difficulty that Nahar had receiving decent services after her attack does not represent an isolated case but rather one that has been common for survivors of acid violence. Bina Akhter was treated poorly by DMCH staff after she was taken there in the middle of the night following her attack in August 1996. Since the burns unit did not have enough beds to accommodate her, she was given a place in the balcony outside the general ward. Even there, space was short and she was asked to take the bed of a woman who had recently died of severe burns. According to Bina, the staff did not even change the sheets of the bed before assigning it to her. Even at that state, Bina refused the bed before it was cleaned, and the staff put her in a trolley where she remained for days. The doctor did not appear until several hours later. When he did arrive he asked that her family purchase pain medicine because the hospital did not have any. They bought both her pain medicine and bandages, which were applied on her burns, not by the hospital staff but Bina's mother. When her family members complained after the doctor did not reappear for three days, the medical staff responded, "Why don't you perform your own surgery if you have so many requests?" (B. Akhter, personal communication, February 21, 1997). Throughout her several-month stay at the hospital, the dressing would be changed only when the family tipped the nurses and not otherwise. Bina pointed out, "Because I was poor, I wasn't of any value" (B. Akhter, personal communication, December 27–28, 2004). Without the financial means to pursue private facilities, acid survivors and their families have been routinely objected to medical maltreatment and emotional harassment.

At that time, the Dhaka Medical College Hospital was the biggest hospital in Bangladesh, occupying an area of 4,50,000 square feet in the heart of Dhaka city. It houses the most prestigious medical school in the country and the professors there are the senior doctors in the hospital. Although the sanctioned number of beds at DMCH is 800, including 582 general and 130 paying beds, because of heavy demand the number of total beds have been raised to 1,400 with attendant problems of congestion and unhygienic conditions. As a public facility, it caters mainly to people from low-income groups, and the majority of women survivors of violence who went there are from disadvantaged groups.

According to a research study by Naripokkho, when a poor patient with severe burn wounds objected to sharing a bed with another patient at DMCH, the attitude of the hospital authorities took a turn for the worse. Most of the women acid burn patients who were interviewed reported they were scared of the hospital staff, were frequently shouted at, and were treated badly (Azim, 2001). This report further notes that although the burns unit was supposed to have intensive care unit (ICU) conditions to protect the patients by limiting exposure to germs, such conditions were not maintained. Almost anybody could walk in, and the No Shoes sign on the door was routinely ignored by the doctors themselves.

During my own visits there in 1997 and 1998, I observed that the air-conditioning did not work. (It is worth noting that when a state minister announced he was visiting the facility, following the 1997 acid workshop, the air-conditioning was quickly repaired.) My conversations with the doctors of the burns unit revealed that they felt overworked and under a great deal of pressure (most had private practices in the evenings). They only had access to the operation theater twice a week, which caused delays in performing the sequence of operations required for the burns patients.

Difficulty getting adequate medical care for victims of gender violence was not limited to the survivors of acid attacks. A report available from the Ain O Salish Kendro, a legal aid group in Bangladesh, stated that gender bias was generally widespread within the medical profession. A case in point was a woman who worked in a garments factory and was gang raped and left in a ditch. This is an account of her experience when she finally managed to get to a hospital,

> In the hospital, the *ayahs* [nurse's aids] would not touch me. I heard that they do not touch "rape cases" unless they are bribed handsomely. A male doctor checked me while a female nurse was standing by. Later I came to know that I was in the emergency department of the medical college. Here the doctors asked me to go to a private doctor and wrote the address. At about 6:30 p.m. I went to that clinic. A woman doctor checked me there and gave me a prescription. When I went back to the police, I was told that I needed to be "treated" again tomorrow. The next day we went to the police station and from there to the medical college. This time they took me to the forensic department for yet another check-up. I started crying. "How many times do I have to go through this painful experience?" The doctor seemed very irritated and angry. "Why are you crying now? I know girls like you. You do this only to get money from the men. If you do not want it, how can it happen?" The doctor was telling the nurse that there was no indication of any injury on my body. The reports confirmed the same later. What was the use of going through so many tests if nothing could be proved? The rapists were all arrested except one. The case started. But I am told that the medical evidence is the most important, more than my own word. So I do not know what will be the result, and whether those men will be punished or not. (Matin et al., 2000, pp. 29–30)

This same study showed that crucial evidence was often lost as a result of needless delays in the production of medical reports (Matin et al., 2000). Women faced further delays in undergoing tests due to bureaucratic rules. For instance, one such rule asked that forensic tests only be conducted on the deposit of three passport-size photographs of the victim, attested by the officer in duty at the police station. In most cases, it was not possible for victims to produce these, or they were not duly signed or attested. Women's reluctance to undergo forensic tests was caused by the lack of women doctors. Furthermore, women doctors were reluctant to appear in court, where they would face unpleasant cross-examinations as witnesses. The study concluded that the recording of medical case histories and the collection of medical evidence remained inadequate, resulting in serious consequences for investigation of the cases for effective prosecution (Azim, 2001).

In an interview, Badrunnessa Khuku, the director of the Legal Unit at the Acid Survivors Foundation, pointed to the complicated process of seeking justice under the current judicial system. She said that the different groups involved in the process such as investigating police officers, court officials, medical officials, witnesses, and media representatives are often in conflict with one another. Instead of cooperating, they end up obstructing acid cases from moving forward. For instance, witnesses may be threatened or bribed by the accused and fail to appear in court. Medical professionals refuse to travel long distances to testify in local courts. Vendors, refusing to face the bureaucracy and expense involved in acquiring a license to sell acid, often continue to do so illegally despite the new penalties for doing so. Khuku continued, "Abuse of power occurs at every level. The investigation process takes anywhere between 4–5 years, so pending cases fall on the wayside. One rarely sees cases reaching completion" (B. Khuku, personal communication, April 2003). Thus, while acid crime cases in theory are now filed and handled by the state, these obstructions frequently make the process ineffective.

Bina Akhter's experiences with the police pointed to further abuses endemic to the justice system in the early days of the anti-acid campaign. When Bina was waiting for a bed in the burns unit of DMCH in September 1996, after the acid attack, the first time the police officers came to take her statement was several days after her family had gone to file a report at the station. She later recalled, "They asked me, 'Did they touch you? Did they rape you?' They were not asking about the acid attack. 'Did they touch your breasts? Did they take off your pants?' they probed. I wanted to kick them. I didn't care who they were—police or president! I told them to get out, I did not want to talk to them. He said, 'I have to know what happened to file a case'" (B. Akhter, personal communication, December 27–28, 2004).

Bina has told me that she believes that the police had no intention of pursuing Dano and his gang because they were protected by political leaders and had already bribed the police into silence. The questions they asked were unnecessary, and she thinks they were probably intended to enable the police to distort the facts of the attack. When she was well enough to leave the hospital and go to the police station with Naripokkho activists, they discovered that indeed the FIR did not have Dano's name at all. Instead, it named Pappu, a *mastaan* from a different and rival gang, as the perpetrator. When Bina's family began pursuing the case in earnest with the help of Naripokkho, a senior member of the community came to visit Bina's family with a proposal for marriage from Dano. This scenario where families considered marrying their daughters to the perpetrators and dropping charges against them was not uncommon. As mentioned in chapter 1, I encountered this at other times during my research. For some families this option seemed logical because the assumption was that women with disfigured faces were not marriageable, and therefore would lack social and economic security in their future.

When we examine in detail the stories of acid violence survivors, the inadequate and even abusive responses of the medical and legal institutions to gendered violence stand out in high relief. By keeping in place loose provisions but failing to implement them effectively, the state is complicit in perpetuating and sanctioning crimes against women. Gaps in the medical system prevent women from protection guaranteed by law. Even procedures created to address gender-based abuse often obstruct women's access to the health systems. Further, the medical institutions operate within a patriarchal and class-determined value system, making its practices unyielding to women, particularly poor women who comprise the majority of acid survivors. The failure of state institutions to ensure appropriate care has been somewhat mitigated by nongovernmental organizations, particularly women's groups, and more recently (though not comprehensively) by the international donor-supported organization, ASF (discussed in chapter 1). But as we saw in chapter 1, the non–state actors, and especially the international donor community, cannot be expected to fill in the gaps and compensate for the failure of state institutions on an ongoing basis.

The Role of the State

The official Bangladeshi state narrative on gender violence is critical for understanding the state's role in developing and offering services for women victimized by violent attacks. Meghna Guhathakurta (1985) has argued that the Bangladesh state is a "soft state," that is, a state that has been unable to firmly institutionalize its own state interests. Rather, it caters to diverse, fragmented, and often contradictory interests such as international capital, donor governments, the rural rich, the urban middle class, and certain state functionaries like the army and the police force. Such fragmentation in the state's discourse is reflected in the ad hoc and contradictory nature of many of its policies and practices, especially those relating to women. Guhathakurta characterizes the state as intervening at a superficial level, which does little to challenge existing discriminating practices among gender relations. This intervention consists of state-driven legal and social processes that further the perpetuation, imposition, and internalization of male-dominant values and existing oppressive social structures by which women are subordinated. The soft state in this view functions as an ambiguous power that, on the one hand, sustains discriminatory practices, yet on the other hand, allows spaces for these practices to be challenged. For instance, while there are strict laws "protecting" the rights of victims of acid violence, interpretation, implementation, and even access to those laws are systematically curtailed for women, particularly poor women, not the least because of ideological gender biases inherent in these legal structures.

Since the seventies, Bangladesh has projected itself as an independent, modernizing state committed to equality and justice. Sociologist Sadeka Halim (2003) has argued that irrespective of which political party might be in power, the changing landscape of the state's official stance regarding women (influenced by its contradictory and fragmented interests) shapes the ways in which it addresses gender discrimination. These gender interventions often appear in five-year national plans, which reflect the rhetoric from the 1990s, of the discourse of "women in development," and more recently, catalyzed by global feminist organizing in the 1990s, of "gender and development," and "violence against women."

The Bangladeshi government's handling of the Platform for Action (PFA) adopted in the Fourth World Conference on Women in Beijing in 1995, of which Bangladesh is a signatory, is one example of the contradictory interests at play as activists attempt to use the state in securing rights for women, and respond specifically to gendered violence. The PFA, which emphasizes mainstreaming of women's development into government policies and programs, commands the government and other actors to promote an active and visible gender perspective in all policies and programs. Therefore, before governmental decisions are taken, an analysis must be made of their effects on women and men, respectively. Bangladesh's national plans, reflected in regularly issued documents and strategies for economic advancement, however, do not reflect an active integration of the PFA.

Sadeka Halim (2003) contends that rather than changing policies to integrate gender, Bangladeshi government leaders took an "add-on" approach, bringing some "gender specialists" into projects that have not actually challenged structural subordination of women. Also, because many of the English terms used in these agendas are difficult to translate into Bangla, when officials adopted these terms at the behest of donors, it was often without understanding the underlying assumptions and responsibilities that they entail. For instance, even the term *gender* is not translated into local language in many official documents and training manuals, but is simply used in the context in which it is often conceptualized in western countries. Another example is the translating of "gender violence" in Bangla as *nari nirjaton* (torture of women), which implies very distinctively specific meanings in the international and local contexts and does not capture the full complexity and diversity of physical and structural violences affecting women.

Sadeka Halim (2003) further points out that in Bangladesh the gender mainstreaming agenda has been the hostage of political shifts in the country. During the Bangladesh National Party (BNP) government of the late 1970s, the Department of Women's Affairs was raised to the level of a full-fledged ministry. Later, the department was demoted to a department of the Social Affairs Ministry under President Ershad in the 1980s. It was reinstated as a ministry when the BNP returned to power in the early 1990s. These frequent shifts have resulted in an unclear mandate and deficiencies in staff, financial resources, and administrative privileges. Currently, the Department of Women's Affairs is part of the Ministry of Women and Children Affairs. The Ministry's formal mandate combines an advocacy role with a program implementation role. In the mid-1990s gender mainstreaming "focal points" had been formally identified in thirty-three ministries or divisions. However, more than a decade after the government of Bangladesh in 1997 declared national policies on women, no discernible changes have taken place in terms of implementing the proposed national policies through these focal points. These focal points remain in most cases inactive. Thus the policy of gender mainstreaming did little to challenge the prevailing socioeconomic and political structures within which the programs were to be implemented.

While implementation of existing seemingly egalitarian laws toward men and women is certainly deficient, equally problematic is the limited scope of international conventions—in particular the U.N. Convention on the Elimination of All Forms of Discrimination Against Women (CEDAW), to which the government of Bangladesh has formally subscribed—in conceptualizing the differing impacts of gender discrimination on diverse groups of women.

Often, women from certain class, ethnic, and religious backgrounds suffer more from physical, and sexual violence than do women with greater social status and privilege. Failing to analyze gender through an intersectional lens limits CEDAW's implementation (I revisit this discussion in greater detail in chapter 5) (Halim, 2003, pp. 113–14).

In a comparable study of gendered violence in India, Shelly Prasad (1999) suggests that violence against women in India is sanctioned by ancient religious texts and perpetuated by contemporary social practices. Despite public awareness campaigns, criminal laws, and the rise of antiviolence rhetoric, violence against women has remained an acceptable form of dominance and control that supersedes the rule of law. These observations are also relevant in studying violence against women and the state response in Bangladesh where, despite laws to protect women, cultural biases in state practices seem to inhere in addressing cases of violence against women. Prasad finds this willful negligence of the state indicative of a widespread belief that women are the property of men and therefore they are poised to be sexually abused and physically brutalized without state interference (Prasad, 1999, p. 479).

In Bangladesh, state authorities have been known to commit acts of sexual violence against women themselves (Pereira, 2002). So while laws exist that aim to address violence against women, such laws fail to punish the perpetrators of violence against women due to ineffective implementation by the state and inherent conceptual defects. These laws are thus at times useless, ornamental additions to the statute books. Lack of funds for collecting and preserving evidence, protection of the victims and witnesses, improper documentation of testimony, and a lack of understanding and sensitivity of violence against women among police, judges, doctors, and social workers contribute to the failure to punish the perpetrators of violence against women and inadequate redress for the victims of such violence.

During my research in 1998, I visited the state run Shelter for Oppressed Women in Dhaka, where many survivors of violence stayed during their medical, legal, and rehabilitative processes. Although called a shelter, the atmosphere of this building was more like a holding cell. When I repeatedly rang the bell at the locked, tall, gray steel gates of the facility, a young woman peered out of a barred third-floor window and yelled, "Come back in half an hour. The guard has gone for tea." The residents of the building were locked in when the guard went for meals or errands. I was allowed in half an hour later by the guard, a scrawny-looking fellow who did not appear as someone who could protect the formidable fortress in which the women were kept. On examining my "security pass," which I had acquired after a long and bureaucratic process from the Ministry of Women and Child Affairs, he unlocked the gate to let me in.

My conversation with the Social Welfare officer revealed that ninety women were in residence at the facility although it only had provisions for fifty-two. Shelter rules commanded that women who were poor and home-less, or "oppressed" were eligible to stay for a maximum of six months. Some acid burn survivors were housed in this facility. While at the shelter, they received vocational training, namely in learning how to use a computer, typing, and sewing. At the end of the training, each woman was presented with a sewing machine. A medical doctor also resided in the facility. Women also had access to legal aid from the "head office," which was located in another part of the city, although the women were not allowed to leave the premises without permission, even for "urgent" matters. Children attended the in-house school. I was neither allowed to speak with any of the residents alone, nor be given a tour without supervision. Rina, a survivor of acid burns who was at the shelter during my visit, mentioned that she hoped that the Women's Ministry would find her a job. She had ended up at the government shelter because her family had exhausted all of their financial means in pursuing a legal battle with her husband who had attacked her because her family had not been able to provide the dowry he had asked for. Because the attack had left her blind, she had not been able to take the training courses and did not know if she could operate the sewing machine.

As briefly discussed in chapter 1, in 2002, as a result of lobbying and advocacy by ASF and various women's NGOs, the government of Bangla-desh passed two new laws. These laws, Acid Crime Prevention Law 2002 and Acid Control Law 2002, provide stringent measures against acts of acid throwing and selling and strengthen existing provisions of the Women and Child Repression Act on acid throwing ("Two Laws on the Anvil," 2002). An Acid Control Board and Special Tribunal were introduced, provisions for bail for the accused during trial were eliminated, and if convicted a fine of Tk 1 lakh (U.S.$1,500.00) was required, in addition to life imprisonment or death if the victim in question was dead, had lost eyesight or hearing ability, or was injured in the face, breasts, and sexual organs. If other parts of the victim's body were burned, the accused faced a maximum of fourteen years in prison with a fine of Tk 50,000 (U.S.$714.00). For attempted acid throwing, the accused faced a minimum of three years and maximum of fourteen in prison with a fine of Tk 50,000. The new laws also prioritized acid cases and ensured speedy trials under Special Tribunals. Many women's groups in the region, however, have criticized these laws for punishing the accused according to the grade of injury, and not charging them with attempted homicide and hate crimes against women regardless of the severity of the damage they inflicted.

ASF research has shown that despite the introduction of the Special Tribunal requirement commanding completion of case investigation within thirty days and the trial within ninety days following the filing of the First Information Report, the reality on the ground has been very different. On the one hand, because investigative officers were charged with legal actions if they were unable to complete the investigation within the allotted 30 days, more often than not an impossible task given their heavy case loads, they produced substandard work. On the other hand, the ninety-day trial stipulation in the Lower Court almost never worked because cases were often sent to Higher Court on appeal, where they sat indefinitely. Moreover, guilty verdicts for the accused passed in the Lower Court were sometimes overturned in the Higher Court, where a lone judge would rule by reviewing the case file, only without the benefit of hearing witness testimonies (B. Khuku, personal communication, April 2003). Given the patriarchal structure of the legal system, this did not work in favor of women survivors.

It is important to note that aside from the gendered obstruction in accessing available legal provisions for punishing perpetrators of acid attack crime, women in Bangladesh are also subject to broad discrimination in the application of laws (Pereira, 2002). Although the Bangladesh Constitution grants equal rights to women and men in all spheres of public life, in matters such as marriage, divorce, custody of children, and inheritance, Personal Family Laws prevail, which are discriminatory against women. It should be noted that the government did not fully subscribe to the UN CEDAW, and expressed reservations on critical articles concerning women's equal rights in all family matters. These included articles 2 and 16, which are two defining articles of the Convention. In spite of strong demand from various women's groups to adhere to these provisions of CEDAW, no significant change has occurred.

The acid laws, though an important victory for the campaign, only function to punish the crime once committed. They do not seek to prevent such gendered violent crime by challenging or changing the subordinate status of women in society, which would require massive re-education. To illustrate the depth of the additional changes needed, I draw on a story from Guhathakurta (1985), which describes an interview with a state official: When the minister for women's affairs is asked what could be the chief cause for the recent trend of acid-throwing on women, she replied that the cause is mostly "unrequited love"; or when a woman quarrels with her husband or divorces him, the chief concern of her relative and friends is almost always to try to send her back to her husband. Maintaining social respectability seems to be the foremost consideration, as well as a deliberate attempt to "keep the personal from becoming political" (Guhathakurta, 1985, p. 83). In other words, as long as women's subordination under existing social relations remains unchallenged, very little can be achieved through legislative measures. If laws operate to simply "patch up" issues while keeping intact existing social relations, in the long run they reinforce the subordinate status of women in society.

The posture of the Bangladeshi state toward women is paradoxical. On the one hand, the state has offered spaces for discriminatory practices toward women to be challenged; yet, on the other hand, it has allowed those practices to continue by not intervening strategically or systematically. The Constitution ensures equal rights to all citizens, yet discriminatory practices such as male violence against women prevail and are often perceived by state-funded institutions such as the medicolegal establishments as acts of individual brutality but not as symptomatic of gender discrimination. Despite laws to protect women, and policies requiring gender analysis as integral to program planning, state negligence and misconduct in relation to cases of violence against women has often appeared to be the norm rather than the exception. Such misconduct is indicative of systematic and institutional beliefs that women are the property of men and can therefore be brutalized without fear of state reprisal. Often, the state apparatus itself is the violator. Laws tend to be ornamental as perpetrators receive inadequate redress for their crimes and the medicolegal system fails to respond appropriately to women's needs.

The Activist Role of the Women's NGO

In the context of a state failing to address gender violence, non–state actors, namely women's NGOs in Bangladesh, provide crucial support by creating alternative strategies and visions for victimized women's recovery and empowerment. In the decades following the independence of Bangladesh, the NGO sector has seen remarkable growth. In part, the state has promoted the image of a modernizing nation in order to garner development funds, as well as promote women's participation in development programs (Karim, 2004). Women's increased participation in the workforce has also been catalyzed

by funds and programs generated during and since the U.N. Decade for
Women (1975–1985). These trends have created new networks as well as
forms of dependencies between the state, donors, and NGOs. According
to the NGO Bureau, in Bangladesh currently there are more than 17,000
NGOs. These NGOs have stepped in to provide many of the services traditionally provided by the state, such as credit, education, health care, voter
education, legal aid, and literacy. NGOs and women's rights organizations
have been in the forefront of challenging intersecting local, national, and
global socioeconomic, political processes that reify women's subordination.
The urban, educated, middle-class national women's movement operates
inside the structure of the NGO with its links to the government, donors,
and other NGOs. These institutional structures provide women activists with
opportunities while simultaneously impeding feminist praxis autonomous of
the same structures. Naripokkho's interventions to combat acid violence can
be seen within these networks of dependencies and strategic alliances with
state and non–state actors.

Patricia McFadden (2005) has referred to this characteristic dependency
of women's movements in the global South as a consequence of distinctive developmentalist frameworks prevalent in "underdeveloped" countries,
where only particular kinds of women's movements and other civil society
activism such as those structured by NGO politics are likely to occur. She
suggests that the politics of such women's movements are in collusion with
the neocolonial state, international capitalism, and the international donor
community. These NGOs seek to define their goals within the framework of
development, which itself can be seen as a regime of repression. Nonetheless,
as Obioma Nnaemeka (2003) has observed, one cannot underestimate the
power of women's struggles, limited as they might be, to effect social change
through accommodation and negotiation rather than conflict and disruption.
While the women's movement's agenda in Bangladesh may be perceived as
donor and development driven, and thus compromised to an extent, women
are simultaneously able to resist some of those same historically constituted
structures and networks of dependencies.

At present, in Bangladesh, the success of the acid campaign can be
measured by the creation of the Acid Survivors Foundation (ASF), as a result
of women activists' negotiations with the state and international donor community. Financed by international aid agencies, ASF provides consolidated
and coordinated services to the survivors of acid violence. The success of
the acid campaign can also be measured by the passing of new and more
stringent legislation by the government criminalizing the sale of acid without

a permit and the creation of the National Acid Council with branches at the district levels. Further, the level of engagement and interest from international media and organizations reflect the grander scale and scope of the campaign in the present day. These successes, however, are ambiguous. The creation of the Acid Survivors Foundation, the proliferation of services for acid survivors, the diversification of actors involved, and the passing of new legislation reflect the culmination of Naripokkho's networking and advocacy on a national and global scale. This has enabled transnational coalitions of nongovernmental, governmental, and intergovernmental actors to exert pressures on one another and other influential political bodies in order to invoke desired policy changes on the ground. Yet, at the same time, these same transnational coalitions have co-opted the local women's issues and agendas and led to the deradicalization of these issues and agendas.

As I have described in chapter 1, Naripokkho's approach was woman-centered, emphasizing the empowering of survivors of violence so that they were able to avail services, make informed and meaningful decisions about their own lives, and participate in leading the campaign against acid violence. At ASF, in contrast, the survivor-centered campaign that Naripokkho developed has transformed into a welfarist one that does not always resonate with the lived experiences of the women who have endured acid attacks. Survivors have been treated as passive "clients" who are channeled into various productive schemes designed by the rehabilitation program of ASF. In the absence of real choices, women are placed in service positions. This does very little to disrupt global, national, and local systems of hierarchies based on gender, class, race, and nationality. Nonetheless, it would be misleading to see current developments in the movement simply as a reinscription of power inequalities because it has facilitated the emergence of a national network of services for acid survivors. It is in this paradoxical space where women's agency is often negotiated.

The paradox of the success and limits of women's transnational organizing through NGOs has been usefully identified by anthropologist Sally Merry (2006) at the crossroads of two distinct yet converging approaches to human rights regarding gender violence (p. 138). The first, a social service approach, is mainly utilized by feminists and social workers and focuses on offering social services to victims. This group is comprised of middle-tier professionals, academics, and activists. The strategies used are often the same and "transplanted" from other geographical contexts without adequate attention to local realities. The second, human rights advocacy, is primarily pursued by legal and political elites and focuses mainly on policy and legal reform. Both tiers ultimately rely on global norms with limited success in "indigenizing" programs to grassroots concerns. This limitation is built into the structural dependence of NGOs.

It is also important to recognize that there are varying kinds of NGOs, some that are more powerful because of stronger infrastructure or through the legitimacy of the state or international aid agencies, and others that are more in line with local issues and populations. Naripokkho was well-positioned for its campaign because its leadership is comprised of influential, urban, educated, professional members of society who are well situated within the national women's movement as well as connected to influential national and international networks of other kinds. At the same time, there is considerable competition among NGOs for limited resources, which hinders collaboration among them. Women's groups are often vying for the same pool of money and are forced to shape their agendas to match the donors', who may not be all that connected to realities on the ground. The inter-NGO dynamics of competition enhances the dependence of NGOs on external interventions and compromises their agendas, autonomy, and possibilities of meaningful collaborations.[3]

In addition to the structural dependence of NGOs and the patriarchal leanings of the state, anti-acid activists also faced a deep distrust of NGOs at all levels. An ASF staff commented, "Many government officers and even the public perceive NGOs in a negative light. They express cynicism regarding our work, they openly air rude comments about us" (ASF staff, personal communication, April 6, 2003). This distrust, she believed, was connected to the disruption that NGOs were causing in entrenched belief systems, especially as related to gender. NGOs had contributed to bringing more and more women out in the public spaces and in to the labor force and thus were suspect in the eyes of the "moral guardians" of society. For instance, a 2003 survey conducted by the daily newspaper, *Prothom Alo*, interviewed 100 men from various professions about their ideas regarding definitions of a "good woman." The top ten responses were:

1. Women who do not provoke and betray men
2. Women who do not put themselves in dangerous situations
3. Women who are accommodating
4. Women who cook well, are good homemakers, are obedient and docile
5. Women who are not jealous or vindictive
6. Women who do not use their sexuality to get what they want; those who are good mothers

7. Women who are modest and adaptable
8. Women who have beautiful minds
9. Women who are obedient and not demanding
10. Women who do not go to extremes (Nazneen, 2003)

When asked about women who were not desirable, the popular answers included women in the public or entertainment industry, specifically dancers, actors, models, and stage performers. Next on the undesirable list were women lawyers, journalists, and nurses. Undesirable characteristics in women were listed as the following: aggressive, wayward, outgoing, independent minded, manipulative, ambitious, straightforward, lazy, disobedient, and nonreligious. Women who have romantic relationships before marriage were considered problematic as well.

Presumably, the purpose of the survey was to weigh public opinion regarding desirable characteristics of a "marriageable woman," and the responses indicate these to be passivity and obedience. In addition, most men seemed to have negative opinions about women in public roles. Ironically, *Prothom Alo* did not conduct a comparable survey polling women on the definition of a "good man."

In April 2003, *Prothom Alo* published another feature story that helps us understand societal views of gender, this time with regard to a "good man." This story was titled, "An Afternoon at the Home of Acid Burnt Rumana." It featured a "great[*mohan*] policeman," Harun, who was endlessly praised for marrying Rumana despite her "unfortunate" circumstances. The story reveals that Harun had been married with a child at the time he was investigating Rumana's case. His first wife was very ill. According to the story, she "readily agreed" to Harun's proposition to marry Rumana who could be a second mother to her children (Rahman, 2003). Therefore, the article attributes the first wife's acceptance of her husband's second marriage to her "inner maternal instincts." Harun is celebrated as a great man for marrying a victim of acid attack, Rumana—who in turn is implied to be lucky to have found a husband at all. And the first wife, driven by maternal instincts, blessed the union. The article thus celebrates the "good" masculine traits of Harun for accepting Rumana despite being a victim of acid violence, and the self-sacrificing maternal instincts that leads his first wife to accept the second wife. It however does not touch on possible alternative interpretations: that, in a social context where beauty is assigned as a woman's greatest asset, Rumana's implied luck is associated to securing a marriage despite having lost that asset. Furthermore, the socioeconomic vulnerability of women outside the marriage contract is not commented on as a possibility for both Harun's first wife's acceptance of Rumana, and the latter's agreeing to the marriage. A discussion of women's devalued status in society, their limited choices, and the gendered meanings that could be gleaned from the assumptions made in the story were therefore effectively lost.

Discriminatory attitudes toward women based on gender have been researched by women's groups in Bangladesh in relation to the soaring statistics of violence against women. Mahbuba Huq of Women for Women, a feminist research organization, pointed out that their research demonstrated that women's changing roles in society contributed to various masculinist attitudes that condoned acid attacks against women. Comments from men like, "that girl was acting out of her place," "she was behaving like a man," are commonplace when describing a woman who dared to say "no" (when harassed prior to the attack) or press charges against the perpetrators. "She goes out too much," "She doesn't listen to anyone," and "She is aggressive" are commonly stated descriptions about survivors in the communities where the research was conducted (M. Huq, personal communication, April 2003). Further, the inspector general of the police, in an interview with the Naripokkho convener had said, "Women are like fragrant flowers. It is only to be expected that men will pursue them," in order to normalize masculinist proprietorial attitudes toward women (Convener, personal communication, April 2003). Huq also mentioned that informal *shalish* (village adjudication bodies) were sometimes set up in villages by male leaders in place of formal trials for perpetrators in court.[4] Monetary compensation was sought from the perpetrator and his family by the *shalish* in place of a criminal conviction. Even then, women who were attacked were sometimes not accepted back by their families. Against such a backdrop where women neither receive proper treatment, nor are they valued or respected by the community, the work of NGOs to secure their rights was critical.

Women's NGOs in Bangladesh have compiled a strong record of engaging the state on the broader issue of gender violence. Past interventions by women's groups including Naripokkho have resulted in the Multi-Sectoral Project to Combat Violence Against Women that was developed by the Ministry of Women and Children's Affairs of the Government of Bangladesh in 1998 (S. Azim, 2001). This project involved developing of institutional capacity to work with victims of violence, including legal redress and public consciousness raising. As we have seen in the case of the acid survivors' negative experiences, health services have their role both in providing care and support to the survivors as well as in evidence collection to assist the legal process. Improving the complaints procedures and police handling, also very important for violence survivors, requires training and reform. Prevention of violence necessitates that justice is administered in incidents of violence against women and that the cases are not unduly delayed. This also requires sensitization of the legal system and monitoring. The project would have been implemented by government working groups consisting of representatives from the Ministry of Women and Children Affairs, the Ministry of Health, the Ministry of Home Affairs, and the Ministry of Law, Justice, and Parliamentary Affairs in collaboration with NGOs and women's groups, including Naripokkho, and with financial assistance from the government of Bangladesh and donor agencies, among them, the Danish International Development Agency (Naripokkho, 1998).

These alliances, Naripokkho believed, would contribute to institutional changes including questioning the very fabric of the cultural and social institutions and value systems. Together with the government of Bangladesh and with donor assistance, the Multi-Sectoral Project was designed to educate and raise awareness among medical and legal professionals, state officials, and the general public. Gender dynamics within adolescent relationships would be a high priority because so many of the survivors of acid violence that Naripokkho had assisted in the 1990s were teenagers. First, this initiative proposed a campaign to work with parents and teachers nationally in order to raise awareness about adolescent behavior patterns. Second, the collaboration included plans to work with young men to demystify socially constructed notions of masculinity, thereby hoping to build a climate where accepting rejection was not such a threat to their "manhood." Nasreen Huq, the coordinator of Naripokkho's acid campaign emphasized this goal when she said, "Aggressive male behavior is commonly accepted in Bangladeshi society. We need to change these behavior patterns" (N. Huq, personal communication, April 5, 2003). Third, this project would have focused on changing the treatment of women as "victims" in Bangladeshi society.

Plans were also underway at that time to establish a burns center at Gono Shastho Kendro (GK)—the leading national NGO providing affordable health care to the poor—in order to train medical professionals of all levels to care for burn patients. Many of the acid throwing incidents occurred outside of the city of Dhaka, but Dhaka Medical College Hospital (DMCH) was the only burns unit in the country, thus it was very important to have hospitals and staff in every district that were equipped to care for burn patients. In the 1990s most of the women who survived acid attacks were the rural and urban poor who found it difficult to afford the periodic visits to DMCH and the accompanying long-term treatment. These women needed a hostel where their family members could also stay with them during the treatment. They needed food, and transportation. The Burn Center at DMCH catered to patients with all kinds of burns and was not equipped to deal with the increasing numbers of acid burn cases. In addition to training medical staff, public awareness campaigns were necessary. For instance, Naripokkho activists even in the late 1990s had already started distributing flyers nationwide with instructions for immediate care of acid victims. Indeed, there had been reports of cases where women had heeded these instructions and washed their wounds with water right away thus somewhat minimizing the acid-inflicted damage.

Another factor that the NGO community had to deal with was the changing profile of acid burned victims and their perpetrators. Whereas the initial anti-acid campaign of previous years had laid the strongest emphasis on acid throwing as an act of revenge by rejected suitors against young women, recently more attention was being given to acid attacks in different situations, including unmet dowry demands, land disputes, and family disputes. Young women were no longer the primary targets. Men, women, children, and the elderly were all targets of violence. According to Nasreen Huq, "Acid is becoming a weapon of violence, a weapon of vengeance" (N. Huq, personal communication, April 14, 2003). Thus, the need to cater to increasing numbers of people with acid burns was becoming all the more urgent. Yet services were still inadequate. While the government did pass new laws that prohibited the sale or possession of acid without a license, sulfuric acid is still widely available, especially in auto-mechanic and jewelry shops. In areas where there are few or no vehicles, the sale of acid is close to nonexistent. Once caught, perpetrators are rarely asked where they had acquired the acid that they had used in the crime. Activists believe the sale as well as the acquisition of acid without a permit should be under stricter surveillance and when necessary criminalized.

Many state responsibilities have been significantly supplanted by the NGO sector over time, but activists, even in NGO settings, would acknowledge that this is not a desirable condition. Stronger involvement of the state for the sustainability of services as well as for protecting its citizens from violence and other human rights abuses is essential. Women's rights groups have proposed developing "One Stop Centers" for victims of violence where they can receive medical treatment, legal aid, and counseling. The women's movement has also been active in lobbying with the government to live up to its commitment to the Elimination of Discrimination Against Women. To that end, women's rights organizations have lobbied to introduce changes to the most important law related to women, the Suppression of Violence Against Women and Children Act of 2000 (which, rather than addressing root causes of violence or structural violence, deals with only punitive measures). Women activists believe it is imperative simultaneously to improve the burn care treatment in Bangladesh at all levels. ASF to that end has begun to bring foreign experts to train medical, legal, and social work professionals. Also, attention has to be paid to develop educational materials for schools to raise awareness among students. The Ministry of Education can work on incorporation of relevant literature into textbooks.

Because of successful efforts of the women's advocacy groups like Naripokkho, reporting of acid cases has improved. As a result, there is more information available, and state involvement will ensure sustainability of this ongoing work. But acid attack survivors still have largely unmet needs related to their devalued position as poor, young, and female in Bangladeshi society. Their mobility is seriously hindered. They are isolated and stigmatized. Developing solidarity networks among the survivors is crucial so that they can share their stories and struggles. They also need to be able to collectively politicize those experiences in a public domain access, which is often denied to women with acid burns. In Nasreen Huq's words, "They are not dead people. They have a right to be on the streets without being marked as such" (N. Huq, personal communication, October 10, 1996).

Conclusion

In this chapter, I have mapped the on-the-ground realities of acid violence in Bangladesh, especially in the earlier days of activist organizing, by emphasizing Nurun Nahar's experience as characteristic of the landscape of acid violence against women. I have also examined Naripokkho's efforts to involve important state and non–state actors in mobilizing a social campaign against acid violence, with implications for the larger women's resistance movements against gender violence. Although I have focused specifically on acid attacks, I do not want to minimize other forms of violence against women, or the other struggles of the larger women's movement in Bangladesh. This singular case study, I believe, can be instructive in illuminating some of the individual and community acts of resistance in the face of multiple and complex layers of gender subordination. The role of women's groups in naming gendered violence, and bringing about small albeit qualitative changes to victimized women's lives in Bangladesh are not insignificant contributions in struggles to resistance against multilayered oppressions.

Chapter Three

From Dhaka to Cincinnati

Charting Transnational Narratives of Trauma, Victimization, and Survival

Following the acid workshop organized by Naripokkho in 1997, Bina Akhter took on the leadership role in coordinating the nationwide acid survivors network. Because of the strong leadership qualities she had demonstrated during her association with Naripokkho, she was called the "star of the acid campaign" by Nasreen Huq, the coordinator at that time. Bina was sought out by many national and international media outlets to speak about her experience and to highlight the plight of acid victims in Bangladesh. Nasreen Huq remembers Bina's first public-speaking engagement: "We took her to Patharghata, on World Youth Day in 1997. She gave an electrifying speech—the entire town heard it because speakers were set up in the main square. The town embraced Bina. They kept saying, 'If we are staring at you, it's because we cannot imagine how cruel and inhuman a person can be'" (Welch, 1999).

Bina's prominent role in the acid campaign has led to her story being told in many different iterations spanning the "victim, survivor, activist" trajectory that Naripokkho envisioned women with acid burns to follow. It is therefore important to me to provide a vehicle to present her story as told by her. In this chapter, I want to draw attention to the importance of stories or testimonials in human rights campaigns, the construction of narratives in presenting experiential truths as well as in strategic mobilizing, and the ways in which human rights narratives contribute to both assisting and impeding transnational movement building. I draw on oral history narratives of Bina, which I documented over a span of ten years. I also use interviews with Naripokkho activists who worked closely with her in the campaign as well as television and print media reports representing her story. The use of these narratives is an attempt to further discussions on transnational feminist praxis with regard to gender violence. It is not my intention to present any one narrative as "truer" or more authentic than the other, but rather to bring attention to the processes of narrative construction, interpretation, circulation, and reception and to demonstrate how all of these registers are imbued in power relations.

Theoretically, I frame this chapter within the genre of human rights narrative analysis through the lens of transnational feminism as explicated by scholars like Shari Stone-Mediatore (2003), Kay Schaffer and Sidonie Smith (2004), and Wendy Hesford (2004). Additionally, I draw from gender theorists of women's agency and subjectivity like Alcoff and Gray (1993) and Tami Spry (1995). Scholars of human rights narrative analysis have pointed to the largely unexplored deep political nature of narratives, particularly stories of marginalized groups. According to Schaffer and Smith (2004), "[L]ife narratives and human rights campaigns are multidimensional domains that merge and intersect at critical points, unfolding within and enfolding one another in an ethical relationship that is simultaneously productive of claims for social justice and problematic for the furtherance of this goal" (Schaffer and Smith, 2004, p. 2). Likewise, Stone-Mediatore (2003) draws attention to the epistemic value of "marginal experience narratives" in the quest for liberatory politics. She shows the ways in which narratives circulate by emphasizing that "experience becomes public knowledge through an exchange of stories in which specific people, in the context of historically specific social and cultural institutions, relay their views of events in a particular rhetorical style to a specific audience" (Stone-Mediatore, 2003, p. 5). These practices can reify dualisms of story/truth, experience/theory, narrative/knowledge, which she believes to be the legacy of Enlightenment epistemology seeking to establish objective, rational, masculinized truths. In contrast to poststructuralists, who stress the impossibility of objective knowledge as they characterize its claims as irreducibly ideological, she points to discursively composed histories that are situationally specific and acquire meaning through certain social and cultural scripts. Recognition of the multiplicity of interpretations of knowledge in itself does not change reality, but it can disrupt given analytic categories to open up new possibilities for political thinking and action. A transnational feminist analysis further illuminates the far-reaching relations of domination and resistance in these everyday narratives. Paying attention to the ways in which stories are told and interpreted can provide greater insight into the influences of everyday narratives and shifting relations of power.

In this chapter, then, I juxtapose the narratives of Bina Akhter, an activist-survivor of the acid campaign, with those told through the U. S.-based popular media during the time surrounding Bina's arrival to the United States, with Naripokkho's narrative of campaign objectives and dissolution. This juxtaposition allows us to see the ways in which these various narratives are in conflict with one another at the same time that they further the aims of the anti-acid campaign from disparate locations. Applying a transnational feminist analysis, as explicated above, in particular allows us to recognize the multiple power relations affecting different actors locally and globally, as well as having an impact on the direction of women's organizing.

Bina's Story

Bina has been alternatively spoken of as "victim," "survivor," "activist," and "angel of mercy" in the course of the campaign by various actors. She has been praised as the "star of the campaign," admired and appreciated as a skillful leader, yet also referred to as "selfish" and not entirely truthful by the same organizers. My purpose here is to explore the shifting contexts of her ever-evolving subject positions and how they defy these categorical representations. Her varying positionalities emphasize the need for a broader framework within transnational organizing to speak of women's experiences and choices.

Speaking to the linguistic limits of "telling a woman's story of violence," Tami Spry makes the observation that terms like *victim* and *survivor* are inadequate and curtail the agency of women to make meaning of their complex experiences. These linguistic constructs govern the ways women can structure their own stories and hold women hostage to hegemonic categories of reference regarding violence: that is, "she is victim to *it* or survivor of *it*" (Spry, 1995, p. 27). Further, these constructs deny women the capacity to define their experience in a more fluid way with "narrative agency" (Spry, 1995, p. 27). She urges feminists to move toward a more "liberatory epistemology" to talk about violence, one that will not freeze them in these given and perceived, mutually exclusive categories. Such dualistic framings of women's experience of violence actually pit them as either "losers" or "winners," "weak" or "strong" and disallow tellings, which show women negotiating in their own terms the various constraints and opportunities to make meaning of their struggles. Using Judith Butler's theory of gender construction through performance, Spry urges feminists to conceptualize women's experience as constituted through shifts, multidirectional movements, and in dialogue with her *self* (Spry, 1995, p. 32). Liberatory epistemologies, with all their contradictions and conflicts, can offer "narratives of knowledge" in our quest for decolonizing and creating oppositional knowledges.

Such expansion of our understanding of women's experiences and narratives of violence help us understand Bina's multiple and shifting positionalities over time and space. Since I first met Bina Akhter in 1997 at the workshop organized by Naripokkho, I have had the opportunity to work with her in various capacities. I have followed her life trajectory in professional, social, and personal spheres and formally interviewed her in a variety of settings that have spanned twelve years, four cities, two countries, and two continents. However, I did not want to simply use the information I knew as a result of my over-a-decade-long association with her (even if at various points we have had "formal conversations") for the purpose of my research. Therefore, in December 2004, when Bina visited me in my home in Boston, we tape-recorded over a week a series of conversations about her life trajectory. Here, she recollected events she deemed of importance "to be documented." The excerpts I use below come from these interviews, which were transcribed, translated from Bangla to English, and edited by me for greater readability.

Because I had prior knowledge of many of these events, I often prompted her to elaborate or talk about certain topics that she did not bring up herself. Therefore, Bina's narrative here is not only mediated by me but also organized, remembered, and presented in a certain fashion by herself. Time, location, and audience certainly influenced her (and my) choices in the ordering of the trajectory and the telling of her story. Elaine Lawless (2001) argues that instead of looking for fixed truths in women's memories, it is important to approach their narrations as a process of "transformative re-membering," in which women creatively construct a "sense of self" for themselves, marking the shift from "an early to a later form of self-knowledge" (p. 71). This is an act of power that offers women a new vantage point from which to interpret the past and to redefine themselves, and it offers their listeners an opportunity to do the same. Bina's experiences are mediated by active narrative construction in particular historical and cultural contexts.

I asked Bina, who is no stranger to interviews with researchers, local and global media, activists, state representatives, and civil society professionals, whether she found it burdensome to narrate her story yet again to me for a book that intended to tell a multifaceted story of women's organizing against acid violence in Bangladesh. Her response was, "I don't mind telling it to you because you were there from the beginning." Bina's interest in telling her story at one level was for it to be heard and known by wider audiences in a continuing quest for greater gender justice. On another level, it was an attempt to (re)insert her voice into the larger narrative of the anti-acid campaign from which she had become "estranged" as a consequence of the circumstances of her immigration to the United States. In this regard, telling this story for her was also an attempt to reach out to Naripokkho activists in Bangladesh with whom she felt deep affinity, yet to whom she felt obliged, and guilty. Because I was someone who had witnessed these shifting relationships, Bina saw in me a trusted vehicle to transmit her complex story. This is reminiscent of Lal's argument on which I drew in the Introduction: that subjects of research self-present/construct themselves in a way to meet the needs of their own agendas (1996, p. 204).

As briefly recounted above, Bina was fourteen and a student of class X (roughly tenth grade in the U.S. system), living in Hazaribagh area of the city of Dhaka on August 26, 1996. That night, Dano (a local "*mastaan*" who had acquired the nickname by making homemade bombs out of Dano milk containers) and his gang broke in to her home with the objective of abducting Mukti, her older cousin. These men had brought along acid with the intention of using it if Mukti's family resisted. Bina's face, hands, and feet were burned in the struggle when she tried to protect her cousin. Here is how Bina, age twenty-two, recounted that night:

> We were all sleeping in one room that night because our things were packed up in the other room. We were moving houses soon. It was a hot summer night, so we were lined up on a bed sheet on the cool cement floor—Shobuj, Shumon (my cousin brothers), *khala* (mother's sister), Ma, me, and Mukti Apa between me and the wall. *Khalu* (uncle) was sleeping on the bed in the same room. There were two gates, the main one leading to the house, and a second to our apartment. The gate to our house had a broken lock, and we had slid a thick wooden stick through the iron rungs on either panel to keep it shut. There was no electricity that night. Dano and his friends entered around 2:30 a.m. I woke up when I felt the flashlight on my face. I saw a man wearing a black mask moving towards my feet searching for Mukti. I called out to my mother. They may have sprayed the room with chloroform because everyone was still fast asleep. Nobody had heard anything, not even these men cutting the

heavy wooden stick to get in. Their plan was to abduct Mukti. They assumed *khalu* was out of town. They had brought along the acid in case the rest of us woke up and tried to stop them. The acid was intended for the family, not for Mukti.

I saw the men with a bucket and a jar advancing towards Mukti. I shook her awake. At that moment the contents of the jar splashed on my outstretched hands, and the bucket on my feet. I screamed, "Mukti *Apa*, they have poured hot water on me." Then, Dano poured the entire contents of the bucket on my face. I felt my ears burning and touched it. The skin was peeling off in to my hands, and the acid was dripping in to my mouth—I could taste it.

It was like the room was alight with fire. I cannot describe, and you cannot imagine what it was like. I tried to grab the man, and in the struggle, Dano's mask fell off. I grabbed the necklace hanging from his neck. I think he also got burnt by the acid on my hands. At that point, he took out a pistol and aimed it at me. "If anyone tries to stop me, I will shoot you. Just look outside," he threatened. There were at least 10 more men outside the house in addition to the four inside the room. I let go of him. I thought, if I lived I would be able to get him later. But, if he shot me and I died, my family died, nobody would be able to do anything about the crime that had just taken place.

Contrary to many assertions by actors involved in the campaign who we learned about in the earlier chapter, we see that Bina was not the "living dead," even at the moment of the attack, but a living thinking and acting person. Contrary also to the way victims of violence are often represented without agency, in Bina's self-narration, we see how she simultaneously experienced and interpreted the circumstances surrounding the attack both at the time it took place and in its aftermath. It is interesting to note here, according to Bina, the intent of the acid attack was not to disfigure Mukti, whom Dano desired, and could not "have," but to use it as a weapon against her family. Bina continued,

We did not recognize any of the other men. I was screaming as they left. My *khalu* ran after them with a knife. The acid felt like thick honey on my face. Neighbors were starting to gather around the house. My mother poured cold water on me, and it was as if the water sparked fire all over my body. I begged her to stop. I was jumping like a cow being slaughtered at Eid [*qurbanir gorur moto*]. My nose, eyebrows, eyelids, lips all peeled off in to my hands. I held on to the skin and flesh thinking the doctors would be able to reattach it. I ran out of the house in the midst of all this to search for my uncle. At least 50–60 people, mostly men, were gathered there. Some men were beating my *khalu*. I threw myself on top of him and the beatings started landing on my back. Some of these men, I am sure, had accompanied Dano earlier to our house. One of them yelled at the crowd, "Go to sleep, all of you. If you don't, we will do the same to you." People started scattering. Nobody came forward to help us.

Bina and her family were renters in a house that was owned by one of Dano's relatives. Dano and his family resided in a house just down the street, and several of his relatives also lived on that street. One of his relatives called an ambulance, which never came. He then took Bina, her mother, and her uncle to Dhaka Medical College Hospital at 4:00 a.m. Because there was no place available yet in the burns unit, she was given a bed on the balcony outside the general ward where she stayed for several weeks.

It was when she finally was transferred to the burns unit that Bina first met Naripokkho activists, who came by twice a week to speak to acid burn patients. They told her encouragingly, "Bina, your life is not over. We see a lot of talent in you; you have a lot to teach us. You will come out of this, and use your talent to help others. Think of yourself as someone who has a lot to offer. You don't have to depend on anybody when you come out of here, we will be there with you." In her 2004 interview with me, Bina later commented:

> I understood that I had to stay strong, but felt weak and vulnerable when they [Naripokkho members] left. I could not understand why this had happened to me. What had I done? What kind of sin had I committed to deserve this? I became very close to Naripokkho members. They helped me regain my strength and I told them that when I got out of the hospital, I wanted to work with them. I did not want to go home and do nothing. I would help Naripokkho support other acid-burned girls because I had experienced the trauma, and knew how to help others.

Exposure to and support from Naripokkho activists coupled with her own strong will led her to become heavily involved in the campaign. Bina was in and out of DMCH for months undergoing multiple skin grafting surgeries and treatment for severe burns. During this time she became more and more interested in working with Naripokkho and began spending time in their office and getting to know the members and their various projects.

Following the workshop in 1997, she was offered by Nasreen Huq—who recognized and wanted to further encourage Bina's leadership skills—the position of the coordinator of the acid advocacy campaign. She describes her job below:

> I used to file articles reporting acid attacks from the newspapers, and then contact the victims and follow up with their case. I went to the hospital to talk to them and their families to lend emotional support. At Naripokkho, I worked with the staff to organize events and rallies. We did a big rally on International Women's Day in 1998. I would go to the court with the Naripokkho lawyer, and every two weeks meet with the police inspector general. My activities were not limited to Dhaka, I went all over Bangladesh. I gave public talks to educate people how to deal with acid attacks—simple things like washing the face with water right away can help a lot to minimize the scarring. With Naripokkho, I also worked with UNICEF and was selected to go to an international forum in New York. Another organization sponsored me to give interviews in the UK on this topic. Many youth victims of violence were present at the forum in New York. I spoke about my experience in both events, and a lot of people were very impressed and encouraged me to continue my work. At the time, I used to cover my face because I did not want to step out in front of all these people with my face exposed. Talking to all the people at these forums gave me the strength to take off the cover. In the UK, I met a woman with a disfigured face who worked for a woman's rights organization. She used to dress up and put on a lot of makeup. She was an activist, and helped me to accept my face. I am grateful to all these people and Naripokkho for their support and love. I became bolder in confronting what had happened to me. In Dhaka, people would pass comments when I walked in public. They would call me "*bhoot*" [ghost] and "monkey." They would say, "Look, at this monkey. We don't have to go to the zoo. The monkey has come to us."

I understood that I had to build my own life; other people could not do it for me. What had happened to me was not my fault. People who did this to me should be ashamed, not me. It is not my shame. So, I stopped covering and would talk back, "Yes, you don't have to go the zoo. Why don't you pay me like you would pay to see animals at the zoo?"

As Naripokkho's campaign became more international and offers of assistance came in from various locations, Bina went to Italy with six survivors for medical consultation and a holiday sponsored by a team of doctors who had visited Bangladesh earlier to perform reconstructive surgeries. Bina's own international exposure was growing, as were her relationships with a wide network of survivors and Naripokkho activists. She expanded her correspondence to burn victims in Sri Lanka, Indonesia, and countries in Africa through e-mails, letters, and telephone calls. A group of six survivors was sponsored to go to Spain for surgery and efforts were underway for another team to go to the United States for medical treatment. When the team returned from Spain, Bina was impressed by the treatment they had received, in particular eye surgeries had restored full or partial eyesight to some of the survivors. Earlier she had forgone the opportunity to go to Spain because she was weary of surgeries after having had so many in DMCH already without significant results. The attack had left Bina blind in the left eye.

When I saw the girls return from Spain, I realized I wanted eye surgery too—I wanted a chance. I am not sure how my trip came together but I know that Healing the Children [The U.S.-based NGO that sponsored Bina's trip] contacted Liz [Liz Welch, the journalist who wrote the story on Bina for *Ms. Magazine*] and ABC Television [for the *20/20* episode on Bina's story]. These people contacted some Bangladeshis in the U.S.—these were Khan *Apa's* [a Naripokkho member whose name has been changed at her request] relatives in the U.S. Together, they worked out the details of our trip to Cincinnati. Two years of organizing went behind this trip.

It is worth noting that although Bina was intimately involved with the acid campaign, her comments above suggest that she did not know the details of the organizing in Bangladesh that enabled her to travel to the United States for medical treatment. In this interview, Bina tended to emphasize the details of the international organizing, rather than the arduous work of the Naripokkho activists in organizing this certain trip. Much of this organizing of course had occurred while Bina was still working at the organization as the campaign coordinator. While it is possible that she has forgotten some of the groundwork laid in Bangladesh, this omission may also reflect her later perspectives on her own decision to remain in the United States, as well as her relationship to Naripokkho, as I will discuss below.

Connie Chung's *20/20* camera crew followed Bina and fellow survivor Jharna to the United States. Bina recounted:

> ABC television followed our journey to the U.S. They introduced us to our host family in Cincinnati. We were nervous if they would love us, but they were very warm and loving and so happy to see us! We were sad to have left our families in Bangladesh. They had prepared a beautiful room for us with identical twin beds. They showed us the bathrooms, the towels. We couldn't speak English, so it was hard. That very night, we went to watch a baseball game.
>
> Many Bengali families in the area contacted us. Maksud Bhai and Kaneez *Apa* [a local Bengali family with contacts to Naripokkho], and the Zaman's [a pseudonym used for Ms. Khan's friends residing in Michigan who had helped sponsor the trip] contacted us right away. We began our medical treatment at the Shriner's Burns Hospital for the burns, and the Children's Hospital for the eyes. I learned that the damage to my eye was irreversible; I would not regain my eyesight. This was devastating for me because I had come to America specifically to seek treatment for my eyes.
>
> Months passed, and I had reconstructive surgery on my face and scalp. This was a very difficult and painful process. I would be very ill at times, and weak and depressed. Twice I tried to kill myself. But, I knew that I had a family who loved me and that there was a beautiful world out there of which I hadn't seen anything. I also wanted to live.

Adjusting to life in Cincinnati had its own ups and downs. Bina's and Jharna's trip had been made possible by a number of actors including Naripokkho, UNICEF, Healing the Children, Shriner's Hospital, and the Children's Hospital in Cincinnati, their American host family, the media such as ABC network, and various individuals like the Zamans (a pseudonym referring to the Bangladeshi family who had helped organize Bina's and Jharna's medical treatment in the U.S.). The two girls felt pressured by the expectations of these supporters and funders. Life in Cincinnati, thus, was not always the "fairy tale" it had been made out to be by some of the parties involved.

Both girls were enrolled first in language classes, and then in school. The condition of Bina's health made it difficult for her to go to school regularly. Her host family, however, was very keen on the girls adhering to a strict routine in the household, any aberration from which would often lead to conflict. Tensions frequently arose around cultural expectations. For instance, mealtimes were strictly maintained and this was a hard adjustment because in their own homes, as in many Bangladeshi households, they followed a more leisurely and flexible schedule. The girls were often not hungry at the times the host family ate their meals, particularly dinner, which was a very early affair by Bangladeshi standards. Snacking between meals was strictly forbidden, and the girls could not just eat something from the fridge if they were hungry in between meals or later in the evening. Moreover, the girls were not allowed to cook Bangladeshi foods in the house. Because of these various changes in eating habits, they both lost significant amounts of weight in the first year. Bina recalled one particular incident:

One day I was very hungry before lunchtime because I could not eat breakfast as early as our host family did. Their kids were visiting so the house was full of people. There was a plate of cookies on the dining table, and I took one. Their son told his mother, "Mom, Bina took a cookie." I was outside on the deck eating the cookie when my host-mom charged towards me and asked, "What's that in your hand?" She took the half-eaten cookie from my hand. "Did you ask me before taking the cookie?" This was hurtful. I thought of all the food at home that I wouldn't even eat when my mother asked me to and here, I had to ask permission to eat a cookie!

Later, when I came inside for lunch, my host-mom apologized and said, "I am sorry. I didn't intend to be mean. I didn't want you to eat a cookie and spoil your appetite before lunch. In my house there are rules, and you have to follow them." At the time, my English wasn't so good so it was hard for me to communicate. She could have asked me nicely. Usually, she always addressed me as "sweetie pie." She could have explained,

"Sweetie pie, this is lunchtime. Don't eat a cookie." But, she
didn't do that. I didn't like the way she came at me. It was the
same issue when I was too sick to go to school and she would
get angry. She would make me work in the garden in the sun.
That made my headaches worse. She would say, "There are rules
in this house, and you have to follow them." Sometimes, when
the family wanted privacy, they would ask us to go outside in
the cold! Why couldn't they send us upstairs to our room? We
were not allowed to talk on the phone, or watch more than half
an hour of TV a day, and that too only the Christian channel.

Religion became another source of tension. Bina and Jharna were
required to go to church with their host family despite their own Muslim
faith. Bina recalled that

Very soon after we arrived in Cincinnati we had to start going
to church with them and then to Bible reading classes. When we
objected, they said they could not leave us alone in the house. I
was seventeen at the time. We didn't have a choice in the matter.
We were scared; we didn't know many people here. If they got
angry, who would take care of us? Our medical treatment was
the most important thing, we couldn't risk having them upset. So,
we didn't open our mouths. I asked them to take us to a mosque
once, but they refused. One day, I was talking to my uncle in
Bangladesh on the phone when my host family was getting ready
for church. They wanted me to finish my conversation so we
could leave together. Because it was an important conversation,
and my uncle was leaving town for a month and we would not
have another opportunity to talk for a while, I asked if I could
stay back to talk to him then. But, the family got upset. My *khalu*
(maternal uncle) got upset when he learned that I was going to
church. He hung up the phone.
    My host family wanted me to convert to Christianity. They
said everyone who came to their house to live must convert. I
was very scared when I heard this. They took Jharna and me
to separate rooms and talked to us about converting. They said
our families did not live in America, so they would not come
to know that we were going to church. The pressure was quite
intense, so we called Kaneez *Apa*. She tried to explain to them

that we were Muslims, that we love our faith and did not want
to take up Christianity. Another reason we did not want to go
to church was that all kinds of people would come and afterward
try to hug us. This made us very uncomfortable, we were not
used to hugging strangers, especially men. Some of the older
men would even fondle us! We did report this to our host-mom,
and she followed up on this at church. You have to understand
that the family loved us and took very good care of us. I too
loved them, and still do. I am sure they had their own reasons
for doing these things, but I am explaining to you the situation
from my perspective.

In relaying these stories Bina did not want to unduly blame her host family
but wanted me to understand that conflicts naturally occurred between them
and that she was relating to me her perspective, knowing there were other
legitimate ones as well.

According to Bina, it was this friction over going to Church and
converting to Christianity that led their local Bengali friends to intervene
and request that HTC find alternative housing for the girls, perhaps with
a Muslim family. After living with the American host family for eighteen
months, the girls were then moved to a Pakistani family that HTC had
imagined to be Muslims but were actually Parsi. They lived not far from
the first host family, so the girls continued to keep in touch with them and
visit occasionally. Here, they enrolled in GED programs, and learned to
commute to school on their own by bus, which Bina appreciated. However,
similar issues began to arise when the girls were still not able to go to the
mosque, which for them would have been an opportunity to meet with their
community of Bengali Muslims. There were also conflicts over the limitations
involving when and what the girls could eat and having to do almost all
of the household chores on top of keeping up with school and the medical
treatment. Moreover, this family was not as diligent as the first host family
about the girls' medical treatment and missed many appointments.

A significant development in these months was Bina and Jharna's decision to explore their options for staying in America. Bina explains that HTC
had sponsored them to be in the United States only for two years, but at
the end of this time their medical treatment was not complete. In fact, the
doctors recommended that Bina remain under their care in the interest of
her long-term good health. In addition, Bina felt that she and her family
were at risk in Bangladesh from Dano and his associates. Her family had

received several threatening phone calls and even visits by Dano's friends during the time Bina was in America. Naripokkho lawyers were building a case against them. The media exposure surrounding Bina had provoked a backlash from these men.

In 2000, in the first year of her stay with the American host family, Bina applied for asylum status in the United States, thus defying the terms of her contract with Healing the Children. When a letter from the lawyer's office with the details of Bina's immigration application reached HTC, the sponsoring parties were upset. The Zamans, the Bangladeshi family in Michigan who had helped organize the sponsorship, having heard from HTC, contacted Naripokkho. Nasreen Huq tried to persuade Bina to rethink her decision and try other options for staying in America, like looking for academic scholarships. Bina's relationship with both organizations became very contentious. One HTC staff member moved Bina and Jharna in to her own house with the intention of sending them to Bangladesh. According to Bina, they were not allowed to leave the house or talk on the phone. Both girls' passports were taken by HTC staff. Bina described one difficult conversation:

> They [HTC] asked me, "Why did you apply for immigration?" I said, "I need security in my life. Here in the U.S. I can study, get a job, and help my family. I love my life, and I want to be safe." They said, Naripokkho informed them that I had lied about my situation in Bangladesh. That my family was not in any real danger. I said, "I am not interested to hear what Naripokkho and others said about me. I don't want to hear about it." I am sorry that because of what I have done, other girls cannot come to America for medical treatment. Because our contract with HTC specified that we cannot stay here. I am sorry other people will be hurt because of what I did. But, I decided that I would not think about HTC, about Naripokkho, or other acid-burned girls. I did this for myself. When I filed for immigration, HTC informed Naripokkho. These two organizations had a lot of problems because the promise was broken, the understanding was broken. I did this for myself—I did not think of them. The contract was between the two organizations. I don't believe that I should be blamed for the terms of the contract and what happened to the other girls. I think they [the sponsoring organizations] did the *beymaani* [betrayal]. Thousands of people are coming to this country in various ways. What had I done that they had to prevent all the other girls from coming here for treatment? Why

blame me? "Whoever comes here will stay back," they said! That's not true. Not everybody wants to stay here. I stayed because I had my own issues. HTC punished us by punishing all these other girls. Why should that be my responsibility? Naripokkho was angry with me because their campaign suffered. Everybody was doing business with me, using me. I am not a thing to do business with. Go everywhere and do interviews! I am not a toy. So, I stopped doing interviews.

My relationship with Naripokkho was ruined. It had been a long and beautiful relationship. I don't know if they will forgive me; I broke their heart. They loved me a lot. But, I did it for my own life. I thought of myself. If they don't understand that, I can't do much about it.

Eventually, my lawyer contacted HTC and said that I was now under the protection of the government, and that they couldn't forcibly send me to Bangladesh. During the time we were in her house [the HTC staff member], we couldn't go to our doctor's appointments, and when we finally left her house they withdrew support for our treatment.

It was the understanding of her sponsoring networks that by staying back she would, (1) jeopardize chances of any other acid violence survivor to come to the United States for medical treatment; (2) be responsible for Naripokkho's loss of face in the national and international advocacy communities; and (3) betray the trust of the international community, which had come forth with assistance. Further, in Bina's absence, a trial could not be held to prosecute her attacker, which activists of Naripokkho believed to be a serious setback in the acid campaign. Because Bina's story had received media coverage nationally and internationally, this trial would have been particularly significant for the larger campaign.

About the trial she said she requested her uncle not to appear as a witness until after her immigration was finalized. "If I am alive, Dano will pay. If we cannot take him to trial, God will do it. I did not want to take the risk. So, we did not proceed with the case. I know Naripokkho wanted to help but the fact is they will not always be with us. Other organizations cannot always protect us. My life would not be secure in Bangladesh" (B. Akhter, personal communication, December 27–28, 2004).

Bina realizes the grave consequences of her action. As an organizer in the anti-acid violence campaign herself, she understands the setback suffered by her peers in Bangladesh, and particularly the young women who were denied medical treatment in the United States following Bina and Jharna's "defection" from the terms of agreement. She continues to believe, however, that her sponsors should also take responsibility for drawing up a contract that was limited in considering the realities of her situation. Also, she believed that her life would be better in Cincinnati, and that her sponsoring organizations could never guarantee the kind of economic and social security she wanted if she returned to Bangladesh. This did not necessarily mean every other survivor would feel the same way. In fact, my conversations with several survivors in Bangladesh who had gone for treatment in European countries indicated that they had had no intention of seeking to immigrate there. They had missed their families and home too much to even think about it.

As she and her lawyer embarked on processing her asylum papers, Bina moved in with a Bangladeshi expatriate family in Cincinnati. Although Healing the Children abandoned the sponsorship of the two girls and tried to return them to Bangladesh, truncating their medical treatment, the doctors at Shriner's Hospital continued to care for them pro bono.

It was a lonely life in Cincinnati, yet Bina Akhter believed that she could continue to contribute to the campaign against acid violence in Bangladesh from the United States. On her eighteenth birthday, Bina moved into her own apartment, and began to attend high school courses by night and a nursing assistant program by day. She had begun touring the country, sharing her own experiences and giving presentations on violence against women's and girls' education programs in Bangladesh. In the spring of 2002, she was a speaker at Boston University's Take Back the Night rally. Bina's effort to tell her story gained her international fame. She had the ability to draw crowds, to stir emotions, and to question people about their own assumptions and beliefs. These same characteristics had made her the leader of the acid survivors' network in Naripokkho. Nasreen Huq had said as much during an interview, "Bina gave the acid campaign its stature, she was the star. One has to own a certain degree of leadership qualities in order to do the job that Bina was able to do" (N. Huq, personal communication, April 12, 2003).

The Faces of Hope Story

One direct consequence of internationalizing the anti–acid violence campaign was the television report titled "Faces of Hope," featuring the story of Bina Akhter's "arrival" in the United States. Connie Chung, a reporter, and Teri

Whitcraft, a producer of ABC's *20/20*, had traveled to Bangladesh to research a one-hour segment on acid violence. Various western publications such as *Ms.* (Welch, 1999) and *Marie Claire* (Brooker, 1998) and TV networks and programs such as CNN (1999), BBC (1999), and Oprah Winfrey Show (1999) had already reported on acid violence in Bangladesh. Thus, although not the first program but influential nonetheless, "Faces of Hope" held the promise of generating further attention from an international community. Yet it is also crucial to remember that the use of personal narratives of suffering in mass media venues can both bolster and impede human rights campaigns, by emphasizing certain aspects—for instance, sensationalizing "distant suffering" and implying that such suffering is a consequence of other inferior and foreign cultures—while obscuring others, such as the agency of local actors and contributions to "local" suffering made by global relations of power. A transnational feminist analysis of trauma narratives presented by such mass media venues therefore gives us important insight into the contradictory roles such narratives can play in human rights organizing.

Connie Chung's trip preceded Bina and Jharna's departure to the United States for medical treatment, and this fact ultimately influenced the angle of her report, which was spun as a "story of arrival." Chung's opening remarks were conscientious in reminding the viewers that the report in no way implied that acid throwing was a "cultural practice" of Bangladesh or an Islamic tradition. Despite the disclaimer in the beginning, however, acid throwing is framed as a crime of the poor in a patriarchal Muslim nation, through the use of specific terminology and visual images. As the narrator describes desperate poverty, city scenes reflect men performing *uzzu* (ablutions prior to prayer) and praying in mosques. Women (the victims) are shown staring at the camera behind wire fences and walking on the streets clad in dark *burqas*. Thus Sherene Razack's analysis, to which I alluded in the Introduction of this book, of the triangularly organized allegorical figures of the "dangerous Muslim man (or, nation, or culture)," "imperiled Muslim woman," and "civilized European" anchored the visual dimension of the narrative of this report.

Moreover, in Chung's voice-over, the escalating phenomenon was described as one of revenge committed by spurned suitors and common among the poor. Bina, one such "victim," around whom the story revolved, was introduced as a "brave" young woman living a "desperate" life in "one of the world's poorest nations," who awaited the help of "American surgeons to reclaim her shattered life." John Morrison, the British expatriate philanthropist who was appointed by UNICEF as director of the Acid Survivors Foundation at its inception, said, "This is one of the most barbaric acts there can possibly be. What it does is not only disfigure a woman for life, but it also ruins her life" ("Faces of Hope," November 1, 1999). Morrison's words precede a clip showing Chung in the dungeons of Dhaka Central Jail, interviewing three male prisoners sentenced to life in prison for committing acid attacks. Huddled together in a row, the lighting seemingly intentionally dimmed, the three men appear pathetic and puny in the face of Chung's pointed and sophisticated questions. The men, who had "avenged" the slighting of their masculinity by ruining the "offending" women's faces, in this scene are shown as deliberately emasculated.

By assigning people featured in the report predetermined roles, "Faces of Hope" deployed the victim-savior-savage prototype narrative I alluded to in the prologue. Moreover, by evoking images like burqa-clad women, the use of *azan* in the background, and the presentation of the prisoners as diminished men, the producers (even if unwittingly) make use of Orientalist rescue narratives concerning the Muslim woman as the ultimate victim subject, and the Muslim man as aggressor yet feminized, and John Morrison as the white male savior.

The same kind of rescue narrative framework appears in other media presentations of the acid violence story. For instance, in 2002, the "Foreign Relations" desk of the *Daily Star*–Bangladesh ran a press release on behalf of the British High Commission on John Morrison's anointment as "Officer of the Order of the British Empire (OBE) by Queen Elizabeth II, on the occasion of the "Birthday Honors" in her Golden Jubilee year. The Press Release reported that Morrison, "was the motive power that brought together various Bangladeshi organizations to provide help and assistance for those injured and disfigured by acid violence" and that because of "his efforts, the Acid Survivors Foundation was established" (Queen Elizabeth Honours, 2002). The article affirmed ASF as having "a high domestic and international profile" where Bangladesh nationals work "ceaselessly under the direction of Dr. Morrison" (Queen Elizabeth Honours, 2002). True to this heroic representation, Morrison (the white male savior) asserts in the "Faces of Hope" report the need for "urgent action," and is seen at work with top executives from fifteen national and international nonprofit organizations. Connie Chung then introduces Nasreen Huq, the activist who was so instrumental in developing the anti–acid violence campaign in Bangladesh, *after* Morrison's call for "urgent action." Huq, portrayed as the "women's activist," explains the motive behind the suitors' act of revenge: "Most men actually look at women as property. And you're not supposed to have an opinion about whether you want to be with him or not. If he wants you, you are damn well going to be his." Chung goes on to narrate the details of Bina's story, at one point reaching toward the younger girl's face and touching the toughened skin on her forehead ("Faces of Hope," November 1, 1999). The juxtaposition of the earlier scene in which Chung is shown at a cold distance from the male perpetrators of violence, with this one, in which she is empathetically reaching out to the female victim, offers a specific gendered/racialized reading. The intended American audience can empathize with the distant (Muslim) female victim, yet remind themselves that the act of violence is of a "foreign" patriarchal culture and religion, seemingly far removed from their own.

Alcoff and Gray (1993) point out that television reports work to (re) produce dominant narratives of "survivor speech" through a variety of narrative strategies that sensationalize and objectify survivors and serve to put emotional distance between the audience and the survivor. Wendy Hesford (2004) calls this an "empathetic unsettlement" whereby the audience as "secondary witness" experiences empathy "but not full identification" with victims (p. 113). This distance is important and often achieved through inserting "expert voices of interpretation," such as John Morrison's narrations in to the television segments. These voices, as Alcoff and Gray (1993) point out, are often of the elite and professional class. In this case, we see the white male voice stamping acid violence as "barbaric"—a term widely reserved for third world "savagery," particularly pertaining to women. The historical connection to colonialist deployment of the same logic in its own legitimization cannot be lost here. It also serves to validate and reify acid violence as a "distant" problem and suffering from which the American audience is not only removed but implicated only through the role of the savior. After all, in the United States American surgeons will correct Bina's face and she will be "safe" in her new "palace" like home.

Chung describes Bina's home in a Dhaka slum with piteous awe as the viewers watch seven members of her family huddled on one bed. The viewer is clearly supposed to feel a certain level of horror as Bina's happy home is diminished to a third world hovel. Chung describes Bina as "poorest of the poor," by whose standards, however, we are not sure. Meanwhile, on the screen, we see the concrete walls of Bina's residence, a television set, and ceiling fans, and in the report, we also learn that Bina participated in South Asian regional sports events and attended school, and that her uncle runs a small business. None of these pieces of her life are indicative of someone who is the "poorest of the poor" in Bangladesh.

In the report, Chung continues to trace the beginning of Bina's providential journey to Cincinnati, the place that holds the promise of American surgeons "repairing her ravaged face." Chung's crew accompanied the two teenagers through tearful good-byes at Dhaka International Airport on their way to "a new home, a new family, and perhaps a new face." So, the story of arrival unfolded. "Thanks to the generosity of so many Americans, Bina is about to taste a life she never imagined," said Jack Ford, Chung's coanchor. An announcer's voice stated, "A journey to America brings new hope" ("Faces of Hope," November 1, 1999). From the one-room "hut" in Hazaribag, Dhaka, shared by seven family members, Bina arrived at her new home, likened to a "palace" by Chung, that raised "her hopes higher than they've ever been" ("Faces of Hope," November 1, 1999). Viewers watched Bina accompany her host family to view the sights of Cincinnati and to participate in the quintessential American experience of a Cincinnati Reds baseball game. Bina, the narrator tells the viewers, "was happier than she'd ever been" ("Faces of Hope," November 1, 1999).

The program presents Bina as facing the news of her irrevocably damaged eye with grace and heroism. Finally "free" from the repression of her past, it is implied, she is ready to face anything. "As long as I'm here for the treatment, I'll be safe," she says. "If I were still in Bangladesh, I might have been kidnapped or killed by now." Chung's voice-over says, "For the first time in a long time, she wasn't afraid." We watch "Windy," Bina's nickname among friends in Bangladesh, for her athletic talents, running in slow motion on screen, and her voice-over of hope saying, "America is a big country. If we all work together and stand as one, we can conquer the world" ("Faces of Hope," November 1, 1999).

"Faces of Hope," then, imagined Bina as a grateful recipient of aid, and therefore a "good" victim. It indicated an inability to understand the lived reality of her situation or to see her as a complex subject who actually participated in the negotiations that brought her to Cincinnati. The program gave wide exposure to a critical human rights campaign, while simultaneously reproducing colonial images of victimized third world women being rescued by benevolent first world institutions. This narrative did nothing, of course, to challenge the historically asymmetrical relations of power and authority that usually frame such representations by western media of the "third world," but instead reinscribed such power dynamics. Bina's own role in shaping her future was obscured, as was the role of the advocacy work done by Naripokkho members.

From Bina's interview, discussed above, we know that she had declined an offer of going to Spain because she had not felt ready. The decision to accept Shriner's Hospital's invitation was, thus, well thought out. By Bina's own admission it was the result of two years of work, mainly by Naripokkho activists, and not a sudden stroke of sheer luck. Bina chose to come to America, primarily for treatment for her damaged eye—and not to acquire "a new face," as the *20/20* report repeatedly emphasized. Surgery to restore the victim's "original face" seems to be the miracle cure offered by the west for which the victim has to physically leave the place of suffering and travel to the place of freedom. Other more pressing needs and wants that are always prioritized by the survivors are not mentioned at all in this report. The terms of Bina's "arrival," stay, and treatment, as we saw in Bina's story, were also carefully dictated by the sponsors and the hosts and were not altogether "rosy," as confidently predicted by the televised story. The fiery Bina Akhter, who spoke out against women's oppression, demanded justice from the government, and delivered impassioned speeches at women's rallies, was reduced to a childlike figure dazzled by America. At the end of the report, we hear Bina using the imperial language of "conquest"—"we can conquer the world"—as if to make her transfer, and transformation, to the "free world" complete.

In 2002, I had the opportunity to interview Teri Whitcraft, the producer of the ABC *20/20* segment, who explained some of the narrative choices for the segment:

> I was doing an Internet search one night on violence and social justice issues, when I stumbled upon an article on acid violence against women in Bangladesh in *Ms Magazine.* I knew then that we had to do this story. Fortunately for us, we entered at a moment when Bina was poised to leave for Ohio. Thus, we were able to film her arrival. This has been quite a journey for us and one that hasn't yet ended. We have continued to film various events in Bina's life. For instance, I sent a team for one of the first surgeries. We have so much footage. And, we plan to be there when Bina gets her citizenship. That's going to be the end. You see, a story such as this needs a proper ending. People want to know what happens to her, and we're going to be there till the end. (T. Whitcraft, personal communication, November 23, 2002)

The producer's focus on Bina's citizenship as the "proper ending" to her story serves to draw the narrative focus of the anti–acid violence campaign away from the activism in Bangladesh and elsewhere, to United States citizenship as the ultimate solution. It implies that Bina's story, like all good immigrant stories, ends with citizenship. The irony here is of course that the road to that citizenship is paved with many contestations, not the least of which is the United States' granting of a limited visa to victims of violence, and taking away that victim's right to treatment if she happened to transgress the strict codes governing the contours of her stay in America.

Scholars such as Schaffer and Smith (2004) as well as Wendy Hesford (2004) have developed definitions of life narratives that can help to contextualize the ways in which the international media contributes to spectacularizing "third world violence," often in the service of generating public response, yet at the same time reinscribing problematic and simplistic generalizations. Schaffer and Smith (2004) define life narrative as a broad term encompassing a range of personal storytelling based on the experiential (p. 7). Wendy Hesford (2004) locates the deployment of the genre of life narratives, or "testimonio," specifically within the transnational human rights movement. These testimonials, often by victims of gender violence in third world contexts, play a key role in advancing an international human rights agenda by mobilizing diverse publics into action, even as they further romanticize spectacularized renditions of the speaking subject. Hesford (2004) cautions that scholars and practitioners must account for the "*ungovernability* of trauma and the methodological and ethical crises posed by its representation" (p. 106). This means recognizing that documentations, interpretations, circulations, receptions, and representations of trauma narratives cannot be contained and are always incommensurable. Hesford (2004) terms this instability of narrative genre a crisis of reference to mean "the inability of representation to capture, as in fix or make static, the truth" leading to difficulty in using these narratives within human rights campaigns to persuade legal and social action (p. 107). The mediated nature of life narratives or the intersubjectivity of them has pushed transnational feminist studies to consider not only the social location of the writer, or the "speaking subject," but also the circumstances in which the text is produced. The critical negotiation involved in the struggle within which trauma narratives are told, listened to, and interpreted occur within "available cultural and national scripts and truth-telling conventions" (Hesford, 2004, p. 108). The discursive subjectivity and agency of the narrator, and the ethical responses the narratives evoke from diverse actors are shaped within such rhetorical conventions.

While reports such as the *20/20* segment presented certainly catalyzed social and legal action (outpouring of support on behalf of Bina and Jharna; the endorsement of ABC journalists for Bina's asylum case in the United

States), these are incommensurable narratives that are primarily about rescue and salvation. One might ask at what cost are these narratives publicly
reinscribed? Is there room to talk about internal struggles like the ones
that unfolded between HTC and Bina, or Naripokkho activists and Bina,
in such narratives, and more generally within human rights narratives that
so categorically imagine its victims and saviors? Even as such colonialist
narratives are deployed by western media with the effect of obscuring the
power dynamics shaping transnational relationships, how might these same
ungovernable narratives also open up space for transgressions?

Schaffer and Smith (2004) point out that in the west, trauma narratives have been told primarily through the lens of psychoanalysis, a tradition that is ineluctably tied to the rendition of victimization processes of
the Holocaust. This paradigmatic status of Holocaust stories for explicating
remembering, witnessing, and recovery experiences of victims, they argue,
has limited the understanding of trauma in other contexts and histories of
suffering, obscuring gender, racial, and national differences. This western
paradigm, they argue, prioritizes the telling of and understanding trauma
through individual and collective stories of suffering of Holocaust survivors,
which make up a significant portion of the western field of human rights
literature. Schaffer and Smith go on to challenge psychoanalysis as the predominant interpretive frame for understanding trauma, and the Holocaust
as the quintessential experience of trauma. They open up a discussion of
diverse cultural, historical, and experiential understandings of trauma and
its rootedness in cultural, institutional, and political structures (pp. 22–23).

Further, the individual emphasis in human rights narratives in the western
context is also connected to the rise of global capitalism, which champions
individual rights and uniqueness. For instance, sensationalized stories of
individuals triumphing over their sufferings, such as the one furthered by
the ABC "story of arrival" and future plans to culminate a report with the
"proper ending" of Bina's American citizenship, have been endlessly popular
in media circuits. These frames have been harnessed by transnational actors,
including human rights NGOs, to package their own campaigns and agendas.

Of particular interest to this discussion are the ways in which "distant"
narratives of trauma and suffering are mediated within international human
rights regimes, as are the strategies and methodologies that render intelligible
the experiences of "foreign subjects" in local and transnational sites. Pointing
to the success of linking local campaigns of gender violence to transnational
movements of human rights, Schaffer and Smith (2004) remind us that "In
these instances, transits between the local and global and within pockets

of modernity involve complex negotiations of traditional and modernist discourses and practices. In other instances, stories may be framed within traditional, communal, religious, or philosophic frameworks different from, but arguably consonant with, modernist aspirations for human dignity and social justice" (Schaffer and Smith, 2004, p. 17). In other words, trauma narratives located at the intersection of local and global spaces might rely on "common sense" scripts but also throw into crisis existing paradigms of cross-border communications.

These narratives, then, hint at the paradox of representation for human rights activists, what Wendy Hesford (2004) calls the dilemma of speaking or staying silent, given the mixture of empowering and voyeuristic elements of these actions. One has to recognize the role reports such as "Faces of Hope" serve in raising awareness and generating support for campaigns against gender violence, and even providing opportunities for victims and activists to state or overstate their own particular angle in order to further just one aspect of transnational campaigns, which are inevitably multi-faceted. This positive dimension is achieved, even as the overall narrative of such western media representations tends to reinforce reductive Orientalist categories. Weaving together the multiple narratives of Bina, Naripokkho, and the western media's versions of the anti-acid campaign can offer a necessary disruption that does not claim any one as more true but points to the complex rhetorical and negotiation processes entailed in the telling and remembering of events/lives.

I do not mean to overstate the importance of the *20/20* report, or deny that audience readings of it can be multiple. The *20/20* report appeared among a host of news reports in the United States following Bina's "coming to America" story, all of which came at it from similar angles. For instance, the *Cincinnati Enquirer* credited "Healing the Children" as "an international charity that seeks high-tech care for children from developing nations" (Bonfield, 1999). The *Honolulu Star Bulletin* described it as "hard to look at Bina" the "subject of a fascinating story," who had acid thrown at her while "asleep one night in [her family's] Bangladesh hut" (Chang, 1999). *The Cincinnati Post* quotes Bina from the ABC news program as saying, "From the moment I arrived in Cincinnati, I felt like I had stepped into a dream world," and notes that the "women are already gaining a sense of hope from just being in the United States" (Conte, 1999). The article goes on to explain, "In Bangladesh, women generally survive through the support of husbands, and these women are typically doomed to a life of extreme poverty." Stories of acid victims have continued to appear in the American press with titles such as "Victims of Acid Attacks Find New Life in the West," and "Fort Myers Surgeon Lends Skills to Repair Third World Horrors" (Wu, 2002).

While it may be true that coming to the United States offered Bina certain opportunities, it is also true, as we learned from Bina's story over the years, that such an "arrival" is riddled with contradictions of loss as well as gain. Lost in this portrayal of the grateful Bina are her day-to-day negotiations of adjusting to a new life that, on the one hand, promised a recovery, but, on the other hand, expected obedience to cultural traditions that were not her own. Again, Bina's own story suggests that obedience is often a result of fear and desperation since the survivors have nowhere else to turn in a foreign country. For instance, Bina admitted that she had no choice in attending church services and enrolling in Christian education classes because her medical treatment depended on adhering to HTC, and by association her host family's rules. Because Healing the Children espoused Christian values, they placed the survivors in the homes of a family who expected boarders to abide by those same standards. When Bina's actions turned her in to a "bad victim," she was in a manner of speaking "kidnapped" from her so-called place of safety (home of the host family) and held in the home of the HTC staff member, who tried illegally and against her will to return her to Bangladesh, which would have ended her medical treatment. This is a different story from the one of benevolence, which does not fit neatly into the paradigmatic representations of survivors and their advocates, particularly ones that come from the other side of the global divide. Indeed, as Hesford (2004) has explained, this version of the story is what is lost in the crisis of reference, and the crisis of witnessing in such narratives as spun by the *20/20* report. Also lost in this is Bina's own agency and shifting sense of self throughout the course of the campaign.

Naripokkho's Story

Naripokkho's own work related to the acid campaign saw significant shifts in the years following Bina Akhter's departure for the United States and the establishment of the Acid Survivors Foundation. Paying close attention to its narrative allows us to further complicate an understanding of transnational human rights movement dynamics, and to observe the effects "back home" of the process that Friedman (1999) has called "transnationalism reversed." This section weaves together the at times dissonant voices of different activists involved in the campaign, and thereby continues to point to the partial, contingent, and constructed nature of narratives this chapter wishes to illuminate. Simultaneously, it offers a critique of some of the organization's strategies and vision deployed with regard to empowering survivors of acid violence.

In 2003, when I visited the Naripokkho office during a research trip, the only area of the campaign that they still maintained was the legal arena. Advocate Kamrun Nahar explained that the current work on acid violence was part of a larger project titled Beyond Beijing: Building a National Network of Women's Organizations and Undertaking a Pilot Study on Violence Against Women (K. Nahar, personal communication, April 11, 2003). This project was supported by the Canadian High Commission, the Royal Danish Embassy, and the Royal Norwegian Embassy. The study that Naripokkho was undertaking had two primary purposes, both related to the organization's activism on gender violence. One was to address issues of institutional reform and the other was to conduct a national survey on gender violence. Many of the key activists who had coordinated the acid campaign in the mid-1990s, she told me, had moved on to other projects and organizations, several taking positions at the ASF.

Speaking with some of these activists revealed that the organization's diminished role in the acid violence campaign also had to do with an internal "falling out" among members, in part a consequence of Bina Akhter's decision to defy the terms of the contract for medical treatment for acid violence survivors in the United States, and the subsequent negative effects on the campaign in Bangladesh. One example was my interview with Ms. Khan.

A member of Naripokkho, Ms. Khan, had been instrumental in organizing a pipeline of twenty survivors to receive medical treatment at the Shriner's Hospital in Ohio.[1] She had been key in mobilizing Bangladeshi medical professionals in the United States, who had in turn set up a sponsorship program with Healing the Children. In her view, Bina Akhter's decision to seek asylum "jeopardized" the pipeline of twenty survivors set to come to the United States for medical treatment and upset the former relationship between Naripokkho organizers and Bina. The organization felt Bina had acted selfishly and ruined the chances for the rest of the survivors who were awaiting the opportunity for medical treatment in Cincinnati. These differences between Bina and Naripokkho, which took place in early 2001, affected Bina's health mentally and physically to the extent that her host family at the time had made concerned phone calls to Ms. Khan and asked her "to leave the girl alone." This phone call in turn had infuriated Ms. Khan, who, as one of the principal organizers of the pipeline of survivors going to Ohio, felt she had very legitimate reasons to challenge Bina's decision. Subsequently she had severed all ties with Bina and withdrawn from the acid work altogether.

Bristi Chowdhury, who had once shared a deep bond with Bina and had supported her throughout her stay at DMCH and accompanied her to the Amnesty Youth Leadership Summit in New York in 1998, also shared Ms. Khan's discontent over what she called "Bina's utterly selfish decision to stay back in the U.S. in flagrant disregard of Naripokkho's concerns" (B. Chowdhury, personal communication, April 14, 2003).

Ms. Khan described some of the meticulous organizing that had enabled the campaign to internationalize:

> An old family friend, who is a physician practicing in Michigan, United States, came for a visit to Dhaka in the summer of 1998. He wanted to help once he learned about the situation in Bangladesh. So, we put together a dossier of pictures and case studies for him to show other physicians in the U.S. He mobilized the expatriate Bangladeshi community and approached Healing the Children and Shriner's Hospital. These institutions came forward with the offer for free treatment for twenty acid-burn survivors. Vast amounts of time and effort went in to this process. A very important part of the agreement with HTC, however, was that none of the girls could stay back in the U.S. If they did, it would terminate the program there and then. This was an agreement with the U.S. State Department for acquiring the requisite visas for the survivors. Dr. Zaman and his colleagues had put their own names on the agreement, they had given their personal assurances to the sponsoring agency. This [some survivors staying back in the U.S.] had always been a concern—however, I just didn't expect it to be the first two! In fact, when our physician friend in Michigan was trying to enlist the Bangladeshi community, some people had said to him, "How do you know that people will not throw acid on themselves just to have the opportunity to come to America? How do you prove a case is genuine?" But he disregarded those concerns. (Khan, personal communication, April 14, 2003)

Ms. Khan had been in a particularly tricky position, being the key liaison among all the actors: the expatriate Bangladeshi community that mobilized sponsors in the United States, the attendant organizations that sponsored the acid victims for treatment, Naripokkho organizers, and the survivors. The fall-out occurring among all of these parties left her understandably frustrated and angry. Her comments above, however, are revealing for us as we come to see the various power structures that were navigated in this campaign: for instance, it was the U.S. State Department that laid out the terms of the contract, and we might also critique the class-based assumptions of the Bangladeshi community that people in Bangladesh would be willing to self-inflict acid injuries just for an opportunity to immigrate to the United States. It should also be acknowledged that Naripokkho's virtual withdrawal from the work that it initiated is not unprecedented in studies of intraorganizational dynamics in women's advocacy groups. For instance, Honor Ford-Smith (1997), a member of the Sistren Collective, an organization in Jamaica that worked with women both culturally and politically, describes the crossroads that members of well-intentioned women's groups often encounter. Despite goals to work in the interest of social justice, women's groups can operate within, or reenact themselves, historically determined power relations in new forms. As she has argued, colonial narratives often work to regulate the production of the unwitting "development worker" in the image of the missionary (Ford-Smith, 1997).

Later Ms. Khan relayed the following story:

When I heard about Bina's plan to seek asylum, I called her. She gave me all sorts of excuses. She did the same to her host family, telling them that her family was in danger in Bangladesh. What danger? If her family was in danger, how come Mukti [Bina's cousin who had been the target of the acid attack that left Bina burned, and who now worked at ASF] was going to work every day? If you come to think about it, nobody is "safe" in Bangladesh. There is so much crime here. Bina's family is in no more danger than the next person. I just said one thing to Bina: that she would be responsible for stopping the treatment of eighteen girls. The next day, her host family called and accused me of shouting at Bina. They said she was very upset. I told them I had not shouted at her. "Is she lying to us then?" they asked me. I told them, "We are the people who sent her." They were yelling at me! My son was in the next room, and when he saw how upset I was he asked, "Why are you still talking to them? You have done enough for these girls." (Khan, personal communication, April 14, 2003)

Having access and connections to the medical community in the United States, Ms. Khan was able to mobilize a sizable expatriate initiative to help Bangladeshi survivors of acid attacks. This, as she points out, had been a risky initiative with the ever-present possibility of someone along the way defecting and thus jeopardizing the entire program with the possible humiliation of the organizers among an international community. When precisely that happened, the organizing group dissolved, turning accusatory eyes on those who needed their assistance. Ms. Khan and her fellow organizers spoke from a position of economic and social privilege when they speculated that the girls need not have applied for asylum because there was no real danger facing them in Bangladesh, or when they debated whether poor Bangladeshis were desperate enough to douse themselves with acid in order to avail themselves of opportunities to go to America. Having "done enough for these girls," in the formulation of Ms. Khan's son, they were able to withdraw from the acid violence work altogether. It was hard for them to accept Bina's disobedience to the rules of the agreement, not unlike the response of HTC.

This turn of events illuminates both the inter- and intranational cultural differences within women's organizing. In a conversation with Jenny Sharpe (2003), Gayatri Spivak shows how international civil society crosses borders in the name of "woman," and develops policy on development and human rights, which they profess to be for the benefit of the lowest strata of those living in the developing world. The reality on the ground, however, is quite different. In this instance, the international collaboration resting on the U.N. mandate for helping victims of violence enabled Naripokkho members to organize a pipeline of twenty acid survivors to go for medical treatment to America. When the pipeline fell through, the euphoria and enthusiasm of the activists dissipated along with their interest in supporting the "lowest strata," in this case the survivors of violence, because of a failure, I would argue, to understand the realities of the survivors' lives on the ground. It is not my intention here to pass judgment on Bina's or other Naripokkho members' actions and decisions. However, at the end of the day, it is she (and the 18 survivors who were not able to go to the United States for treatment), who bore the most painful consequences of the international and intranational negotiations.

Although ostensibly advancing gender justice and seemingly adapting democratic practices, Naripokkho was not only mired in asymmetrical power relations within transnational circuits, but also within its own organizational hierarchical and often class-based regulations. Activist scholar Honor Ford-Smith (1997) argues, "A language is needed that will help to analyze and address the contradiction between the emancipatory goals of groups and their internal practice, between their interest in transforming social relations toward liberatory power relations and the tense, conflicted organizational culture of many women's groups" (p. 216). There is need for language that can address the complexity of the conflicts that shape complicity and resistance in feminist spaces, both locally and globally.

Further, Ford-Smith (1997) discusses the contradictions of funding that often dictate the development of women's organizations and how those can consequently affect the group's democratic practices. The insistence on delivering "products," which are measured in technical terms, coupled with the often contradictory perennial search for the "grassroots women" by funding agencies, contribute to a cycle of eternal dependency. She says, "A rhetorical emphasis is placed on funding grassroots women's work and on building up the productive capacities of women's groups when, in fact, the way that the agencies operate lead to exactly the opposite results" (Ford-Smith, 1997, p. 216). For instance, to be able to expand and to function efficiently within a globalized environment, organizations need to attract members with a certain kind of skill set, who then train those lacking these skills. However, acquiring those skills would automatically mean that they were no longer eligible for "grassroots" funding. Such is the tricky situation for many women's groups. Thus, a hierarchy inevitably surfaces between those group members with the desirable skills (e.g., social connections, efficiency in English, western-educated, etc.) and those without. In Naripokkho's work we see glimpses of Ford-Smith's observations. The members of the organization are women with a set of skills and access to resources that enabled them to mount a campaign transnational in scope. In the process, survivors—particularly Bina—often if unwittingly took on the role of the grassroots organizers who, if and when "transgressive" from their "good victim" conduct, became the ones responsible for losing both international and even local support.

This hierarchical scenario is recognizable in the "dissolution" of Nari-pokkho's involvement in acid work, which I contend occurred not simply because of the emergence of ASF but rather resulted from a combination of interconnected events. Bina Akhter, the so-called grassroots beneficiary and activist, had provided currency to the organization and helped bring unprecedented national and international support. When she had ceased to be "grassroots," she also lost the nurturing relationships with both her sponsor, Healing the

Children (and by association ASF, CIDA, and UNICEF), who had found the measurable product of their work in Bina, and with her mentors at Naripokkho, who had found in her the star of their campaign.

Yet Bina's defection only served to quicken the disintegration of Naripokkho's involvement, as internal conflicts were already underway. The acid campaign had been designed by a small group of activists who had gradually gained the support of many key institutions. Just as the Naripokkho campaign had gained its legitimacy because of a few, if influential actors, the organization's role also disintegrated because of the withdrawal of the same few. That is the risk of campaigns that are not mass based, but rather instigated by few committed, if influential, members of society. Although the organization planned for an eventual mass-based campaign by involving more and more actors, especially survivors of violence, the full range of the campaign was not ultimately realized. Moreover, donor-funded campaigns such as this one, are mobilized within institutional spaces (such as NGOs) that inhibit mass-based collaborations.

Again, this problem is not singular to Naripokkho. Honor Ford-Smith (1997) asserts that women's groups often act on ad hoc strategies due to external pressures; for instance, donor agencies that respond to challenges in an ad hoc manner instead of allowing for more systematic and long-term solutions. She argues that the dictates of international funding agencies exacerbate internal contradictions among structures of race and class, specifically on issues having to do with power and authority. As a result, the organization can become constrained in terms of what it offers the community, as well as in its capacity to develop clear and effective organizational support, and its ability to satisfy members' needs (Ford-Smith, 1997).

While the acid campaign can be defined as successful because of the emergence of ASF's coordinated efforts, it lost one of its critical characteristics: the involvement of Naripokkho. This, perhaps, was inevitable once the proliferation of discourses and diversification of actors was underway. The benefits of the proliferation in discourse had led people like Ms. Khan to successfully organize a pipeline of survivors to receive medical treatment in a western country, but it had set certain limits on the same opportunities, which had unintended consequences—an example of "transnationalism reversed" (Friedman, 1999). What might be considered successful in one scale of the organizing, that is, mobilizing upward and internationally within transnational feminist organizing, can also have lesser-known consequences at the local front, which is an example of transnationalism reversed. Significant in this equation is who had the privilege to abdicate from the organizing. And class privilege was certainly one of the key factors, in tandem with others like the emergence of ASF, for Naripokkho's reduced involvement. When asked why the organization had discontinued its work against acid violence, Ms. Khan stated,

> The campaign just got too big. Naripokkho works on a volunteer basis, they don't have the time or the resources for work of that scale. Naripokkho can raise awareness; it can work as an activist organization. It couldn't provide all the services that the survivors needed. We are more equipped to do the research work. Besides, ASF is doing it now. ASF is quite well off, they can give the kind of support needed for this work. We didn't want that level of involvement. (Khan, personal communication, April 14, 2003)

In contrast, according to Bristi Chowdhury, the campaign stalled because of both internal and external politics within the Bangladeshi women's movement. She said,

> I think the way we first launched the campaign could have been better orchestrated. We got ahead of ourselves. We should have done more research, but then there just wasn't enough information available. Second, and this is connected to the first, we could have avoided an ASF. Instead, we should have gotten involved with other women's organizations. We tried, but "in-politics" both within our own organization and amongst various women's organizations kept us from it. No other [women's] organization came forward to work with us and neither did we seek them out before or after the acid workshop in 1997. Third, Naripokkho's Executive Committee could have been in the know from the beginning. We didn't have clear goals and we kept changing our plans and strategies. Most of the time, a few of us made the decisions according to the needs of the moment, based on what was going on at that moment. So, much of the blame also fell on us when things went wrong. (B. Chowdhury, personal communication, March 9, 2003)

By "in-politics" here Chowdhury refers to the competitiveness among women's organizations for funding, which led them to keep their agendas distinct from each other. In an earlier interview, Chowdhury had talked about how other organizations had come to visit some of the acid survivors at DMCH when she was going there biweekly to follow up and informally counsel them. "One day, we found out that [a women's NGO] had made a visit to the burns unit and had talked to some of the girls. One girl said to us that the representatives of this organization had asked them not to talk to us [Naripokkho staff]. This was strange because we were trying to help the girls, and this kind of rivalry is quite unnecessary. They [the women's NGO], however, never came back to the ward again, so the issue did not come up" (B. Chowdhury, personal communication, March 9, 2003).

Her reflections turned to Bina's role as a vital part of the changing direction of Naripokkho's work:

> I believe it was a mistake to choose Bina as the Naripokkho intern. We should have groomed someone else. We knew from the outset that she was a star. But, she was also a child. We should have known better. Nonetheless, Bina also did a lot of good work for Naripokkho. She brought a lot of glory to the organization. And, it's better that she tells her story than John Morrison, who goes around representing barbaric brown practices. It's like a white man coming in and saving poor brown women. If Bina had stayed on track, if she had come back to Bangladesh, she could have become the director of ASF one day, had she stayed and been properly groomed for it. (B. Chowdhury, personal communication, March 9, 2003)

Chowdhury questions her own organization's decision to put Bina in such an important role in the campaign even if she had proven to be a skillful organizer. Ironically, a touch of organizational ethnocentrism can be detected here, as Bina's ability to properly represent the campaign was questioned when the authenticity of the knowledge of middle-class feminists was not. And, even though Bina was an integral part of the campaign, here she is represented as someone needing "proper grooming" by the Naripokkho organizers, hence, setting up a clear division between women leading the campaign, and those who were mere participants.

In these comments, Bristi Chowdhury berated the donor community for hijacking the acid campaign and undermining the work of the local women's advocacy group—as exemplified by her indignation expressed at John Morrison—but left her own organization's representational choices unquestioned. She believed that Naripokkho's work reflected a truly organic approach where Bangladeshi women worked with Bangladeshi women and the survivors of acid violence worked to help themselves. Yet simultaneously, she believed that Bina, the star of the homegrown campaign, needed to be guided and groomed by her better-educated and more savvy older sisters. Bina was being shunned as the "uncultured" activist, one who had not "stayed on track," because she had acted as the ungrateful and wayward child of the campaign: the very campaign that had brought her into the limelight. From Naripokkho's point of view, Bina had betrayed the campaign because she had chosen to put her own needs over those of not only fellow survivors of violence, but also of the women's advocacy group. She had chosen to overlook the collective good of the campaign in order to advance her individual gain. And, if indeed Bina was the "child" that Bristi made her out to be, it was a tall order to expect her to be the only accountable one for the loss of her survivor sisters' opportunity for medical treatment in the United States. This appears to be a misplacement of responsibility, which should also be placed with the various structures governing the terms of Bina's contract, not the least of which is the U.S. State Department.

The subsequent conversations I had with other activists complicated the story of Naripokkho's diminished role in the campaign further. I learned that internationalization of the campaign introduced into the equation more troubling power relationships not only between "funders" and "recipients," but also within organizations and among individuals. For example, in 2003, Nasreen Huq no longer worked with Naripokkho and had taken the position of country director of ActionAid, a British development NGO in Bangladesh. She described her own decreasing involvement with Naripokkho as in part resulting from internal struggles that often singled her and her projects out as "too high profile" and "getting too much exposure." She described herself as someone who gave 150 percent to her projects, and who was critical of others' approach to their work if it seemed lacking in commitment (N. Huq, personal communication, April 5, 2003, Dhaka). In 1999, when Bina left for the United States, Nasreen Huq nominated another staff member from the organization who had served as the medical coordinator of the campaign in Naripokkho, to take on the position of the overall coordinator.

Earlier, I alluded to the unspoken hierarchy between those members of the organization who were mostly urban elites with western educational backgrounds, who worked for the organization on a volunteer basis and often brought in the grants for projects, and the full-time paid staff, who were not from the elite classes and were locally educated. The members were mostly in leadership positions, whereas the staff saw to the day-to-day operations of the organization. The medical coordinator was one such staff member, and her nomination by Nasreen Huq did not meet with approval from other members, an occurrence in contradiction with the organization's professed democratic governance process. Huq's desire to appoint the medical coordinator to the new position was a part of a longer chain of disagreements between herself and other members, some of which she believed to be class based. In the interview with me, Huq explained,

> Back in 1995, when I wanted to begin the work on acid vio-
> lence, Naripokkho was not really interested. I told them that I
> would do it anyway and did so under the auspices of Naripokkho
> even though they did not lend me much support. Only when
> Bristi joined as the intern, I finally had some support to do the
> groundwork like research, documentation, and follow up with
> medical and legal organizations. When the campaign gained
> in prominence, however, everybody benefited. The organization
> earned a lot of fame. I wanted to keep ASF within Naripokkho,
> but the in-politics did not allow me to pursue that direction. I
> was obstructed. (N. Nasreen, personal communication, April 5,
> 2003, Dhaka)

Here, as Bristi Chowdhury did in the earlier interview I discussed above, Nasreen Huq refers to "in-politics" that "obstructed" the formation of a more broad-based local response to gender violence. Speaking of these intense internal disagreements was by no means easy for Huq, as at this point of the interview her voice trembled, she wiped tears off her eyes and fought to remain composed. Turning to the later struggle over the consequences of Bina's decision to apply for immigration, Huq pointed out,

> In my opinion, Bina's actions led to two tremendous losses. First,
> Healing the Children withdrew sponsorship for the remaining
> survivors of acid violence. Second, we lost Bina's case in court.
> We faced so many challenges in organizing her case in court,
> even Dano who had been sheltered by Haji Selim the Awami
> League MP, had been apprehended and had been in prison for
> two years. But, Bina's *khalu* repeatedly failed to appear in court
> when he was being summoned for his statement. Dano has been
> released since then. It's really unfortunate. If the case had gone
> forward, because of Bina's international stature it would have
> had a really high profile and it would have been good for the

campaign. The sad thing is we lost her case after all that work. But, it didn't happen. Bina said to me, "What would that justice have given me? I have a better life now."

If Bina had returned to Bangladesh, she could have had a major role in the movement against acid violence. But, she would still be in the slum. I tried to explain to Naripokkho members: "You tell me, how many others have left [Bangladesh] and not returned? Students do it all the time when they decide to stay on and get a job. Bina did what was possible for her. She claimed asylum. I don't blame her. I am not angry with her for leaving. I am angry with her for not being entirely honest. She could have done it [applied for permanent residency in the United States] differently. She could have enrolled in school and gone about the process differently. I would have advised her to do that, but she did not tell me about her plan in the first place. (N. Huq, personal communication, April 5, 2003, Dhaka)

Nasreen Huq points to the class-based bias of some Naripokkho organizers in her comments about the concerns regarding Bina's decision to seek U.S. citizenship. Huq also mentioned that when she was negotiating with the U.S. embassy to secure visas for Bina and Jharna to travel to the United States, another member of Naripokkho had requested her to negotiate her nephew's student visa as well. Huq shared with me, "Because I had connections at the U.S. embassy, I didn't mind helping out. But, nobody was concerned whether this [Naripokkho member's] nephew would decide to stay back in the United States like they were with Bina and Jharna" (N. Huq, personal communication, April 5, 2003). Another feminist researcher I talked to pointed out that when students are granted visas to study in the United States, it is not normal practice to put conditions on their stay and demand, for instance, that they not fall in love with an American and stay back. Therefore, she asked, in the case of these two young women who were granted visas on medical terms, how could the U.S. State Department stipulate such expectations so as to regulate their long-term actions?

Huq continued to explain the complicated reasons behind her, and Naripokkho's lesser involvement with the acid campaign. Although Huq was initially on the Advisory Board of ASF she eventually stepped down from that position. She explained,

I became more of an obstruction than a help as I did not see eye to eye with the staff. John Morrison had good intentions but he was just not well informed about what needed to be done on the ground. He didn't understand the context. I was not happy with some of the appointments the organization made. Its agenda is very much donor determined. Survivors are being placed in embroidery school for training—there is no strategy to empower survivors to be activists. ASF basically does charity work. It serves a purpose, but they do not have much of a vision. As an organization, it is still insecure about its position—and therefore, it erases Naripokkho's involvement with the acid work. They were getting competitive with Naripokkho. Besides, any movement is bound to lose its more radical vision when it becomes mainstream. It was time for me to step down. It was becoming too much of an individual thing. An activist should know when to exit, when to back off. They have to make their own mistakes and learn from them. You have to give them that space. (N. Huq, personal communication, April 5, 2003)

As Huq states, the primary narrative that Naripokkho projected about its work on behalf of acid-violence survivors and for its overall organizational agenda, was of a woman-centered campaign for and by Bangladeshi women. When the ASF shifted the campaign's focus to skill building rather than community empowerment, Naripokkho activists felt disconnected from the work.

At different points in the campaign, then, we have seen the various participants use a particular subjective narrative to bolster and/or subdue certain goals, whether it is for the greater good of the individual or the group as a whole. The disagreements between Bina, western NGOs, and Naripokkho activists are certainly cases in point. It is important to recognize the different parties' diverse understandings of their choices, in order to illuminate the multilocational complexities of gender violence as revealed in the contesting narratives of this campaign. It is this dissonance—the tension, ambivalences and outright conflicts—which are so important in stories of transnational feminist praxis. They are stories often neither told nor analyzed within feminist scholarship, but doing so leads us to a more realistic understanding of feminist organizing.

Certainly, as the various stories relating to Bina indicate, the simple "victim-survivor" binary does not give a complete understanding of the complicated and changeable experiences of those who have been the targets of gender violence. As Tami Spry (1995) has said, women's experiences of violence have too often been paradigmatically represented in the dualistic framework of victim and survivor. It does not allow for a deeper understanding of shifting and fluid subjectivities that diverse women may craft in multiple contexts that interact in a dialectic rather than linear fashion. In other words, women may be one or both of these things at any given moment, and can switch between these subject positions contingent on the particularities of their situation.

The differences in Bina's and Huq's versions of the story shows how human rights narratives in the service of mobilizing campaigns are subject to multiple renditions and contingent on the prevailing discourses of the locations in which they circulate. For instance, the "local" discourse of Naripokkho activists revolves around the losses that the campaign suffered and the organizational in-struggles. On the other hand, the circulation of Bina's story among the media and NGOs in the United States has concentrated on the potential dangers to Bina's family and the acquisition of medical services, which the United States can provide. These became contesting narratives of the transnational campaign.

Further, stories of the survivors' experiences were to be central in both local and global actors' development of strategies to respond to gender violence. This was reflected in the way each group, particularly Naripokkho, saw the survivors' experiences unfold in the spectrum of victim-survivor-activist roles. Specific value was attached to women's—and, in this case, victims of violence's—ability to speak and act for themselves as a symbol of personal transformation and empowerment. On the other hand, the international media representations offered a rescue narrative where victims also became agents capable of action and speech, but only once they were extricated from local oppression through western intervention (we saw this in the manner in which Bina's travel to the United States was cast as a "story of arrival" by various western media reports, and in the contours of the Yale Club event I wrote about in the Prologue). The act of speech by the (victimized) woman, then, is crucial for both the local and global visions of empowerment. In complicated ways, both these logics share a material and symbolic economy of patronage—a transactional system in which the woman rescued is always a client—never coeval in these efforts of "empowerment." To illustrate with an example, I highlight a conversation with Bristi Chowdhury regarding the "transformation" that was key to Naripokkho's vision for acid survivors. She explained:

> I think becoming a survivor is a process. You travel a long road. A person goes through stages of denial, depression, of not knowing if they want to live or die. One doesn't immediately become a

"survivor" the day of the event. The second time I saw Bina at DMCH she was sitting up on the bed and smiling. The bones on her forehead were visible, but she was smiling. This is a survivor. Becoming a survivor involves a complicated emotional process. She was no longer a victim. She didn't kill herself, or lie down and die. Of course, she required help as most of the girls do. It is possible for them to slip into depression but they get over it. There was a day when I visited Bina at DMCH when she threw herself on the bed and wept, she wanted to die. But she didn't. The fact that you decide to get up every day and get on with it means that you are a survivor. That you choose to believe that there is still meaning to your life whether or not you have a perfect face. A victim, on the other hand, lies down and says, "My life is over. I will never live. There is no point to my being." Something terrible happened to the girls. What the guys did to them is vile but the girls refuse to be victims. We have to acknowledge that refusal. Look at Nurun Nahar. It is not in her nature to be a victim. If you ask her, she'll say, "I went to school, got a job, got a counseling diploma—so what makes me a victim?"

Chowdhury's comments illustrate her organization's view of the ways in which survivors go through their own internal emotional shift from victim to survivor. However, this view not unlike the western rescue narrative, but minus the travel westward, is still mired in a linear understanding of the transformation that victims of violence experience, and a certain assumption that victimized women are able to exert agency merely through the act of speech. Indeed, the same logic inheres in the use of individual narratives of suffering in activist circuits as alluded to earlier in the discussion of the deployment of stories of trauma in mobilizing human rights campaigns. It is Bina's arrival to the United States, and the perceived "freedom" she acquired by doing so that was emphasized in the various global media reports. In their essay "Survivor Discourse: Transgression or Recuperation," Linda Alcoff and Laura Gray (1993) draw on a Foucaldian analysis to demonstrate that while speech can be seen as a locus of power in movements of social change, it also stands the risk of submission by being inscribed into hegemonic structures. Therefore, speech that aims to resist and transform existing power relations cannot automatically be read as liberatory. What then, we might ask, are the implications for survivor discourse particularly within transnational circuits?

At the very least a recognition that human rights life narratives can be both recuperative and transgressive of hegemonic norms, and an admission of that which is "statable" and not necessarily that which is the "truth." Alcoff and Gray (1993) conclude that "arrangements of speaking" need to be transformed such that spaces are available for women to be "both witness and experts, both reporters of experience and theorists of experience. Such transformations will alter existing subjectivities as well as structures of domination and relations of power" (p. 282). Rigid categorizations of victim and survivor, and the movement of individuals from one category to another, such as the victim turned survivor or the survivor turned activist, cannot do justice to the multilayered, overlapping, and shifting positionalities of women who were part of the transnational anti-acid campaign. In light of Alcoff and Gray's analysis, it seems more appropriate to read Bina as witness—both experiencing and interpreting her life events, and not linearly progressing from a victimized state to that of a survivor or activist. Similarly, this analysis calls for the language for women to better express their capacity to transgress the fixed roles of the good and obedient victim/survivor to influence more nuanced understandings of their experiences of violence and agency. This might also free Bina from being interpreted alternatively as the good and bad victim/ activist by other campaign members on both sides of the geographic divide, and potentially recognize that her (Bina, and more broadly speaking women survivors/activists of violence) actions and subject positions are contingent on various shifting circumstances.

Further, as Marnia Lazreg (2002) has argued, speech serves as the privilege signifier of empowerment within development discourse (and global feminism, I would add), where primarily "third world" women are brought into "modernity," "action," and "agency" through it often by the already modern, active, first world agents. Thus, structurally, these progress narratives are positioned such that they transmit powerful values of western-dependent development and global feminism. As part of civil society, these narratives have enforced the shift from viewing women as beneficiaries to participants in development. The subject status of "Other" woman participants in global feminist schemes is governed by a powerful script of confessional narrative modes. Transforming women's lives into discourse, these stories assign to their speech the sign of "empowerment" and describe women's survival stories as linear processes of victimhood to empowerment. These primarily individualistic and heroic narratives are recognizable in global feminist discourse as interchangeable across geographic locations. Gayatri Spivak, for instance, in an interview with Lyons and Franklin (2004) adds a cautionary note regarding the use of testimony/institutionalized truth-telling within human rights praxis, calling it "a literalization of a Christian model" (p. 206). Alcoff and Gray (1993), and Hesford (2004) in turn suggest that we recognize that the confessional mode implies an "objective" listener being confessed to—in the case of feminist transnational work of the kind we are talking about here, this is often the "savior" entity—the elite activist, or the Northern-based researcher whose own subjectivities in reinterpreting the "confession" gets obscured in the equation. Rather than considering survivors in terms of the "confessional mode," these scholars encourage us to think of them as *witnesses*, or subjects who both experience and interpret their life experience in acts of self and self-knowledge creation.

It is the absence of this concept of role fluidity and a level of unacknowledged privilege among some Naripokkho activists that contributed to positioning the survivors and the activists of Naripokkho in a patron-client relationship, contrary to their egalitarian vision. For example, when Bina ceased to be the "good victim" by breaking the sponsoring organizations' trust, she was not treated as an agent who made the choice that she deemed as better for her. Rather, HTC, the American partner organization of the acid campaign, withdrew their support of the broader campaign and wanted to immediately send Bina and Jharna back to Bangladesh. And, Naripokkho activist, Ms. Khan's response was territorial when she said to Bina's host family, "We are the people who sent her." Similarly, Bristi Chowdhury's response was to suggest that Bina had not been properly groomed to be an activist. Neither Khan nor Chowdhury interrogate their differential positions that may lead them to come to different decisions and priorities in life and instead dismiss Bina's concerns about her and her family's long-term security in Bangladesh. Nor do they reflect on their own infantilization of Bina—attributing her choices to a childlike selfishness. The trouble with the dualistic framing of women's experience of recovery from violence in terms of victim/survivor, survivor/activist, or both is that it assumes a linear progression from one to another, often signified by the culminating achievement of agency, when victims speak for themselves. This does not allow for complex narratives to emerge, where a woman can be all of these things at the same time, or to shift from one subject position to another while negotiating her own terms. This is why it is important to hear the more complex stories of the individuals involved.

In comparing the multiple narratives of the anti-acid campaign, we see how Bina's and Naripokkho's more complex and ambiguous stories were transformed by the western media to a heroic "rescue narrative," in which Bangladeshi women activists are aided by western benefactors in their struggle for gender justice, and victims of gender violence acquire "freedom" by arriving in the United States. In addition, we also see that Naripokkho activists, including Bina strategically used the dominant rescue narratives in furthering both their own campaign and members' own individual agendas. The use of these narratives at times bolsters the mobilization of transnational forces and at others impedes the autonomy and agency of local actors. Further, paying attention to the multiple narratives illuminates the role of the researcher—that is, my own multisited location as the "insider/outsider," and further mediation of the stories. That is, it alerts the reader that even as I offer competing narratives of women's activism, each narrative was shaped by the particularities of my shifting relations with the various actors: Sometimes I was considered part of the movement, at other times I was thought of as a researcher based in a Northern institution wishing to study the movement, and having allegiances with individuals and institutions in conflictual relationships—that is, Bina, and Naripokkho, UNICEF, and certain local NGOs. By disrupting the victim/survivor, victim/activist, western benefactor/third world victim, researcher/researched binaries, we move closer to a different kind of (self-)knowledge about women's experiences of violence and the ways in which we come to learn about them in diverse contexts.

Another theme that emerges from these conversations is that the internal struggles within women's organizations are often exacerbated by transnationalization of campaigns. Despite the appearance of democratic vision, there were divisions between members and staff, activist and survivor, patron and client, based on level of education, social class, and professional skills. Jealousy and competition among members, the expectation of almost filial respect, loyalty and service from staff and clients by members belie the egalitarian, mutually reciprocal governance relationship that the organization has professed. These factors show that women's organizing needs to pay closer attention to class dimensions of gender in framing and operationalizing their agendas.

Conclusion

In this chapter, I have aimed to broaden our understanding of the logic of local versus transnational women's activisms. Within this dynamic, "local" women's issues have often been represented as a monolith, but this conceptualization hides the intramovement dynamics, which may be at once ambiguous and contradictory. For instance, it was arguably the internal disagreements and class-based divisions within Naripokkho that unwittingly hindered the campaign from moving forward. At the same time, if and when the terms of contracts negotiated by Northern and Southern NGOs go awry, the consequences are often the most severe for actors from the South. While it is possible that the ability of the Bangaldeshi expatriate community in the United States to organize effectively around issues of gender violence in the future might have been compromised, the more severe losses are borne by the survivors (such as the ones who were denied entry to the United States altogether) and the organizers in the South.

In this particular story of acid violence, the campaign had consistently struggled with issues of class, power, and imperialism. The campaign had been birthed by a group of middle-class, urban, socially committed women located in Bangladesh, who had been "moved" by the social injustices meted out to younger, poorer women. The implicit strategy of the campaign had entailed the transformation of the young survivors, nurturing them into becoming activists for women's empowerment. This construction of the paradigm of victim-survivor-change-agent, however, did not completely represent the complex subjectivities of the survivors in question. Although very keen on helping the survivors, the activists leading the campaign had been acutely aware of their own role as "guardians" and "educators" of the young girls. When that role was tested, for example, by Bina, who had decided to defy the terms of the agreement put in place to help her, the system of support crumbled. Bina, who was once commended as the independent-minded "leader" of the acid network, was then shunned for being too self-serving. We must also remember that global inequalities lead to such impossible situations where victims are bound by contracts between nation-states with asymmetrical relations of power. It is unfortunate that Bina's defiance of the contract resulted in the severe loss for other victims. Yet, I would argue that Bina's decision and its consequences must be understood in the context of larger global inequities and not simply as her personal decision.

Bina's role as the "self-serving" survivor had defied the sociocultural perceptions of a "good" victim that are often perpetuated through transnational feminist organizing. Powerful assumptions of womanhood and class-based directives of "appropriate" female behavior governed the movement actors' understandings and expectations of how a "good victim" should act. Naripokkho campaign leaders' indignant responses to Bina were also reflective of their disapproval of her disobedience as well as of the fact that her action jeopardized other survivors' medical treatment. In the process, Bina's complex agency, including both complicity and resistance, were undermined. Also missing in these responses by NGOs and activists alike is an understanding that women who form alliances in transnational movements are differentiated not only by the North-South global divide but also by the South-South class divide.

This analysis has broad implications for understanding local women's groups' relation to transnational feminist politics. In the case of Bangladesh, a complicated national and transnational web involving a diverse set of actors, influenced and redefined acid violence against women. In her discussion of the campaign, Bristi Chowdhury pointed out the dependency on international aid agencies as a failure of the campaign. After all, western aid is not a long-term solution for creating autonomous and sustainable local movements for social change. The appointment of John Morrison as ASF's first executive director and his subsequent recognition in the UK as the force behind the anti-acid organizing was perhaps one of the most blaring examples of the disconnect between the visions of local and international actors. Even as Nasreen Huq has recognized his "good intentions," circumstances around his appointment have to be seen within larger imperial historical processes.

Donors and NGOs in the global South supplant a weak and inefficient state in providing social services within the expanding neoliberal development rubric and are thereby able to gain direct access to the public and private lives of ordinary citizens. This has been noted by Kendall Stiles (2002) as an intrusive form of foreign aid and a new means by which transnational elites govern subordinate populations. In addition to helping us see the challenges of transnational organizing around gender violence, the multiple narratives described in this chapter shed light on this new form of intrusion that brings together differentially located actors in transnational campaigns for justice.

Chapter Four

Feminism and Its Other

Representing the "New Woman" of Bangladesh

The current moment in contemporary Bangladesh is witnessing a shift in the representations of ideal womanhood from earlier anticolonialist and nationalist era when the middle-class woman was considered the epitome of spirituality, domesticity, and the essentially nonwestern core of an authentic Indian culture (Chatterjee, 1989, pp. 240–43). This chapter explores and analyses constructions of new womanhood, feminist solidarity, and women's organizing against gender violence in contemporary Bangladesh. I look at cinematic representations of the "New Woman" in the postcolonial woman-oriented narrative of the 2006 telefilm *Ayna (The Mirror)* in order to engage an analysis of the sociocultural issues it dramatizes, specifically the changing notions of gender oppression within a transitioning society.

My analysis will take on the concomitant new subject positions required for women as well as modes of feminist mobilization and activism constituted in this human rights advocacy film. Through a textual analysis of the film, I want to illuminate how feminist advocacy can be shaped and bolstered by hegemonic power dynamics that at times can perpetuate inequalities between women, a phenomenon we have also witnessed in the anti-acid campaign dynamics discussed in the previous chapters. Showcasing a discussion of this film, an instance of education-entertainment promoted by human rights activism, this chapter contributes to a better understanding of the kinds of transnational organizing mobilized locally and the ways in which these are influenced by and embedded within larger global processes.

The social construction of the identity of the "New Woman" in colonial and post-colonial Bengal has been the subject of feminist theorizing for some time. Partha Chatterjee (1989) has noted the ideal woman in the nationalist context was constructed as an elite woman in stark contrast to both the uneducated, downtrodden, and backward women of South Asia's poorer classes and her sexually liberated, modern, and amoral western counterparts. A variation of the Victorian "New Woman" of England, the ideal nationalist woman's counterpart in colonial and postcolonial Bengal and post-independent Bangladesh has had diverse applicability across the domains of class and the rural-urban divide. Sonia Nishat Amin (1994) refers to the "New Woman" in the context of Bengal as "layered," "a composite of many women," and "elusive" (pp. 137–40). At first sight, discontinuous from the colonial rescue narratives and anticolonial and nationalist representations of the normative middle-class respectable woman (*bhadromohila*), contemporary constructions of the "New Woman" are nevertheless shaped by discourses of development and modernization. Utilizing narratives of "women's uplift" and emancipation as the benchmark of progress, native/local women are now put in the contradictory positions of both the downtrodden/victim and the modern/savior. These competing constructions of the "New Woman" serve larger progress narratives of both the nation and western-global feminism. They replicate the victim-savior trope of colonial feminism by assigning agency to the emancipated local woman (as the human rights activist) while simultaneously representing her as merely the beneficiary of modernization schemes. These two distinct figures are coconstituted yet emerge as competing representations of the contemporary "New Woman."

The invention of "third world woman" as a category to be "intervened" on and "empowered" by western experts and technological interventions through global development discourse and practice has influenced both governmental and nongovernmental development initiatives in countries of the global South including Bangladesh (Escobar, 1995). Women's issues in contemporary Bangladesh are linked to and shaped by the linear progress narratives of development and global feminism. In these narratives, poor women oppressed by local patriarchal religious and cultural practices are uplifted by their integration into global capitalist development initiatives, like the garments industry or NGOs. These two sectors, one with an explicitly economic and the other a social mission, have both been facilitated by global restructuring. Together they have revolutionized women's participation in the labor force and their emergence into public spaces as economic agents (Feldman, 2001). At the same time, the NGO boom has benefited the middle class by facilitating the creation of a local cadre of development professionals and staff in the service of "uplifting" and "empowering" the poor. This new professional class is perceived as enlightened, highly educated, urban, and liberated. Including both men and women, this group works within the liberal-nationalist mission of the nation-state and the liberal-humanitarian mission of NGO-led development initiatives. The relationship between the local agents of social change and the "beneficiaries" of development constitutes a new type of colonial dependency similar to the one discussed in the introduction of this book with regard to new forms of NGO dependency. *Ayna*, a woman-oriented telefilm, centers around two women, one an acid violence survivor who is uplifted by the advocacy of the second, a human rights lawyer. The film, which animates a discussion of human rights advocacy, aired multiple times in prime time on the private channel NTV Bangladesh in 2006. *Ayna* is certainly not alone in the genre of woman-oriented films with a social message, but the fact that it was written and directed by Kabari Sarwar, a prominent activist and film star who reigned over the silver screen for three decades, gives it special appeal. The feature film is currently available nationally in DVD produced by Impress Telefilm, a leading media production house in Bangladesh, and has been widely disseminated by G-Series, a private enterprise that markets popular film and music.

The use of video can be effective in presenting complex social realities by invoking empathy and creating an ethical community. Narrative strategies are used to make "the message" palatable for a wide audience. In an interview with *New Age* newspaper, the director, Kabari Sarwar said, "I opt for such kind of scripts, because there are lot of similar incidents happening in our society on a regular basis. I would like to make people aware through cinema" (M. Khan, 2005). Sarwar's comments reveal the activist intent of the film, and in this chapter I offer an analysis that applauds the use of social media in human rights advocacy, and the way the film draws attention to feminist issues. At the same time, however, I critique how the film, perhaps inadvertently, furthers a neoliberal script of development and women's empowerment.

Ayna can be read as a text that reveals the ways in which dominant scripts of globalization, gender oppression, and women's emancipation are both reinscribed and subverted. In her essay "Global Feminisms and the State of Feminist Film Theory," E. Ann Kaplan (2004) traces the shift in feminist film critique in the early 1970s that moved from prioritizing issues of the gaze, psychoanalysis, and sexual difference between men and women to an emphasis on cultural differences between women racialized by historical discourses, traditions, and power relations (p. 1242). *Ayna* provides a particularly good example of a film that invites this kind of feminist analysis. It provides an opportunity to analyze cultural differences—as well as inequalities arising from colonial and globalizing forces—between women that both instigate yet hinder effective organizing by and for women. *Ayna* acts as a script that translates the shifting socioeconomic trends in contemporary Bangladesh into a social text, thereby generating dialogue and knowledge through providing a "palatable" message for mass viewership.[1]

Anthropologist Cymene Howe (2008) calls the transmission of social messages through television "televisionary" whereby education-entertainment impacts shifting cultural values as opposed to more traditional, nonmedia forms of advocacy geared toward policy change (Howe, 2008). A recent study conducted by Mai Do and Lawrence Kincaid (2006) found that the impact of entertainment education television dramas on health were successful in generating knowledge and dialogue among the viewers on issues such as the transmission and prevention of HIV/AIDS in Bangladesh. Making use of the dramatic format, messages are inserted at appropriate moments and desirable health behavior is modeled through the characters. The authors claim, "Social modeling allows the audience to experience vicarious motivation, observation of consequences of the modeled behavior, vicarious reinforcement, and parasocial interaction when the audience becomes emotionally involved with characters in a drama" (Do and Kincaid, 2006, p. 304). In this type of film, key ideas are integrated into the plot with the assumption these will trigger interpersonal communication, especially among friends and within families.

My analysis enters an ongoing conversation exemplified in a series of essays published in 2006 in the *American Anthropologist* on the visual culture of human rights. Several critical questions have been raised here about NGO-generated human rights discourse and practice in the global South, the cinematic representations of human rights (advocacy and suffering), and the engendering of solidarity and action through media. In this collection, Meg McLagan (2006) notes that the proliferation of organizations and venues producing and disseminating rights-oriented media also facilitates connections between filmmakers and members of grassroots, nongovernmental, nonprofit, and governmental communities. She draws attention to the social processes through which human rights media representations are produced and circulated, and she compels readers to question the political and social backdrop of the critical generation of human rights visual culture as well as modes of mobilization encouraged by such media (McLagan, 2006). Speaking on the power of visual media as a tool for activists, Leshu Torchin (2006) posits, "Film can visualize abject conditions or humanitarian mission work for a broad audience while stories and images marshal the sentiment of vast and dispersed spectators to generate empathy, encourage action, and . . . raise money for political and relief efforts" (p. 214). Sam Gregory (2006) expounds on this point by noting that human rights advocacy films tend to utilize two main discourses: legal (including national and international human rights laws) and transnational (including both transnational empathy and solidarity). These discourses privilege policy advocacy and generate support for human rights by placing issues in the "global morality market." A globalization of local contexts occurs within such framing, he argues, so as to maximize impact among multiple actors: funders, international NGOs, the state, and the multiply located audiences in the local-global nexus.

The growth of social media as a field within the larger development agenda has created venues for transmitting messages with regard to social uplift and nation building (Abu-Lughod, 2005). Writing about images of women in the media in postcolonial South Asia, Rajeswari Sunder Rajan (1993) has commented that women figure in primarily as either victims of social injustice and violence or confronters of social injustice, and thus "their relationship to the social structure is marked as external and adversarial rather than as integral and ambivalent" (p. 138). An exploration of the multiple representations of womanhood in *Ayna* allows us to understand how these intersect with larger pervasive social and economic structures, like globalization, neoliberal development, and NGOization, that form the backdrop of transnational human rights advocacy films.

By centering native/local women as agents, custodians of nation and culture, and moral guardians, texts like *Ayna* avoid some of the earlier traps of west/nonwest colonialist works while simultaneously replicating aspects of the colonial relationship within a local context with new actors. The film uses the dominant structure of human rights advocacy (scripted in discourses of global feminism, liberal nationalism, and neoliberal development) to represent gender oppression, while attempting to mediate feminist consciousness and solidarity with popular appeal. This results in an inevitably ambivalent narrative about female subject construction. Seen in conjunction with ethnographic research, the limits and possibilities of such media representations of the "New Woman," and the disjunctures with women's lived realities of oppression and survival, can be further explored.

Synopsis

The telefilm *Ayna* offers a window into the changing social and economic landscape of contemporary Bangladesh and the complex negotiations of power and inequality across gender, class, and community. It offers an opportunity to unpack the social messages underlying development and modernization initiatives, the new kinds of alliances and dependencies engendered by them, and their multiple and uneven consequences. The film also centrally features categorical representations of the "New Woman" as both the "development expert" or patron/matron of development and the "aid recipient" or client of development. *Ayna* can be read as a vehicle for transmitting educational messages about social ills and as a venue for eliciting political participation by envisioning models for individual and collective social action against injustice. At the same time, the film reinscribes the separate representations of women as either activists or victims, but not as complex agents.

Ayna is about a young woman, Kushum, and the many trials she overcomes with regard to family, community, economic hardship, love and romance, and gender violence. The daughter of a folk singer, Kushum is a beautiful and spirited young woman with a strong penchant for speaking the truth. At the wedding function of her friend, Tuli, she catches the eye of the local *mastaan*, Rameez, when she confronts the bridegroom's father about his demanding dowry and casting aspersions on the bride for her dark complexion. Rameez is unemployed and directionless, spending his time doing drugs, intimidating innocent villagers, and visiting sex workers. Initially, Kushum's father accepts Rameez's proposal to marry Kushum but later changes his mind when he discovers the truth about his character. When Kushum's father rejects him as a suitor for his beloved daughter, Rameez murders him and then attempts to rape Kushum. She manages to fight him off and runs away to Dhaka, where she finds employment as a domestic worker in a middle-class home. There, she is faced with sexual harassment by the male head of the household and is asked to leave by his wife. Desperate and without any knowledge of the city, Kushum meets a group of young women who work in a garment factory. Eventually, she gets a job on the shop floor and falls in love with Dolon, a bachelor of the slum community where she lives, who is an administrative officer in the same factory. As Kushum seems poised to marry Dolon, Rameez reappears in her life and casts a shadow of doubt on her character by claiming that he is her estranged husband.

Ukeel Apa, the second heroine of the film, is a human rights activist/feminist/lawyer who is consulted by Kushum.[2] *Ukeel Apa* gives legal advice to the slum community and escorts Kushum to the police station to report a case against Rameez. Unable to circumvent the law, Rameez takes his revenge on Kushum by splashing her with acid on the night of her wedding to Dolon. The slum-factory community stands by Kushum and her new husband and helps to raise funds for her reconstructive surgery abroad. The arrangements are made by *Ukeel Apa* who also raises private funds and seeks the help of NGOs. She also represents Kushum in court and wins the case against Rameez, who is sentenced to death by hanging. In the end, Kushum returns to her husband and her country after being restored by reconstructive surgery abroad.

Gender and Class

The Bangladesh social context in which *Ayna* is set, as briefly discussed above in chapter 1, reflects a complex set of issues including the gradual transition from agrarian to industrialized economy, urbanization, and the flows of capital, ideas, and people across local and global boundaries. In *Power to Choose* (2000), Naila Kabeer traces the postindependence transition from an agricultural economy to a monetized one in Bangladesh, leading to erosion of the "patriarchal contract," the devaluation of women, the consolidation of the dowry, and the emergence of new patriarchal alliances. Structural adjustment programs driven by western donors and neoliberal development have led to massive rural to urban migration and the growth of export processing zones in Bangladesh. The category "garment girls" has come out of these processing zones to describe the surge in women's participation in the labor force (particularly by young women) and their subsequent visibility in public spaces. Kabeer emphasizes that women enter these newly created occupations from diverse constituencies and under very different socioeconomic circumstances (Kabeer, 2000). In *Ayna*, Kabari Sarwar grapples with some of these changes in Bangladeshi society across gender, class, and community-based cleavages.

The newly emergent monetized relations are reflected in a scene from *Ayna*, in which Kushum's friend Tuli's marriage negotiations go awry because of her father's inability to provide a color television as part of her dowry settlement:

> Tuli's father: I haven't been able to arrange for the cash for a color TV yet.

> Father of the bridegroom: This union (marriage) cannot be forged on credit.

> Kushum's father: I request you to honor his word. Please give him time to fulfill his promise of providing the color TV.

Father of bridegroom: My son's marriage cannot be arranged on credit. This is a matter of honor. I will not be able to show my face to my community if the dowry settlement does not include a color TV.

In this conversation, we witness the changes in the community as it transitions into a capitalist economy. Terms of negotiation are shifting, and one's word or promise can no longer take the place of cash or goods. Notions of honor are now tied to commodities like a color TV, and the promise of future compensations based on one's goodwill is no longer a reliable option in securing marriage contracts.

In earlier marriage practices in preindustrial South Asia, the bride and her family were compensated for the loss of her labor. Newer dowry practices, reflecting the weakening of the patriarchal contract, favor the groom's family, which intensifies women's status as "liability" to her family. This transition is exemplified in the conversation that ensues between Azam Ali (Kushum's father) and his daughter following the above-mentioned scene.

Azam Ali: Tuli's father was able to marry her off. Given my financial situation, I doubt that I can do the same for you.

Kushum: Why do you have to marry me off? Am I a burden to you?

Azam Ali: I am not suggesting that daughters are burdens to their families. However, it is my duty to arrange your marriage. I cannot do it however if the demands are as exorbitant as in the case of Tuli.

Kushum: Why would they be? I am neither dark nor disabled. I am very good at managing the household [*shongshaarer kaaj*]. If my prospective in-laws demand dowry, you can just beat them off with shoes [*joota diye pitay diba*]. I will not enter into a marriage with dowry.

Azam Ali: You are still a child. You don't understand the harsh ways of the world.

Because Kushum is fair complexioned (unlike Tuli), her chances are higher in negotiating a smaller dowry payment by her family. She confesses to her friend Karimon, a young woman of Kushum's age, that she wants to be swept away by love and marry a man who will always stand by her. Karimon, also unaware of Rameez's "true" character, explains to Kushum that she would be doing well by marrying Rameez because "Women are fields for men to plough. It doesn't matter which man ploughs the field, because women are only recognized for how good a harvest they are able to produce." Kushum is none too satisfied with her friend's advice and continues to be doubtful about marrying Rameez. Her father believes at this point that Rameez can be disciplined in marriage to Kushum. Later in the film, he sees Rameez with another woman, and changes his mind about the marriage. Kushum's father is killed by an angry Rameez. Kushum is haunted by her father's cautionary words iterated earlier in the film regarding her innocence in relation to the ways of the harsh world. After Rameez murders her father, Kushum flees to Dhaka city alone, to a world vastly different from her "simpler" existence in the village.

In Dhaka, when Kushum has found work as a maid in a middle-class household, surrounded by concrete and modern amenities, she spends her days pining for the life she left behind in the village. Although her female employer, a housewife, treats her with kindness, Kushum has to fend off the sexual overtures of her male employer. Admitting her own vulnerability, Kushum's female employer compensates her with cash and urges her to find alternative employment. Her parting comment is, "I wanted to help you but I am just as helpless as you are."

Thus, despite her economic and educational privileges, this woman is also shown to be constrained by her gender and finds commonality with Kushum. Ironically, because Kushum is fired, and despite her resulting economic vulnerability, she is able exit the patriarchal contract, whereas her middle-class "sister" cannot. Kushum, having escaped from the moral economy (*shamaj*) of the village, is freer to transgress patriarchal boundaries in the city, where she is relatively anonymous. It is her middle-class counterpart, her former employer, who remains more confined within the patriarchal norms of her community. Her home is her site of oppression and we see her only within the walls of her concrete apartment in the city. On the other hand, later in the film we see Kushum and Dolon enjoying the freedom, mobility, and anonymity of the city as they begin to fall in love and patronize public parks, and restaurants.

Feminist scholar, Kumkum Sangari (1993) has argued that patriarchy is class differentiated and that some women participate and reproduce patriarchal relations in consent and in contract. One way in which this is shown in the film is that Kushum's female employer overlooks her husband's transgression in marriage, as her marriage presumably offers her security. She sustains the patriarchal contract and her position within it by staying in the marriage, and offers only a token compensation to Kushum, despite her recognition of common vulnerability. The potential of female solidarity here is thus bypassed, in favor of individual gain and social and economic security.

After losing her job, a lost and desperate Kushum on the streets of Dhaka is given shelter by a slum community, many of whose inhabitants work in a garment factory nearby. The factory is a source for jobs to mostly young women, and entry into its gated walls as well as survival on its tiered shop floors are heavily negotiated. For example, floor supervisor Khalek must be compensated handsomely by any candidate before securing them a position in the factory. Some women workers in the factory must often do "double duty" by moonlighting as sex workers, in order to keep their jobs and provide for their families. Women in this complex nexus of urban slum-factory relationships are referred to as commodity (*maal*).

When a worker leaves her job in order to get married, Kushum is lucky to bypass Khalek and land a job in the factory through the help of Dolon, an administrative officer at the factory. The process by which Kushum secures her job creates a rift between Khalek and Dolon. The former feels side-stepped in the "chain of command" because he was not consulted and did not benefit by Kushum's employment. The job, however fans the flame of romance between Kushum and Dolon. A grateful Kushum hands over her first month's salary to a woman named Fatima and her new "family," who give her shelter in their room in the slum. The following conversation unfolds when Kushum earns her first month's salary:

> Dulabhai (term used for elder sister's husband, in this case Fatima's husband): Why are you handing us your entire salary? You should save some for your future. Without cash, you won't be able to get married.

> Kushum: I am not interested in buying a husband. It is your responsibility now to find a self-respecting man for your new sister-in-law.

> Dulabhai (to Fatima): Keep some money aside for rent and food and give the rest back to Kushum. I will assist her in opening a bank account with it.

On the one hand, the garment factory symbolizes a place of economic and sexual exploitation. On the other hand, as the film shows, it is also a place where new kinship structures emerge among women, and between men and women, reflecting the fluidity and multiplicities of power structures. Because of such apparent contradictions, Shelley Feldman (2001) has argued for a more nuanced understanding of the emergence of the category "female garment worker" in the context of a modernizing economy in Bangladesh. Feldman's work on globalization and women's labor in Bangladesh helps reveal the unexpected ways in which patriarchies are reconstituting themselves at the intersections of globalization and economic restructuring, as the above vignette from the film also demonstrates. She argues that globalization is constituted through complex and contradictory histories and trajectories of women's lives and not simply in response to external realities such as international donor and state-driven Structural Adjustment Programs (SAPs). Women are actors and determine the way globalization is enacted rather than being simply "impacted" or acted on by its economic flows. On the shop floor, women are the commodities (*maals*) and subjected to multiple negotiations. In the film, the factory is built on their labor but they remain vulnerable to transactions by Khalek the pimp, who profits from their economic insecurity. However, the women shape the informal economy through their triple duty of working on the shop floor, moonlighting, and sustaining the newly emerging kin and community structures in the slum. Kushum's address of Fatima's husband as *dulabhai* (elder sister's husband), the landlord as *nana* (grandfather) illustrates the forging of kinship like community structures among people who are associated not by blood but processes of social and economic restructuring. This potentially wards off sexual tension between men and women who are not presumably protected by familial relations.

The film portrays the changing meanings of kin and community as Kushum navigates the city, the shop floor, and relations in the slum community. These fictive kinship associations of the slum community thrive on the earnings from women's labor. *Nana* (the elderly landlord affectionately addressed as grandfather by the women workers) invests in a color TV with the rent he collects monthly from the workers. This in turn acts as a source of attraction for the entire community, bringing them together, as the women gather at *nana*'s quarters around the television. Now, after returning from the factory, Fatima, Kushum, and other young women pool their resources and cook together. Dolon begins to pay them to provide him with his meals. Thus, the film shows, while patriarchal divisions of labor are not entirely subverted, new kinds of kin arrangements and newer gendering patterns of urban space are forged. The film portrays the changing meanings of kin and community as number D-26 in the factory (Kushum's numerical designation) negotiates the city, the shop floor, and relations in the slum community.

Feminism, Community, and Solidarity

The young, beautiful, and spirited Kushum is undoubtedly the heroine of *Ayna*. The story revolves around her struggles in overcoming oppressive social structures within the family, community, and wage labor while finding enduring love. Her subject position as the woman aspiring for better conditions and availing herself of the "benefits" of modernization poses a stark contrast with Afroza (the human rights lawyer, activist, and feminist addressed as *Ukeel Apa*—using this term here denotes respect for a professional woman of higher social class) who helps Kushum realize her dreams. Forces of modernity enable the contradictory yet necessary coexistence of two heroines, two sides of the contemporary "New Woman." The two heroines with fully fleshed-out social and political contexts in the film embody an analysis of the disparate subjects of contemporary feminist human rights advocacy within a transnational frame.

The creation of the newer subject positions shown in *Ayna* is linked to the proliferation of liberal apparatuses of human rights and neoliberalism. Lauren Leve (2007) argues that the post–Cold War era is marked by a certain global cultural imaginary recognizable in a "constellation of institutions, ideologies, frameworks, structures, forms of knowledge and norms, that acts in such a way as to establish not only the categories of democratic social identities, but the very ontology that underlies these identifications itself" (p. 97). Neoliberal economic development, along with liberal political structures, including human rights discourse and practice, are the venues through which this "identity machine" thrives and creates new kinds of subjects, that are both legible and governable through these liberal structures. In this film, the subject positions of the human rights lawyer and the feminist activist, as well as the beneficiaries of human rights, are legible and governable through the same liberal apparatuses.

Ukeel Apa, the human rights lawyer, NGO leader, and feminist activist, represents a kind of global, cosmopolitan subject who can traverse multiple locales with ease and authority. She is shown advocating for a woman victimized by *fatwa* in a village and doing research about gender violence in urban slum communities. She is an NGO activist who raises funds for Kushum's rehabilitation transnationally, a powerful lawyer arguing Kushum's case in court, and an outspoken feminist who speaks eloquently to journalists about the global oppression of women. On the flip side of her activism are the subjects of her advocacy—the victimized rural woman, the oppressed slum woman, the violated heroine—all in need of her intervention. It is on the subjects whom she tirelessly advocates for that *Ukeel Apa*'s own subjectivity is dependent. These contradictory subject positions are constituted through the liberal apparatus of the human rights identity machine that sets up the agent and client in dualistic opposition, thus perpetuating itself by legitimizing certain kinds of actions and governing structures, such as neoliberalism, global feminism, and nationalism.

In postindependent Bangladesh the woman's question has been framed within discourses of modernity, development, and globalization. Poor women have entered this equation primarily as clients of state, private, and nonprofit sectors. The specific consequences for women as the result of the growth of the NGO sector and the proliferation of neoliberal development programs, in the context of a weak state and western financial institutions' imperatives, have been discussed in chapters 1 and 2 of this book. In addition, Lamia Karim (2004) has persuasively argued that in contemporary Bangladesh, members of the urban-based elite women's movement (the patrons, or more appropriately "matrons") are worlds apart from their rural counterparts who lack both access and resources, and are caught in the middle of the competitive vying for clients among multiple constituencies like the state, NGOs (whether feminist or not), and the rural elites. NGOs, argue Dina Siddiqi (2006) and Shelley Feldman (2001), have taken on the role of the "moral regulator" and "patron," along with and at times in place of older forms of power structures like elite constellations of men.

A neopatriarchal relationship seems to have emerged through NGOs and between their patrons and clients. This is exemplified through *Ukeel Apa*'s relationship to the slum community, and in particular to Kushum, but also to lesser extent to men like Dolon and Rameez. Anne Marie Goetz's (2001) study of "women development workers" points to the emergence of a new category of professional women seemingly morally bolstered by the rhetoric of development that promises to uplift and help the poor, particularly women, out of their backward and uneducated ways. *Ukeel Apa* in *Ayna* must be understood in such a context: she is an enlightened, educated, and empowered NGO activist with access to resources and the voice of morality. The space between her and Kushum, the subject of development initiatives, is ultimately incommensurable because the former's subject position as the patron relies on the latter's abject victimization.

The introduction and integration of Women in Development (WID), followed by Gender and Development (GAD) and gender mainstreaming strategies in global development rhetoric and practice in the 1980s and 1990s, have created opportunities not only for poor women to be integrated into neoliberal development projects but has also led to employment opportunities for urban-based highly educated middle-class women as NGO professionals. Ironically, however, Anne Marie Goetz (2001) notes, the bureaucratization of NGOs and professionalization of development have led more recently to the replacement of local women staff with "efficient," "skilled," and "trained" staff, consisting mostly of men but also of women from urban spaces outside of local communities.

The degree to which these programs actually practice gender *conscientization* and empowerment is the subject of much scholarly controversy. Goetz cites a study conducted by Bangladesh Integrated Rural Development Program that suggests that few of these development professionals are motivated by feminist goals of equality and rights. Moreover, the women studied were uncritical of patriarchal aspects of their own culture and often expressed "patronizing and dismissive" views regarding poor rural women, the very same group that they are in the business of "serving." It is nevertheless important to note that these women development professionals were transgressing social norms and entering traditionally male spaces through what Goetz (2001) explains (using the words of Simmons et al.) is "a strategy of accommodation and reform rather than of confrontation and radical change" (p. 109).

Aditi Mitra and Jean Van Delinder (2007) also studied elite women's work in NGOs in Kolkata, India. Based on ethnographic research in women's NGOs including in-depth interviews, the authors argue that elite women NGO workers perceive themselves as empowering "other" less fortunate women. The interviews also reveal that the process of empowering others is one and the same as empowering the self. The authors see the role of elite women in NGOs as "an extension of and reinforce[ing] their existing status, social class norms, education, upbringing, family values and social networks" (Mitra and Delinder, 2007, p. 355). Additionally, the authors argue, "in the age of transnational feminisms, the way these women define feminism and construct the image of a feminist based on their appeal to feminist ideas helps to analyze the discourse of feminism in the post-colonial context" (Mitra and Delinder, 2007, p. 358). Although women in development as well as gender and development perspectives have argued that women of all social classes are subordinate to men of their social classes, these same discourses have not adequately analyzed the power of women of certain social classes over others. In the age of transnational feminisms, neopatriarchal relations among differentially located women can reflect a consensual and contractual structure much like the ones between men and women. These hierarchical and codependent relations among women, exemplified by the two sides of the "New Woman" in *Ayna*, begs for critical interrogation of feminism, community and solidarity by, about, and for women. It raises the question, "What does feminist solidarity look like, and whom does it benefit?"

The women NGO workers in the Mitra and Delinder study gave their own perspectives on this question:

> Family thinks this kind of work does not bring in any kinds of rewards—monetary or any kind. Initially, my in-laws were not at all approving but now . . . when I was always being quoted in the newspapers and was being interviewed and all that, then they started saying "oh, we are so proud of our daughter-in-law!!" (Mitra and Delinder, 2007, p. 369)You know, let us face it in the present society around the world if you don't earn too much, then your work is not seen as important. In my family, everybody is earning in five figures [denoting high salaries]. Because of this (low) earning possibly, there is little contempt I can feel, although people don't tell me. But also they think that I am doing important, at least somewhat they accept and my daughters also think that this work is important.

> [But] there is a plus point of this work; where I work there my work is very much appreciated. As I said, starting at such an old age, I found it difficult to be accepted in other places, including one women's NGO, but here I have been very well accepted. The girls I work with I feel they love me, they love me. . . . and that is a very great thing. (Mitra and Delinder, 2007, pp. 371–72)

> This is my life. If one gives me the choice . . . it gives my life some meaning. (Mitra and Delinder, 2007, p. 73)

It is clear from these statements that these elite women working in NGOs feel validated through their work on behalf of other women. Yet the position of social privilege that these women possess can lead them to unwittingly exert social control over those groups they strive to empower. This is not to suggest that the goals of the women are somehow completely contrary to feminist goals, or that there is anything wrong in finding appreciation and meaning in the work that one does. These narratives, however, often obfuscate power relations within transnational women's networks that unwittingly reproduce the patron-client dyad. Here poor women are perceived as objects of intervention rather than as agents in their own right. The dependent relationships between elite and nonelite women are framed primarily through self-validating moral terms of "doing important work," rather than being examined from a critical transformative angle. They seek to empower "other" women, rather than to work for the mutual liberation of all women. These power relations can perpetuate social inequality and gender oppression between women as well as women and men of different classes.

In *Ayna*, *Ukeel Apa* acts as the feminist counterheroine to Kushum. The film opens with a shot of her walking through rural Bangladesh accompanied by a local woman NGO staff member who carries her water bottle for her and helps her climb into a boat to travel to a nearby village, where they are investigating a fatwa-related attack against a woman. *Ukeel Apa* makes her second appearance when the setting of the film shifts to Dhaka. In this scene *Ukeel Apa* is seated in her living room where a journalist is interviewing her on the status of women and children in the world. She pontificates earnestly:

> *Ukeel Apa*: Many works of fiction prose and poetry have been written worldwide on the situation of women in patriarchal societies. I remember reading about a Vietnamese folk song that compares the fate of women to rain. Like drops of rain, women may land in a palace or a ditch. We talk about progress and civilization but all that is empty rhetoric. In reality, the majority of women in the world are in vulnerable situations.
>
> Journalist: As a human rights advocate could you say something about the situation of children?
>
> *Ukeel Apa*: In our country, the lion's share of children are deprived of their basic rights. Societal inequality, poverty, superstition, illiteracy, ignorance, etc. are responsible for the dismal situation of children. This is a big challenge for our political leaders.

This and a number of scenes described below serve to introduce *Ukeel Apa* as an influential member of the urban, progressive activist community. Sometimes she is shown in her own element in an urban modern apartment, at other times navigating villages and slums for her advocacy and research projects. Each of these scenes creates distance, both physical and economic, between *Ukeel Apa* and the women and communities that she is helping.

In her third appearance in the film, *Ukeel Apa* is seen among the slum community where Kushum finds shelter. She and her assistant, another female NGO staff member, are conducting a research study in a number of Dhaka slums about the various ways that working women are victims of abuse. It is clear that she garners respect and authority among the community who look up to her as someone who has the means to provide justice, particularly to women in vulnerable situations. She makes her fourth heroic appearance precisely at the moment when Rameez has come to abduct Kushum, under the pretense that he is her lawfully married husband, thus casting doubt on her virtue and character among the community members who are arranging Kushum's wedding to Dolon. Rameez claims that Kushum ran away from him because of a minor domestic dispute and that he is now trying to make amends and take her home. In this scene, the arrival of *Ukeel Apa* in her shiny new car conveys the power she wields as an NGO professional. (NGOs are often criticized by the public in contemporary Bangladesh as running businesses rather than welfare-oriented work and for using donor funds in order to acquire material objects like fancy cars and computers rather than serving their constituencies.) She placates a hysterical Kushum, who falls at *Ukeel Apa*'s feet, by asking her to "calm down." Her intervention is framed as neutral and fair and through the objective arm of the law. She asks Rameez for proof of his marriage to Kushum, and she demands that Kushum produce proof that he (Rameez) indeed is her father's killer. As both parties are unable to provide proof, she takes them with her to the police station to open a case file.

When Rameez fails to provide proof of his marriage to Kushum, *Ukeel Apa* urges the slum community to go ahead with the wedding preparations for Kushum and Dolon. With much fanfare and jubilation the two are reunited. The camaraderie in this community brought together by the factory is depicted in the following song:

> We don't own gold bangles, we don't have famous friends
> We don't own homes, cars, or wealth
> We work in the factory and live in this slum
> Our only asset is the love in our hearts
> We don't have the means to fulfill our many desires
> But we can enjoy the beauty of the full moon
> Our friend has married such a beauty
> We wish them a happy life together
> Our dreams may not be fulfilled
> But we find peace with the one we love

This song, representative of the class divide between the slum community and the elite, presents a different kind of support network, one not as centrally emphasized in the film. *Ayna* shows divergent notions of feminist and community solidarity. To explain this point, I draw on an assertion by Kumkum Sangari (1993) that the "consent" of women to patriarchy across different classes is nuanced differently contingent on the specific situation of their social subordination. As the film shows, the solidarity between *Ukeel Apa* and Kushum is shaped by the latter's consent to the contractual relationship offered by the former; that is, access to formal institutions of power such as the legal system and NGO community. The terms of this relationship, however, are determined by *Ukeel Apa*. Thus, as depicted in this film, neoliberal establishments like NGOs and the state become the saviors of the poor and the victimized, and offer only the kinds of support legible and governable through those apparatuses. Other kinds of support once provided by the community—love, emotional solidarity, even financial support—are assumed to be and represented as secondary. The horizontal reciprocity and informal systems of support practiced within the slum community are not intelligible through the politics of neoliberalism or the kind of feminism depicted in the film. Yet, reading against the grain, the film does show that it is the community that sustains Kushum by giving her shelter, a job, and ultimately love. She in turn provides for the community by cooking and caring for the children. *Ukeel Apa*, on the other hand, extends a needed helping hand through moral and legal directives. And by empowering others, she empowers herself.

Ukeel Apa and Kushum represent two sides of the "New Woman" in contemporary Bangladesh, one the urban, educated patron of development and the other rural, simple recipient of development. It is curious that while Kushum's female subject position is formed in relation to her family and community, the film constructs *Ukeel Apa* without either. In this way, the film seems to imagine "independent" women like *Ukeel Apa* as lone heroines. This portrayal is in direct contrast to the reality of feminist organizing, which often happens within communities of women as we have seen in earlier chapters featuring the history of Naripokkho's organizing. Additionally, her sexuality or sexual vulnerability does not appear to be of much significance in the plot; Kushum is repeatedly cautioned about the "dangers" lurking around every corner for young women in the city (presumably from some men), but *Ukeel Apa* does not face similar questioning while traversing multiple urban and rural sites. As a matter of fact, she is often shown with men, such as the male journalist who interviews her, and a male assistant. As a powerful woman, she has male subordinates as well as female. Significantly, her only friend in the film is a young male artist who donates the money from the sale of his art to Kushum's cause. In one shot *Ukeel Apa* is seen in bed alone with her papers and reports. Thus the film implies that her class and educational privileges allow her to transcend her gender vulnerability, yet leave her without family and community.

The feminist human rights advocate in *Ayna*, then, appears to be in a lone struggle to serve the nation. *Ukeel Apa* is devoid of family, kin, and community, whereas Kushum's subject position is intimately influenced by these relationships. To help explain this contrast, we might turn to Purnima Mankekar (1999), whose analysis of women-oriented narratives in postcolonial Indian television, suggests that the figure of the emancipated woman represents progress, in that her service to the nation supersedes that to the family. At the same time, the "uplift" of women is often seen to be a nationalist project in taking the nation forward into the twenty-first century. The socially conscious, strong-willed, and loyal modern woman is the custodian of morality and integrity of the nation. In this representation, Mankekar claims the "woman's question" in the postcolonial context is subsumed within a liberal nationalist, and I would add liberal feminist, framework, that is not oppositional but reformist. Similarly, *Ukeel Apa* in this film is a provider and arbiter of justice, representing NGOs and the state. *Ukeel Apa* is the modern emancipated woman who serves the nation, as opposed to Kushum, who is more tied to the family and community. By providing both iconic women figures, the message of the film is made more "palatable," as it does not unilaterally reject femininity or women's position and roles within the community.

Victimization and Agency

A feminist consciousness of oppression and resistance to it is evident throughout *Ayna*. For example, Kushum vocally complains about the ills of dowry and the obligations placed on women through marriage. *Ukeel Apa* conducts research about gender violence and advocates for women victims. The slum community expresses a class-based consciousness in the song that was discussed previously, as well as through their modes of mobilizing on behalf of Kushum. Yet, these modes of resistance in the film are still couched within the dominant discourse of neoliberalism, where *Ukeel Apa*, as the symbol of a transnational identity machine, represents justice through law and NGO-driven organizing, rather than collective social empowerment. Resistance in the film is trapped within dominant ideologies, namely globalization, neoliberalism, and patriarchy.

Following the horrific acid attack on Kushum the night of her wedding to Dolon, the slum community rushes her to Dhaka Medical College Hospital and makes a single call to *Ukeel Apa* for help. She meets Dolon and others at the hospital where the doctor tells them reassuringly, "The patient is in our care and we will do everything to make her well." *Ukeel Apa* presides over a gathering at the slum with the police where she tells them, "The incident has been covered by the press. The entire country knows about it. You must not let the culprits get away. . . ." The community becomes agitated and starts shouting at the police, but they are placated by *Ukeel Apa*, "That's enough. Am I not by your side?" Thus, rather than allowing the community voice to be heard, *Ukeel Apa* takes control of the situation.

Later *Ukeel Apa* also takes charge of fixing Kushum's acid-ruined face. When a desperate Kushum tries to commit suicide by throwing herself in front of a speeding train, but is saved by Dolon, she cries to *Ukeel Apa*, "What is the use for my staying alive?" *Ukeel Apa* reprimands her, "Your life has not become meaningless. The benefits of modern medicine have provided many unfortunate women like you the chance to live again. We will help you." Dolon begs, "Please help us get Kushum's old face back. I will arrange for the money." *Ukeel Apa* promises to enlist the help of NGOs. She says, "About three months ago, some NGOs sent a group of victims of acid attacks abroad for plastic surgery. These girls now have regular jobs!" The solution to Kushum's problem is represented through a physical restoration of her former self, rather than empowering her to live as the person she has, however unwillingly, become.

With the help of NGOs, *Ukeel Apa* raises funds for Kushum's trip. Dolon's boss in the factory donates Tk 50,000 (roughly U.S.$714.00), and the workers in the factory raise an additional Tk 25,000 (U.S.$357.00). Unable to come up with the rest of the money, and beside himself with anxiety about Kushum's deteriorating mental health, Dolon shows up at *Ukeel Apa's* house with a leather briefcase he hijacked from an ostensibly "rich man" on the street. Demarcating the difference between the two is the large black iron gates separating *Ukeel Apa's* house from Dolon and the street. She arrives at the scene in her shiny black car and issues a stern moral directive to Dolon: "Neither you nor I have the right to what's in the bag. We need to return it to its rightful owner or hand it over to the police. Do you honestly want to restore Kushum's beauty by such dishonest means? Could you find peace then when you look at that beautiful face? This [restoring Kushum] is our problem, and we need to solve it." Dolon's attempt to help Kushum through the only means available to him is thwarted by *Ukeel Apa's* moral authority. Moreover, in this conversation, the emphasis on beauty, rather than on other possible attributes, is representative of the obsession with female beauty under patriarchy. The physical becomes all encompassing, prohibiting the characters to see beyond that and to heal Kushum inside as well as out.

As fate would have it, the leather briefcase belongs to Shuvro, *Ukeel Apa's* artist friend, whom the audience met in the opening shot of the film. When *Ukeel Apa* was traversing across rural Bangladesh doing research on *fatwa*-related violence against women, Shuvro was roaming the same rustic roads in search of subjects for his art. Unbeknownst to Kushum, he had spotted her running along the fields and by the trees and imagined her as the perfect subject for his art. In Dhaka, he re-created the image of Kushum and sold the painting in an art exhibit, which bought him a large profit of Tk 1.5 lakh (U.S.$2,140.00). When *Ukeel Apa* and Dolon come by to return his stolen bag, Shuvro is moved by Kushum's story, and he donates the profit from his sale for Kushum's plastic surgery abroad. A grateful *Ukeel Apa* marvels, "I am at a loss for words to appreciate your compassion. You have set an extraordinary example as an artist." Shuvro responds, "If my earnings come to use for those in need, that is the greatest satisfaction I could ask for. I hope I can continue to serve the people in this way." *Ukeel Apa's* subject position as the human rights activist (one side of the "New Woman") is shaped by saving Kushum (the flip side of the "New Woman"). Interestingly, the resources that contribute in "restoring" Kushum were earned by the use of her indirect "labor," or by posing unknowingly for Shuvro's painting.

Later, *Ukeel Apa's* dazzling performance in court leads to sentences of death by hanging and life imprisonment for Rameez and Khalek, respectively. Feminists and human rights activists are ambivalent about the death penalty, yet the film loses an opportunity to make a critical comment about the legal system here, and how pushing for conviction inevitably means doing the same for a death sentence. The film however upholds these sentences (as stated in chapters 1 and 2, acid violence crimes can carry death sentences in Bangladesh based on the degree of injury to victim) triumphantly and as a fitting end to the struggle for justice. The film draws to a close with her voice-over asserting, "The Kushums of this world want to live," as we witness Kushum's return from a presumably western location fully recovered—her face showing no scars from the attack or the reconstructive surgery—and into the welcoming arms of her country and husband. *Ukeel Apa's* subject position as the savior is reinforced by her authoritative voice in the background helping to restore Kushum, the counterheroine—to her place as the protected wife and daughter of the nation.

Ayna is a part of a larger media discourse about women and development. As we have already argued, women figure into development narratives primarily as victims and saviors, and are often represented in the media either as victims of violence or agents of protest against violence. These categorical representations obfuscate a host of other complicated issues. For example, the developmentalist narrative positions women as the barometer of both tradition and modernity—in the latter case, they mediate the attack by proponents of tradition on modernity. The victimization of women is addressed in developmentalist discourse with the modern inventions and interventions of medicine, law, and NGO-organizing. These interventions in turn are delinked from collective and organized political action, such as the role of the women's movement in mobilizing campaigns against violence. Thus the victim (in this case, Kushum) becomes relegated to the status of the grateful recipient and her savior (*Ukeel Apa*) to the status of a lone, heroic, and benevolent activist. Further, the victim of gendered violence is restored through cosmetic surgery in the west and returned to the arms of her loving husband and nation. As an individual bearing no external mark of the physical attack she endured, her reintegration into society is complete, unlike that of other acid violence survivors featured in this film who are not "lucky" enough to get the same treatment. In fact, in the film Kushum looks at them with horror and finds neither support nor community among them.

As a tool to raise awareness on violence against women, the emergence of social message films like *Ayna* are coextensive with the proliferation of a discourse of development and modernization in contemporary Bangladesh. *Ayna* effectively highlights the gendered and classed socioeconomic shifts that have taken place in the recent decades as a result of gradual industrialization, the shrinking of agricultural and subsistence-based economy, the transition to monetized economy, growing landlessness and poverty, rural to urban migration (illustrated by the garment workers in the film), and attendant new gendering patterns of urban space. It also brings out the formation of new kinds of alliances and kinship structures as exemplified by the relationships between *Ukeel Apa* and Kushum and the slum community of factory workers.

The competing and coexisting sides of the "New Woman" in *Ukeel Apa* and Kushum bring to the fore ideas of women's empowerment and objectification, community, sisterhood, and hierarchy, as well as representations of women as both agents in, and pawns of, patriarchies. At the same time, however, these depictions make familiar symbols out of women (heroine, victim), rather than locating them in their multifaceted particularities. *Ayna* ultimately cannot escape the dominant discourse of individual uplift and rescuing of third world victims through modern interventions. Nor can it elude the polar categorization of the victimized client and the feminist matron-patron. As I have argued in this chapter, this powerful dyad of the transnational identity machine creates an apparatus that makes legible and governable only certain types of gendered subjects and agents. Its conceptualization and depiction of what survivors of acid attack need remains within the frame of neoliberal and patriarchal discourses that reintegrate individuals into the productive machinery of the state (for example, by getting them regular jobs) through the imperialist gendered discourse of restoring victims by cosmetic surgery (provided by the west).

In earlier chapters, I have argued that transnational networking, particularly in the 1990s, has led to key policy changes related to violence against women, and has positively impacted global feminist movements on a local level. The case of Bangladeshi women activists mobilizing a successful campaign against acid violence is an example of this networking. I have also argued that the same process of transnationalization runs the risk of delinking social movements from locally informed agendas and supplanting them with neoliberal developmentalist programs. The focus on rehabilitating acid violence survivors through cosmetic surgery in the west, reintegrating them into service sector jobs, and providing for the speedy criminalization of acid-related crimes by donors and the government have not resulted in a sustained focus on the socioeconomic issues underlying the systemic oppression of women and other marginalized groups. In this transnational rhetoric of the NGOs, as we have seen, survivors are represented by a linear narrative that moves from victimhood to heroism. Similar case studies are abundant in the progress reports of development organizations dealing with income generation and victims of violence in Africa, Asia, the Middle East, and Latin America. The intervening organization and its professionals are seen as guardian angels saving "unfortunate" women from their locally based misfortunes.

The rescue narrative where the victimized woman is saved by elite actors—whether locally or globally—also obscures the on-the-ground realities of those surviving acid attacks. Because the focus on WID, GAD, and gender mainstreaming has led to the proliferation of gender-related programming where the term *gender* is interchangeable with *women*, most research reports on acid attacks continue to claim that women predominantly are the victims. At the same time this narrative fits the still prevalent "third world horror" framing of violence against women as "spectacular" and "aberrant" in the global South (Grewal 1998; Rajan 2004). A 2007 study titled "Acid Violence and Rape—Ending Impunity" conducted by Odhikar, a human rights organization

in Bangladesh, shows that in the years 2003, 2004, 2005, and 2006 there
were 181, 191, 104, and 105 reported cases of acid attacks against women,
respectively. However, the report also makes note that in the same years the
total cases of acid attacks were 337, 307, 196, and 161, respectively (p. 3).
It is therefore logical to assume that at least a third of these reported cases
are against men. The circumstances that lead to attacks against men remain
largely unknown. However, the rehabilitation and reintegration programs
continue to be framed around the "typical case" of a young and beautiful
woman being punished by the spurned suitor and subsequently being saved
by benevolent western donors and NGO professionals. Spectacularizing the
violence romanticizes the "saving" of women by western donors and cosmetic
surgery. Such linear and simplistic narratives obscure the complex and critical
organizing of local women's movements in response to gendered violence.

Conclusion

Despite its shortcomings, *Ayna* is an important woman-oriented narrative
tackling feminist concerns such as gender oppression, violence against women,
and women's shifting roles in a developing society. The film effectively portrays the coexistence and intersections of multiple patriarchies with power
structures such as global capitalism and neoliberal development. In doing
so it defies notions of the abject victimization of women by men as well as
capitalism as a totalizing project. The film opens up the space to look at
inequalities between women and class-based disparities among women and
men. However, the film simultaneously sets up polarized images of the native
woman as victims (represented by the economic underclass), and saviors (as
the educated human rights activist) as well as depicting gender violence and
feminist responses to it as simplistic. Its treatment of women as subjects of
social transformation is ambivalent at best, as it offers avenues for women to
transgress patriarchal institutions yet keeps them mired within a neocolonial
frame. Simultaneously, the film is enmeshed in an overarching developmentalist narrative that is ultimately patronizing (and, in this case, matronizing) to
women and the working poor. It reinforces modernist notions of "uplifting"
the disadvantaged through juridical mechanisms of the state, and technical
and professional interventions of the elite and the west while depicting the
poor as gullible, uneducated, and unaware.

Ayna grounds the larger discussion of the emergence and production of
competing notions of the "New Woman" within the context of development,

modernization, and globalization schemes in contemporary Bangladesh. It is an example of the new media interventions that are coextensive with the NGOization of social life and with social movements for change. The message of the film, even as it falls within the genre of human rights advocacy, reflects and proliferates the linear progress narrative of development and constructs for itself the heroine-feminist-savior and the abject victim subject coterminous with the larger discourses surrounding transnational advocacy. Just as it is important to ask "Who does the feminist heroine work for?" in these transnational circuits, it is equally important to investigate where the "ungrateful" recipient of development aid fits into this narrative. How do we talk about the stories of survival and struggle as opposed to misery and heroism?

Bina Akhter's story as described in chapter 3 allows for a discussion of the multiple layers one must pay attention to when designing programs that are meant to "aid" "third world beneficiaries," such as global inequality, power relations between the North and the South, the control of agendas of humanitarian projects, the limits of global feminism, and the people affected when negotiations go awry. Further, it enables a conversation that pushes the good/bad victim/survivor binary, which limits a fuller understanding of women's experiences of violence. Bina navigates the tricky waters of multiple and shifting subjectivities of victim, survivor, and feminist, which are seen as mutually exclusive categories in development discourse. Defying the misery-to-heroism and the victim-savage-savior narratives, she compels a complex analysis of women's lives in struggle and survival—an analysis it would behoove *Ayna* to emulate in delivering a more inspiring political message.

Chapter Five

Transnational Challenges

Engaging Religion, Development, and
Women's Organizing in Bangladesh

As a feminist activist and scholar interested in women's transnational organizing in Bangladesh, I have followed with curiosity a sudden soar in the
western media over the last several years of reports depicting the nation as
alternatively "the site of the next Islamist revolution" and a model developing
nation. The first of these images of Bangladesh was tied to a series of attacks
on NGOs, women clients of NGOs, progressive intellectuals, and leaders
of a secular-leaning political party by Islamist groups, many of whom claim
transnational allegiances with growing networks of extremist organizations
in the region. The second image is associated with the globally acclaimed
Grameen Bank and its founder Professor Muhammad Yunus, winner of the
2006 Nobel Peace Prize. And, more recently, Dr. Yunus was one of sixteen
to be awarded the 2009 Presidential Medal of Freedom by President Barack
Obama—America's highest civilian honor extended to individuals making a
"contribution to the security or national interests of the United States, world
peace, cultural or other significant public or private endeavors" (the White
House, 2009). Professor Yunus was particularly lauded for helping to launch
Grameen-style microfinance programs, integrating women in Afghanistan
into the monetary economy.

Development initiatives empowering poor "brown"[1] Muslim women
through microloans, with Dr. Yunus as the moderate "brown" Muslim
male voice, have gained prominence in the global context of proliferating
discourses emphasizing a stark contrast between western "civilization" and
Islamic reticence to join it. Several questions come to mind in response to
these categorical representations of the third-largest Muslim majority nation:
(1) Why the shift from a developing nation status to that of a moderate/

violent Islamic country? (2) In what ways are women perceived to be the measure of development or lack thereof? (3) In the age of transnational feminism, what kinds of mobilizations and alliances are possible, as women activists in Bangladesh face the multiple challenges of neoliberal development, patriarchy, and rising religious extremism regionally, as well as resurgent Orientalism globally? and (4) How do transnational constructions of gender violence in a Muslim majority country articulate with local feminist responses?

In this chapter I want to situate the discussion of women's transnational organizing in Bangladesh within the larger debates surrounding local, regional, and global feminist activism around gender violence. Like the NGOization of women's activism, another force that is becoming increasingly important to address is rising religious extremism in Bangladesh and its consequences for feminist mobilization. This conversation is not delinked from what the world has been witnessing in the post–September 11 climate, where discussions about women's emancipation in the Muslim world have taken on a new kind of intensity. The agendas of women activists organizing on the ground, and transnational feminist scholars critiquing the various forces shaping activists' responses and strategies can be at odds and create a chasm between the feminist transnational activist and scholar. For instance, the concerns of transnational feminist scholars located primarily in the North can be perceived as overly "academic" (focusing on important and vigorous debates over location, privilege, and colonial legacies and neocolonial relations) and derailing the practical and exigent issues on the ground (such as mobilizing global awareness and resources for constituencies in immediate need of assistance). By looking at Bangladeshi women activists' responses to gender violence within a climate of rising religious extremism—nationally and globally, as well as within the constellation of dependent relationships discussed in preceding parts of this book—in this chapter, I wish to deepen our understanding of more effective transnational analysis and organizing at both local and global levels.

As a feminist scholar occupying multiple and often contradictory locations in both the North American academy and Bangladeshi activist circles, I fully understand the importance of scholarly concerns problematizing Orientalist framings of gender violence in nonwestern locations. Yet I am equally cognizant of the difficult conditions in which local activists organize; conditions that involve time and resource constraints, working with recalcitrant state services and international aid agencies, and making use of transnational networks that can perpetuate unidimensional images of women's oppression under an indigenous patriarchy. These conditions may render irrelevant or suspend the pertinence of scholarly concerns that in theory should inform activist agendas.

Here, I neither mean to reify the activist/academic binary, nor do I intend to suggest that activists are not aware of complex global power configurations shaping local contexts. Rather, I suggest that (1) these debates may very well be more pressing for academics located in the North than for activists or academics in the South, and (2) in the process of instigating urgent action and advancing complex negotiations, they may lose pragmatic relevance. My purpose is to open up a more nuanced discussion around transnational feminist praxis that addresses the troubling yet real disconnect between criticism and urgent action. I also seek to shed light on the question of feminist complicity in, and mounting dissent against, the interlocking hegemonies of neoimperialism, fundamentalism, and patriarchies.

The available literature on Islamization in Bangladesh has focused little on its relationship to the national women's movement, which historically has been aligned with the nationalist movement for liberation. The nationalist movement has remained secular in orientation as a means to create a distinct identity from the colonizing West Pakistani state ideology of "authentic" Islam.[2] In fact, the very visible urban-based progressive movements in Bangladesh have collectively taken a strong stance against Islamization, perhaps at the expense of attention to the complex ways in which the contemporary social and political landscapes have shifted since 1971, leading to a strengthening in national and local-based Islamist politics. Postindependence, the women's movement has been equally influenced by "modernizing" forces of international development initiatives. The secular-nationalist stance of the women's movement, then, generally understands Islamists as a force external to the nation. In turn, progressive movement activists in Bangladesh believe that Islamists are bolstered by those factions in society who collaborated with the West Pakistani state in 1971, which unleashed a genocide on the Bengali peoples whom they considered not properly Muslim. These factions have gained prominence in the political life of the nation over the years and are in leadership positions, particularly within the Islamist political party, Jamaat-e-Islami. At the same time, a certain "purist" strain of religious ideology has also burgeoned among Bangladeshis as a consequence of their increased labor migration to the Middle East. That is, labor migrants who travel to the Middle Eastern states tend to return and propagate a more rigid form of religious identity and values that are different from the historically plural and syncretic nature of Islam practiced in the Bengal region. Further, financial support, and the attendant spread of a more "purist" value system and understanding of Islam, from Gulf Arab states leading to a proliferation of religious institutions and social organizations have also contributed to the changing landscape in Bangladesh, where newer meanings of Islam and Islamism are in motion. At the same time, regional conflicts involving India, Pakistan, and Afghanistan in particular, and global processes of Islamophobia have all fed into reactionary movements across South Asia. A conflux of all of these elements—strengthening of Islamist political parties at the national level, the increasing presence of religion-based social organizations at the local level, and the ripple effects of global politicized religion-based conflicts are interactively shaping the current forms of Islamization in Bangladesh.

The question I would like to engage in this chapter is how the women's movement has responded to these social and political changes in the nation. The Liberation War, and women's important role in it, is undoubtedly an inspiring legacy for women's activism in Bangladesh. However, framing all contemporary feminist struggles in that light—as the women's rights leaders often do—leads to the marginalization of *other* struggles incommensurate with the politics of Bengali nationalism and development.[3] Some Bangladeshi women may see their interests as better served by these other struggles. The challenges that the women's movement in Bangladesh currently confront require an analysis that goes beyond the Islamist/secular-nationalist binary and engages a more self-reflexive lens to acknowledge the linkages that connect disparate power structures, including feminist ones, that have differential implications for differently located women.

It is important to acknowledge that the landscape of contemporary Bangladeshi politics is such that categorical political divisions like nationalist, secularist, and Islamist are no longer clear, if they ever were at all. Historians Sugata Bose and Ayesha Jalal (1998) encourage understanding "regional dissidence" in the subcontinent, as it is manifested in secular democratic as opposed to authoritarian and Islamic government, in terms of the "historical dynamics of the transition from colonialism" (p. 203). That is, the relationships among seemingly oppositional discourses have to be understood in the context of the colonial past and its legacies in the subcontinent. They point out that historically, these apparently contradictory modalities of governance—democracy, authoritarianism, secularism, and religion-based—"have co-existed if not been thoroughly imbricated" within the nation (Bose and Jalal, 1998, p. 203).

Too often the women's movement (and feminist politics generally) in Bangladesh is uncritically coupled by its participants with the secularism of the civil society or the NGO sector. These groups in turn are deemed to be the progressive voice in the backdrop of a weak state that has dubious allegiances to Islamist parties. Both the state and the civil society, however, are implicated in donor-driven modernization and "nation-building" initiatives, with contradictory consequences that are not always entirely "emancipatory" for women. In such an intricate web of relationships it is difficult to tease out autonomous agendas for any of these constituencies. Further, it is not easy to understand the specific constraints that the women's movement must negotiate, constraints that might involve confronting rather than aligning with so-called secular/modernizing forces of NGOization. Indeed, in my view, the women's movement's attention needs to be shifted precisely to the interface of globalization, national development, and rising militant Islamic politics. Therefore, in this chapter I argue for a more nuanced analysis of Islamist/ secularist politics in Bangladesh, with a focus on the class-based women's movement's responses to the perceived dichotomy between the two. Moving beyond this dualistic framework, which I argue serves a narrow and elitist agenda, we must call for more serious attention to the actual and potential links between Islamist and secular agendas. We must begin to imagine feminist dissent that is more accountable to those constituencies, such as poor women, that seemingly "benefit" from, yet are also abjectly affected by, the promise of secular development.

Women's NGOs: Complicit, Dissident, or Both?

Women's NGOs, like mainstream NGOs, occupy a complex position in Bangladesh as they frame their organizational agendas and vision within the neoliberal development policies of donors and the state, and at the same time push their boundaries. It is at the intersection of this complicity and dissidence that the possibility of a more autonomous space for women's organizing, which I will discuss in this section, lies.

As Najma Chowdhury's (2001) account of implementing women's rights in Bangladesh shows, the impetus behind women's organizing post-1971 reflects the merging interests of the state and its economic development initiatives supported by international organizations such as the United Nations, other donor agencies, and global corporations that bring capital into the country in the form of direct foreign investment. Chowdhury points out that some women's organizations distinguish themselves from NGOs because their service is not salaried but voluntary. Nevertheless, they too solicit donor funds for projects and often partner with NGOs who provide them with the infrastructure to access subjects of development, namely poor women. Hence, even women's organizations who do not strictly identify as NGOs, nevertheless operate within the NGO paradigm to which I alluded in the Introduction. One of the major predicaments for the women's movement is to carve out an autonomous space from colonialist discourses of donor-driven development agendas, the state's conflicting ideologies and practices subscribing to these agendas, and the Islamist visions of a moral society.

Women-specific NGOs, as well as those with a major focus on women, are an important part of the national women's movement in Bangladesh (Chowdhury, 2001, p. 212).[4] These NGOs, however, tend to have specific class-based characteristics. In Bangladesh, the headquarters for women's NGOs are primarily concentrated in urban areas and are largely led by western-educated urban elites who advocate women's rights within a secular modernist framework. This class-based women's movement—a legacy of the secular nationalist politics of the Independence movement that is integrated in to the cultural underpinning of the progressive urban ethos—is highly visible and active in the public arena. On any given day, if one were to look through the national newspapers there would be a plethora of seminars and workshops on topics related to women, gender, and development and featuring the familiar names of professors, lawyers, researchers, NGO advocates, and professionals who circulate with high frequency in national and international conferences.

To complete the picture of the background against which Bangladeshi women's organizing takes place, we should emphasize that women have been heavily implicated in the nation-building project, and they play important roles in government. Leaders of the two major political parties are women. The position of Prime Minister has been held alternately by these two women almost exclusively from 1991 until present. Bangladesh has a Ministry of Women's Affairs; Women in Development focal points; a National Policy for the Advancement of Women; reserved parliamentary seats and nonprofessional, clerical, and custodial posts for women; and a national umbrella women's organization entrusted with improving conditions faced by women. However, these opportunities for government service continue to come from and benefit mostly certain sectors of the population, namely educated and urban-based women (Karim, 2004, p. 301). Outside of the urban centers, the large rural population in Bangladesh is mostly poor, illiterate, unemployed/underemployed, and alienated from the nation-building project.

Women's NGOs in Bangladesh have been able to exploit the globalizing force of human rights and women's rights ideology by taking on the mandates and implementation of the Convention on the Elimination of All Forms of Discrimination Against Women.[5] While Bangladesh is a signatory to international treaties and therefore obligated to protect the human rights of all its citizens, the various successive governments remain ambivalent regarding policy on gender, and ineffective in operationalizing gender mainstreaming.

Chowdhury reports, in preparation for the U.N.'s World Conference on Women in Beijing in 1995, that women leaders in Bangladesh participated in the formulation of national plans of action, monitoring tools, and measurable targets for gender mainstreaming with tremendous enthusiasm even though the implementations of these have been met with tepid response by the government. The Bangladesh National Preparatory Committee Towards Beijing, a coalition of over 200 individuals and organizations encompassing civil society, women activists, researchers, professionals, workers, development organizations, grassroots workers, cultural organizations, and human rights groups, engaged in awareness raising and mobilizing for nearly eighteen months prior to the conference. The main agenda items of this committee included lobbying the government to withdraw reservations pertaining to CEDAW and spotlighting violence against women. Post-Beijing, national workshops and taskforces were formed which broadened access to government-level policy making to civil society advocacy groups.

The tangible outcomes of these alliances have included strategies to strengthen the capacity of law-enforcment authorities and agencies to deal with crimes of violence against women, but there has been minimal intervention in the social arena that inhibits the majority of the population's access to such legal machinery (Chowdhury, 2001, p. 217). Critiquing the festival-like organizing stimulated by transnational forums such as the Bejing Conference, Suzanne Bergeron (2006), citing Gayatri Spivak, likened the U.N.-sponsored World Conferences on Women held in Beijing in 1995 as representing a kind of "global theater," where a show of global unity is produced in spite of continuing colonialist power relations, and where subaltern women remain invisible. Bergeron (2006) notes that according to Spivak these conferences further the image of global unity while obfuscating the premise of the conferences, which is the "unspoken assumption of the U.N. that the South is not capable of governing itself" (p. 161). Women's groups at the conference rallied around issues identified by the global platform, rather than allowing for issues to be defined by local groups based on their specific situations.

Urban-based women's rights organizations in Bangladesh are using the U.N. mandate for gender mainstreaming and international human rights treaties to put pressure on the government to implement more gender-sensitive policies. Moral shaming of the government in the global community by pressuring it to comply with the international treaties has been an effective mobilizing tool for women activists in the global South, even as it means integrating gender mainstreaming, as an "external" discourse rather than an organic "internal" one, to define movement agendas. As Liz Kelly (2005) has suggested, mainstreaming a gender perspective into development and human rights discourse and practice has been more of an exercise in mainstreaming activists than ensuring gender mainstreaming's methodological incorporation at all levels. It implies a "rhetorical absorption of a gender perspective" rather than a meaningful infusing of gender discourse and transformation of gender relations (Kelly, 2005, p. 472).

Transnational organizing thus often follows the mandates of global feminist advocacy, and are further shaped by the way these figure into national government priorities, instead of identifying diverse local concerns. This point emerges more clearly when we take into consideration Najma Chowdhury's (2001) observation that as the time for submission of the Bangladesh report to the CEDAW drew closer in 1995, the government surreptitiously withdrew some of its reservations to article 2 (those having to do with equal enjoyment of family benefits and guardianship and custody of children). This decision was most likely made by the government to appear in sync with global women's rights mandates and therefore project a progressive front internationally. However, by not publicizing the withdrawal of reservations and keeping it out of a public debate, the government also chose not to trouble its ties with local groups—such as religious political parties—and, presumably to protect itself from appearing inconsistent (Chowdhury, 2001, p. 226).

The point above is an example of the way that the government has manipulated the "religion card" while simultaneously projecting modernist and Islamist identities for state politicians' own political agendas. As Bangladeshi feminist scholar and activist Meghna Guhathakurta has suggested, Islamization has tended to influence restrictions on women's rights in the legal arena to a greater extent than in the mainstream political and economic spheres, which are more heavily determined by the flows of the political economy than by Islamist ideology (*Eclipse*, 1994). On the one hand, official policies have espoused the Beijing Platform of Action and passed the National Women's Advancement Policy crafted with progressive feminist and human rights groups. On the other hand, in 2004 the Bangladesh National Party government secretly introduced changes to the National Women's Advancement Policy (NWAP) undermining its previous progressive elements, without discussing it either in Parliament or with women's groups (Siddiqi, 2006).

Curiously, adds Siddiqi (2006), the western donor–endorsed Poverty Reduction Strategy Paper still reflects the principles of the 1997 document. She also notes that a group of thirty-five women's and other social-justice–based organizations have formed a coalition, the Shamajik Protirodh Committee, to protest the underhanded revisions to the NWAP. This coalition protests the BNP government's secretive alliances with Islamists. However, it is not equally critical of the limited ways that gender mainstreaming has translated within economic and social arenas, for diverse groups of women.

Moving away from the principle of equality stated in an earlier 1997 document formulated under the Awami League (AL) government—historically more secular in policy and outlook—the revised policy under the BNP government, which came into power in coalition with Islamist political parties, restricts women's rights to inheritance and control over resources, employment, and political and economic autonomy. Dina Siddiqi suggests that, "in terms of employment, the new policy calls for efforts to employ women in 'appropriate' professions. What constitutes appropriate is left open to interpretation" (Siddiqi, 2006). Further, women are barred from holding the highest positions in the judiciary, the diplomatic corps, and key administrative bodies. The government has neither formally endorsed nor rejected the revised documents, but the common understanding is that these changes were brought on by directives from the Islamist parties with which the government was in alliance. Most recently, in its 2008 election manifesto, AL removed all references to the Beijing Platform for Action, which it previously used as the basis for its policies for eradicating gender inequality. However, it maintained that the Bangladesh National Party would not act in contradiction to the Qur'an or *Sunnah* (the second source of Islamic jurisprudence after the Qur'an detailing the way Prophet Muhammad lived his life), consequently making feminist interventions to reform family law quite challenging (Sultan et al., 2010, p. 243). One cannot make too much of the differences in the stances of these two main political parties (the AL and the BNP) with regard to women's rights—even though one has more overt ties to the Islamist political party than the other and that alliance makes it more susceptible, according to progressive activists in Bangladesh, to enact stricter policies with regard to women's rights—because when it comes to gender policy they cannot be significantly differentiated. Both parties have tread a fine line in navigating the competing ideologies of modernization and Islamism, and the attendant interests of the constellation of actors they collaborate with who espouse these seemingly divergent views.[6]

In a recent conversation with a women's movement activist in Bangladesh, I learned that the emphasis on the Poverty Reduction Strategy Paper (PRSP) by the government reflects its class-based top-down approach. The PRSP, developed by member countries along with the World Bank and the IMF, is an imposed agenda, one that is not grounded in country-specific needs and realities. Together with the implementation plans of Millennium Development Goals (MDGs), donor-driven gender mainstreaming overlooks differential realities of women by class, ethnicity, and religion. While the national government historically laid out program goals for development in five-year cycles, that strategy had been replaced by gender mainstreaming through MDGs and the PRSP mandates. This shows a supplanting of the state's development agenda by that of the international development apparatus. Not to mention that matters are further complicated by the competing versions of women's rights initiatives espoused within donor-driven documents (PRSP and MDGs), individual political party manifestos, the Constitution, and family law.

On the national development front, the push for gender mainstreaming puts the Ministry of Women and Children Affairs at the lead for ensuring the integration of gender in other government sectors. This, according to sociologist Dr. Sadeka Halim, is not an effective strategy, given the marginalization of the Ministry of Women and Children Affairs in relation to other ministries. The "burden" of gender integration remains with the Women's Ministry, with its members approaching other sectors for assessment of gender component in their work. Dr. Halim maintains that the onus should actually be on the other ministries to approach the Women's Ministry, which they rarely do, since gender is not seen as a priority for them. Replacing national five-year plans with the imposed agenda of the PRSP is "unconstitutional" according to Dr. Halim, and perpetuates the elitist vision of donor- and urban-based women's development (S. Halim, personal communication, October 6, 2008b).

MDG assessments often do not pay close attention to local complexities of gender relations on the ground. Naila Kabeer (2005) argues that the third Millennium Development Goal of gender equality and women's empowerment is clearly important, yet disappointingly narrow in its vision of implementation. It ignores the crucial reality that unequal social relationships result in differential access to resources that are understood to ameliorate women's participation in education, employment, and politics—MDG's three indicators of gender equality and empowerment. For example, in her report on "Gender Needs Assessment of MDG-3," commissioned by the United Nations Development Program (UNDP), Dr. Halim notes, "Bangladesh has made considerable progress in terms of reducing the discrimination between men and women" (Halim, 2008a, p. 2), and points out that gender parity has been achieved in primary school enrollment. However, the report goes on to reveal that not all regional divisions (there are six in total) have reached the aforementioned parity, and surprisingly the division with the highest literacy rate has not reached gender parity in primary education. In addition, in the last five years, five divisions have shown a negative annual growth rate of primary school enrollment. Although conclusive data is not yet available, Dr. Halim notes that areas with high populations of minorities (defined by ethnic, religious, socio-economic status) might have less parity and enrollment.

This same UNDP document reports that gender parity in secondary school enrollment has also been reached in Bangladesh. In the last fifteen years, enrollment of girls has even surpassed that of boys, and between 1991 and 1995, enrollment of boys witnessed a substantial decrease. Dr. Halim notes that the impressive enrollment of girls in secondary school can be attributed to the government-assisted Female Secondary School Assistance Program (FSSAP) launched in the late 1980s. The program offers cash incentives or stipends to secondary school girls to cover a large portion of direct school expenses, and also provides tuition assistance to the schools. As at the primary level, secondary school–level growth rates also differ according to division, with three divisions noting a decrease in enrollment. Between the years of 2000 and 2005, growth rates in both rural and urban areas witnessed a decline.

At the tertiary level, by 2005 women's enrollment indicators stood at 24 percent. Between 1997 and 2005, female enrollment declined from 31 percent to 24 percent while male enrollment increased from 61 percent to 76 percent. Dr. Halim notes in the report that stipend-related interventions must be available at the tertiary level to address gender parity effectively. In the area of nonagricultural employment, by 2005 the male-to-female ratio reached roughly 85:15. The annual growth rate has decreased for females in recent years. In the area of political participation, the numbers are most disheartening, with women holding only 12.6 percent of the seats in National Parliament (which allocates 30 reserved seats to women out of 330 seats), reflecting a decrease from the two previous parliamentary democracy governments (Halim, 2008a, p. 3).[7]

Much development research indicates that education increases women's ability to deal with matters in the public sphere more effectively as well as exercise more control within the family and community. However, in the context of societal gender inequality, the effects of education may take on different meanings. For instance, where women's roles in society are defined by their reproductive function, education is seen as a means to acquire suitable husbands and take on subordinate roles within family and wage work spheres. Social inequalities are also present in the delivery of education, where gender discrimination leads to lower expectations and achievements among women. Moreover, a hidden content of school curriculum usually is the devaluation of work that is generally taken up by the poor and women. Naila Kabeer (2005) observes that policy makers recognize that educating women leads to the improvement of the welfare of the family, but they neglect to emphasize educational content that is geared toward better equipping women as equals in society. Based on these observations, we can see how even the attainment of MDG goals can be illusory, because the intended effects are not uniformly experienced by all women.

The Millennium Development Goal of employment is another place where more attention needs to be paid to the unique experiences of local women. Kabeer shows that women's participation in wage work increases self-esteem and confidence among women. Wage work is a way for women to achieve greater respect within the family and community as well as acquire skills to negotiate with various actors in wider society and participate in political activities. Women workers in the garment industry have expressed that they are able to negotiate marriage relations and oppressive family and community structures by moving away from home and developing alternative communities of support in their new work and living spaces. However, paid work often involves harsh and exploitative working conditions, with little recourse for organizing against or protesting them. In the area of political participation, notes Kabeer, greater attention needs to be paid to strengthening women's voices in local rather than national government. The latter tends to draw its members from more elite factions of society that may not respond to the needs of poor women.

Kabeer concludes that while the formulation of the MDG might reflect the success of global movements for social justice, the translation of them "into a series of technical goals, to be implemented mainly by the very actors and institutions that have blocked their realization in the past" minimizes their potential for greater change (Kabeer, 2005, p. 22). Policy changes have to allow women to participate more effectively, she suggests, so attainment of goals can be tested beyond the numerical parity of capacity to challenge and question unjust practices. Kabeer believes that the international community has to commit more seriously to building the collective capacity of women at the grassroots. Exercising collective capability is connected to having transformative agency, not hollow "empowerment" indicators.

Lamia Karim (2004) and Elora Shehabuddin (1999) have criticized the urban-based women's movement for either exploiting unequal social relations with their clients or having little understanding of women's realities in rural Bangladesh. These scholars bring to our attention the fact that women who staff and run NGOs lead vastly different lives from the women who are their clients. While not intending to lessen the very important work that women's rights organizations do, it is nevertheless critical to acknowledge that privilege based on religion, ethnicity, and class result in perpetuating the clientelist social structure of Bangladesh and hinder feminist alliances (as we saw in the history of the acid campaign, discussed in earlier chapters).

The consequences of the NGOization of development and women's organizing provide feminists opportunities to mobilize resources and forge alliances in the transnational arena, yet also inhibit forging more autonomous and transformative alliances across class, ethnicity, and grassroots-based agendas. In a 2004 study commissioned by CARE Bangladesh that explores current initiatives for women's empowerment undertaken by the NGO communities, Santi Rozario (2004) convened twenty-five organizations involved in promoting women's rights. An important observation made in her report is the large extent to which the agenda of the groups are donor driven, manifesting in project-based work that is time-bound and product-oriented. Rozario's findings reinforce what the consolidation of ASF has demonstrated in terms of prioritizing certain goals that departed quite significantly from the initial Naripokkho-based agenda. Rather than strengthening local organizing and fostering collaborations among women's groups, the donor-driven agenda engenders a climate of competition among these groups.

The most significant common issue among the groups is violence against women, not surprisingly since the global women's movement has been most successful in leveraging this as a common platform. However, the framing of gender violence within this platform has limitations in enabling a fundamental critique of women's role in society because of the way physical violence (understood as a consequence of patriarchy) is considered as detached from structural violence (requiring an analysis of global capitalism and racism). This delinking of violence against women from its structural causes facilitates publicity and criminalization of spectacular acts of violence, but it has not effectively confronted social conditions that enable gendered violence or dealt with women's lack of access to due process and the ability to lead secure lives.

For instance, Rozario (2004) reports that delivering legal aid in and of itself would not make much difference to the practice of dowry, as is suggested in the statement of a young man: "I can tell you this, if there is one [court] case against dowry from this village, no man will come forward to marry any girls from this village" (p. 18). Challenging patriarchal norms that measure women's worth by her marriageability are as important as providing legal services. Rozario's report makes the important point that despite laws against the giving and taking of dowries, most dowry-related violence cases are only reported when a woman has been attacked because of unmet dowry demands, not when a dowry transaction has been made. This brings home the earlier point made about the dubious success of global feminism and gender mainstreaming in criminalizing violence against women, without also confronting structural violence.

Another striking gap in women's NGO organizing is the lack of solidarity across and even within class lines. Programs that foster competition instead of collaboration perpetuate the patron-client relationship between urban elite feminists who are conversant in the language of global feminist platforms, and their counterparts, women often based in rural contexts or even urban contexts but who lack the professional skills required to be participants in global development apparatus. The competitive model is replicated even in development programs for women who have to become members of NGOs in order to access services. Santi Rozario (2004) reports that while in theory NGOs are supposed to provide services to all individuals of any given community, in reality they do so only to their members, or charge nonmembers higher fees.

The consequences of unacknowledged privilege are also brought up through the example of the women in the Chittagong Hill Tracts (CHT) of Bangladesh by Meghna Guhathakurta (2004). Guhathakurta uses this case to illuminate the contested ways violence and victimization have been understood by the mainstream women's movement, the state, and indigenous community struggles for citizenship. Guhathakurta's work reinforces the idea that the dominant women's movement ignores ethnic and class differences in thinking about violence. While the state conceptualizes violence against women primarily in its physical manifestation, the national women's movement has also located its causes in patriarchal and class-based structural inequalities, whereas the indigenous women's movement has integrated further nuanced intersectional analysis of gender, ethnicity, nationalism, and class in thinking about violence. A critical reading of the writings of Kalpana Chakma, the organizing secretary of the Hill Women's Federation (HWF)—an organization that mounted a powerful response to the state brutalization of the Jumma people—reveals the multiple challenges facing indigenous women against "politicomilitary" interventions of the Bengali state such as patriarchy, poverty, and nationalist struggle to retain cultural identity.[8] Guhathakurta surmises, "Kalpana's feminism also differs sharply from that of her middle-class Bengali sisters because unlike them her life struggles force her to confront and engage military and ethnic/racial domination in a way that is not easily comprehensible to the privileged Bengali" (Guhathakurta, 2004, p. 201). Chakma's writings also frame struggles for gender and ethnic justice within the broader struggle for Bengali democracy, nationalism, and freedom, denying that her ethnic identity excludes her from Bangladeshi nationalism: "We are part of the students' movement who had created '52, '69, '71. And '90!"[9] (Guhathakurta, 2004, p. 202). Although the Jumma struggles were perceived as a threat to the sovereignty of the Bengali nation by the state, this statement casts them as a democratic movement for self-determination within the nation of Bangladesh.

Despite the flourishing civil society sector in Bangladesh, very few organizations expressed interest in the CHT issue. Yet following the abduction and alleged murder of Kalpana Chakma in 1996, and the subsequent organizing among the Jumma people, as well as various human rights reports in the mainstream media, the women's movement joined together with the indigenous women's group, albeit not using the conceptualization of the larger struggles so eloquently defined by Kalpana Chakma. The HWF participated in the International Women's Day Rally in 1994, and went to the NGO Forum of the Women's Conference in Beijing in 1995 (although Kalpana Chakma could not go because of lack of funds), with their slogan "Autonomy for Peace." Yet a description of their struggles barely made it in the summary of the official NGO report. Guhathakurta's study shows that indigenous women would have benefited from global feminist vehicles to promote visibility for their struggle for autonomy but their agenda was not given that visibility in the national women's movement driven mobilizations. Middle-class Bengali organizations are so driven by the development discourse and its narrow conceptualization of gender mainstreaming that there are serious limitations to engaging more critically in questions of ethnicity and nationality as they intersect with gender. While showing support to the Hill women around generalized notions of human rights violations by the state, the same women's organizations failed to interrogate notions of citizenship, nation, self-determination and ethnicity—the very ideals on which the Bengali nationalist movement was mobilized.

In addition to class-based factors, feminist organizations are further polarized along party lines, and this seriously influences the kinds of responses they mount toward other important campaigns such as those advocating a Uniform Family Code, and female students' movements against sexual harassment. There is a tendency for women's organizations, following the general trend among civil society, to line up alongside the Awami League or the Bangladesh National Party), the two major political parties that have ruled the nation for much of its thirty-nine years of independence. Although policies regarding gender do not differ in any great detail from one political platform to another, they do capitulate to alliances with the Islamist parties to varying degrees, thereby consolidating the "Islamic"/ "Secular" bifurcation. The AL was the political party that led the secular nationalist independence struggle and, while both parties have embraced secular modernist development initiatives for nation building, the BNP has made more overt alliances with Islamists over the years. The AL's more recent support of Islamist platforms has been met with harsh criticisms from progressive constituencies, including women's groups. These vacillations clarify the intricate co-dependencies between various state and non–state actors and the need for analysis that recognizes the cross-currents in discourses of religiosity, secular development, and global feminism shaping women's organizing strategies in Bangladesh.

Brahmanbaria Rally—Vying for Social Control

The complex positionality of NGOs and their contradictory relationships to their constituencies are crystallized in two competing representations of a women's rally led by the NGO Proshika in Brahmanbaria, a district in east-central Bangladesh, in December 1998. Namely, one of these representations is furthered by Political Science scholar Ali Riaz and the other by feminist scholar Lamia Karim. Riaz (2004) describes the events of that day as an attack by Islamists on women who took part in an NGO-led rally to celebrate the liberation of Brahmanbaria from the Pakistani Army in 1971 (while the local police failed to intervene). In contrast, Lamia Karim's (2004) account of the same event exposes how democratizing impulses of women's NGOs are in conflict with the clientelist relationship they have with their constituencies, whom they profess to empower. Here, the secular progressive underpinnings of NGOs, which are frequently heralded as democratic and modernizing forces in Bangladesh, come to be seen as making poor women particularly vulnerable to physical and structural violence.

The attack on the women's rally needs to be contextualized within a spate of violence in the late 1990s against NGO staff and women clients, as well as poor women in general. Most media reports portrayed these as symbolic of the threat modernization projects posed to more orthodox factions of society, namely Islamists. Anthropologist Dina Siddiqi's (2006) analysis of *Eclipse*, a film made by women activists in Bangladesh in response to *fatwa*-related violence against women in the 1990s, demonstrates how similar ideas were reflected within progressive organizing as well. She argues that in *Eclipse*, Islam is seen as an "external threat" to the nation and its women, and "Islamist violence" is carried out in the film by those groups who opposed the nationalist struggle of Bangladesh. The film places Islam in a stark binary against both Bangladeshi nationalism and modernism. Analyzing the attack on the Proshika-led women's rally in December 1998 will shed further light on this particular debate pitting Islam against nation, while framing women activists' agendas as secular nationalist.

In December 1998, Proshika, one of the biggest NGOs administering microcredit in Bangladesh, organized a *Mela* (village fair) for its women members in Brahmanbaria. The location is significant because it is the place of a historic victory won by the Bengali Liberation forces against the Pakistani army in 1971. Moreover, it is known as a conservative and influential hub of Islamist political groups and of Qwami madrassas, an important vehicle for teaching Islam that offers free education for poor students. *Mela*s and folk theater, historically associated with Bengali Hindu culture, and often used as tools of grassroots organizing and consciousness raising by NGOs, were considered blasphemous by the Islamist groups in the area, who issued a *fatwa* against Proshika. Subsequently, Proshika changed the *Mela* into a public rally to commemorate the 1971 Liberation War, thus setting in motion an implicit challenge to Islamist groups. Invoking the memory of 1971 symbolically strengthened Proshika's secular progressive positioning, not an uncommon strategy in Bangladesh among the progressive communities.

Karim notes, the rally was attended by approximately 10,000 impoverished women and men. At this rally, madrassah students and clergy launched an attack on the NGO staff, and the women participants in particular. Women attendees were beaten, their clothes were torn off, and insults were hurled at them for daring to gather in public in spite of the *fatwa*. In the days following the rally, NGO offices, schools, and staff homes were looted, burned, and torn down. The police were notably absent, despite existing laws against issuing *fatwas*.

Ali Riaz (2004) and Lamia Karim (2004) see the attack and the subsequent fallout as a result of conflicts between very different forces. Riaz sees the event as a clash between Islamists and secular progressives. According to him, "Their [NGO workers] only crime was that they didn't heed the warnings of the Islamists not to join a gathering deemed 'un-Islamic.' . . . The NGO activists in particular were forced to flee the city. Thus, twenty-seven years after independence, Brahmanbaria returned to the media spotlight, once again as a battleground, this time between the secularists and the Islamists. And this time, the secularists had to take cover, at least for that day" (Riaz, 2004, p. 90). In contrast, Lamia Karim emphasizes the disconnect between the NGO staff of Proshika and their poor women clients. She notes, not without irony, that the leaders of the NGO, rather than staying to support the local victims of the attack, fled to the capital "in their imported SUVs," and began holding seminars to raise awareness and support to mobilize against Islamism (Karim, 2004, p. 306). She further comments that feminist leaders in Dhaka also responded by blaming the gradual Islamization of society as the source of violence against women, while the opportunistic NGO politics in this case remained unquestioned.

Karim interviewed men and women borrowers of Proshika following the rally, who revealed that they had little choice in the matter of attending the rally in the first place, as they believed their loan approval depended on it. What is more, the attendees were unaware of the fatwa issued by the Islamist group against potential attendees, and they did not know that the *Mela* had been changed to a rally by the NGO. Karim further argues that the Islamists' aggressive reaction toward women—particularly poor rural women—was class based, since a women's rally attended by middle-class women activists from Dhaka a few days earlier had gone unchallenged. In a climate of increasing socioeconomic disempowerment of both men and women, and the loss of employment and underemployment of men, "modernizing" forces of NGOs represent a layered threat. The NGOization of society within the context of globalization is perceived at the grassroots level to go hand in hand with westernization and even Christianization (Karim, 2004).

NGOs have become a powerful symbol of change in the domain of gender relations and the social structures of Bangladesh and elsewhere. As Dina Siddiqi (1998) has argued, the hierarchical gender practices that Islamist parties seek to protect overtly clash with the seeming modernist ideologies of NGOs (pp. 216–217). Women NGO staff members, in particular, have been attacked by religious extremist groups, as have NGO schools and offices. Ironically, points out Karim (2004), despite the anti-Christian rhetoric, no missionary schools have been attacked, neither have the more radical NGOs with overt feminist agendas. It is the large NGOs of Bangladesh (such as BRAC, known globally as a model development organization whose education and health programs have been replicated worldwide, and Proshika) that have been borne the brunt of most Islamist attacks.

Siddiqi connects Bangladesh Rural Action Committee's iconic position and visibility to these attacks. She observes, "This kind of movement [Islamist] must ultimately be located within the specific predicaments of modernity, in particular the tensions of the postcolonial nation-state and the contingencies of global capitalism." In the context of Bangladesh, she concludes, politicization of Islam has been state-sponsored rather than a "fundamentalist" people's movement (Siddiqi, 1998, pp. 212–213). In other words, the allegiances forged between ruling political parties and Islamist parties at the national level have emboldened Islamists at the local levels and increased their power.

Like NGOs and state-sponsored development initiatives, Islamist political groups are also invested in mobilizing poor women to bolster their group support. Ali Riaz suggests that these Islamist groups accuse NGO education programs of spreading atheism, and they see western development aid organizations as continuing colonial era structures by transforming existing gender relations to the detriment of the family (Riaz, 2004, p. 123). Digging deeper, Riaz also reveals that the rural power structure in Bangladesh—patron clientelist in nature—is grating against shifting gender dynamics.

The state certainly has been complicit in maintaining the rural power structure as a means to maintain its link to the rural population. Developmentalist agendas of the NGOs, on the other hand, have relied on the active participation of women in credit and educational programs that have directly confronted the rural power structures' assignation of proper female behavior. As Dina Siddiqi (2006) has argued, the advent of NGOs has actually reconstituted local power structures. The patronage system run by religious leaders and other formations of local elites, like rural moneylenders and large landowners, is in the process of being replaced by NGOs providing low-interest loans. Simultaneously, these different elite formations are strengthening their alliances in opposition to the shifting social and economic tides in rural society. At the same time, *madrassahs* are losing students to NGO education programs. The prominent presence of NGOs, their perceived ties with western institutions, in a context where large segments of the rural population feel disempowered, create conditions for a certain type of Islamist rhetoric to thrive.

The state and NGOs have both failed to protect poor women citizens and left them vulnerable to physical violence emanating from power struggles among various interest groups whose existence is legitimized precisely by invoking the rights of poor women. While Proshika depicted women's participation in the *Mela* as democratization, and the religious groups saw it as un-Islamic, the women involved saw it as simply meeting the conditions of their NGO contracts. In this instance, integrating gender into development required their visibility, in the form of participation in a public rally, without ensuring the social and economic empowerment needed to make this participation a real choice. Further, it hinted that the vehicles of women's empowerment, in this case NGOs, are just as interested in self-promotion in a fashion that is ostensibly recognizable by international development structures (galvanizing bodies of poor brown Muslim women in the public space) as in attaining goals of gender mainstreaming. As Liz Kelly (2005) points out, the turn to gender mainstreaming has resulted in increased donor support for NGOs, although not always for feminist ones. Intergovernmental organizations have become major players in choosing large NGOs over smaller, long-standing feminist ones to be their service providers, thus entrenching new hierarchies.

Feminist scholar Chandra Mohanty (2003) has argued that although much of the literature on globalization has marked the centrality of race, class, and gender in critiquing global capitalist development, racialized gender still remains a largely unmarked terrain. In this case, the poor women who are the constituencies of state, NGO, and Islamist group-led social mobilization are subject to racialized patriarchal marginalization in the context of globalization. Further, the political economy of capitalist development brings into sharp focus the intersections of colonialism, capitalism, race, class, and gender as they discipline the labor and public and private lives of the poor in the third world, and of other women of color disproportionately. The abject victimization of the impoverished women and men at the Brahmanbaria rally is an instance where we see the intersecting forces of global capitalist development and religious patriarchy through NGOs who are integrating poor women into the market through microcredit initiatives. Rising religious extremism itself is a complex phenomenon, inseparable from the particular dynamics of modernization and global capitalism. It is this uncomfortable intersection that global feminism in its resolute allegiance to the so-called belief of progressive development may not have given sufficient attention to.

The Brahmanbaria example brings home the point that while Bangladesh has been portrayed both by international and national groups as a site with tension between modernism/nationalism and Islam, the less focused tensions between elite and poor NGOs and their clients are equally palpable, and push us to go beyond the secularism-Islamism binary as we try to explain the dynamics of violence against women. These intranation and intracultural tensions rising largely from class-based inequalities help us understand how the women's movements responses to gender violence cannot be effectual unless they are more fully confronted. This broader lesson is one also drawn from the more specific campaign mobilized against acid attacks in earlier chapters.

Conclusion

In 2000, I was in the audience of a forum in Dhaka, where women activists were presenting an appraisal of the 1995 Beijing Platform for Action, five years after its declaration. Speakers and audience included representatives from prominent national and women's NGOs. Also in the audience were staff and clients of NGOs, many of whom had traveled long distances to be part of a ceremony, which clearly had a celebratory ring. Following a presentation by a representative of BRAC—known globally as a model development organization whose education and health programs have been replicated worldwide, as indicated above—a member of the audience identified himself as an ordinary citizen of Bangladesh who worked hard to provide for his family and who had traveled from Kishoreganj to hear the "national development plan" for Bangladeshis. He said, "I did not come here to listen to a progress report from BRAC. I want to know what plans the NGOs have to improve the lives of the poor?" This man did not get an answer that day, and the stir he momentarily created in the room was quickly suppressed as the facilitator stepped onto the platform and moved on with the program.

As an inside-outsider, I have often wondered about the relative absence of critique by scholar-activists in Bangladesh of development and social mobilization in Bangladesh. I have seen firsthand the difficult challenges of transnational organizing faced by feminists in Bangladesh, even as they sometimes depend on framing issues in essentialist terms to mobilize disparate communities to take urgent action. NGOs occupy such a powerful social space in Bangladesh that they seem to have appropriated the space of dissent even among progressive intellectuals and activists. In fact, much of the organizing, production, and dissemination of knowledge, and social mobilization now occur through NGOs and not against them. NGOs contract professionals as consultants and researchers; organize national, regional, and local forums; employ increasing numbers of graduates interested in grassroots development work; and mobilize constituencies for social and political action. How do we have conversations in this context that can engage the particular ways in which NGOs have become the vehicle of neoliberal governance, control, and the disciplining of postcolonial subjects, even as they do produce new identities and meanings that, on a smaller scale, disrupt the global order?

I would like to return to the question of what kinds of mobilizations are possible as women activists in Bangladesh confront the scattered hegemonies of rising religious extremism in the region, neoimperialism and Islamophobia globally, and neocolonial development initiatives that make use of poor Bangladeshi women's participation to bolster their own sustainability. Although I agree with much of Karim's (2004) analysis of the unequal power relations between NGO-based urban feminists and poor rural women clients of NGOs, I am not comfortable in dismissing urban women's activism as wholly uninformed and clientelist.

The urban-based women's movement in Bangladesh has flourished as a result of transnational networking and availing itself of global feminist instruments. At the same time, such alliances hinder a more nuanced engagement with diverse women's realities on the ground. This contradictory consequence of global women's organizing efforts, whereby new kinds of hierarchies emerge and only certain kinds of organizing are visible, has been noted by Elizabeth Freedman (1999) as an example of "transnationalism reversed." Anthropologist Sally Merry's (2006) ethnographic work on the making and implementing of human rights policy on gender in the U.N. reveals how participants seem to perpetuate an image of an unchanging, essential national culture in which women's status is embedded, in order to maximize the impact of their own claims on behalf of women. Instead of explaining how culture is used in struggles over class, kinship, ethnic, or religious identity, global feminist activists often invoke an essential culture as detrimental to women's emancipation. Sally Merry writes, "In the context of an international setting and universal principles, acknowledging such complexity would diminish the political impact of her [the woman activist's] statement" (Merry, 2006, p. 18). International documents and country reports on Bangladesh are rife with such simplistic "progress narratives" where women are perceived to be victims of culture and indigenous patriarchy, deflecting attention from other kinds of analysis.

Even if feminists use essentializing discourses of gender and culture consciously and strategically, we must persistently ask about the implications for transnational solidarity and praxis. Saba Mahmood (2005) observes that feminism is both an analytic and a political project, and while the two certainly inform one another they ought not to be collapsed in to one. There is value in keeping the possibilities of the analytic project open in the interest of thinking beyond immediate or urgent political action. The expediency of mobilizing campaigns under difficult circumstances may lead to silencing critical voices, as we saw happening in organizing related to the Beijing Conference, as well as the constructing of a nationalist identity to counter an Islamist "threat." Nevertheless, ongoing reflection and dialogue are essential if NGOs are to effectively serve and integrate their constituencies into development initiatives.

In order to understand women's experiences more clearly, feminism and fundamentalism must both be viewed as part of modernity rather than as opposing discourses. In western discourses, the idea of Islamic fundamentalism is linked to the racialization of Muslims as a people without history, the demonization of Islamic masculinity as barbaric, and Islamic femininity as victimized and subordinate. Western egalitarian feminism, on the other hand, is tied to the feminist progress narrative of women's emancipation from backward tradition (often associated with patriarchal religion) to enlightened modernity. This dichotomy disallows an understanding of the complexities of women's experiences as both Muslim and feminist.

Minoo Moallem (1999) sees overlap between feminism and fundamentalism and co-complicity in "perpetuating power relations, either by sustaining the boundaries of a totalistic ideology (in the case of fundamentalist feminists), or by creating restricted boundaries through a replacement of patriarchy with matriarchy, or by limiting women's issues to only one set of relations, and thus putting an end to any constructive sociological discussion" (Moallem, 1999, p. 325). Sometimes both feminists and fundamentalists can be intolerant of other points of view on women's status, yet can function as rivals, but they can also act in similar ways in their rigidified positions and categories of analysis. Subject positions emerging from such fixed formations remain cut off from historical and geopolitical contexts. Several scholars have proposed a transnational discourse that is based on intersecting and interlocking positionalities and power relations. Further, feminism must disrupt its own complicity with perpetuating rigidified analysis of women's oppression within transnational spheres of mobilization. Following this line of thinking, NGO-based organizing, important as it is as a venue for social change, must interrogate this rigid dichotomy between secular development and religious oppression and find more nuanced causes of conflicts such as the one that unfolded in Brahmanbaria.

Binary analysis of women's organizing as secular/Islamist or modern/underdeveloped freezes up conversations that recognize the heterogeneous ways in which women activists negotiate their environments. Instigating action within the structure of global U.N.-based feminism is imbricated within the culture of such a field that inhibits multiaxial analysis of diverse women's positionalities and realities. Raka Ray (1999) suggests that organizations are embedded in and respond to a set of unequal socially constructed structures and relations that ought to be understood "both as configurations of forces and as sites of struggle" that perpetuate yet disrupt existing dynamics (p. 7). She presents the term *protest fields* to imply subgroups and networks that oppose the logic of power relations in the larger political field, even as they are constrained by them. Organizations act, not as free agents, but rather within the context of asymmetrical power relations within a given field. Ray's analysis of women's movements juxtaposed with Moallem's assertion of western egalitarian feminism's (which appears to dominate global feminist scripts of fashioning "other" women's needs and desires in the image of the liberated western subject) complicity in furthering imperialist discourses of modernity and development opens up an important dialogue.

My work here seeks to illuminate intramovement tensions in the context of Bangladesh in an attempt to theorize and imagine feminist alliances that are more equitable and just across borders of nation, class, and community. As feminist activists, scholars, and practitioners we need to be more attentive to the protest field conversations that rupture the asymmetrical plane of political fields and open up more productive dialogue for effective transnational praxis.

Conclusion

This kind of work [transnational feminist solidarity] requires that we ourselves [feminist academics], as well as the institutions in which we work, put equal weight on organizing protest and theorizing our involvement in such activism. U.N. world conferences on women and U.N. policy language and debates have yielded little more than small doses of success for the world's poorest women. They have been far more successful in creating an industry of "studying poor women" that generates a somewhat steady source of funding for middle-class women globally in the name of feminism. This gravy train for middle-class feminists, including Southern transnational feminists based in the North, has reproduced class interests antithetical to the goals of working-class feminist action in the South in particular. We are proposing a different solution: that as feminists in the North we work in the communities in which we are located, making lateral linkages with women across those communities, crossing class boundaries to achieve a more realizable and relevant transnational praxis. (Carty and Das Gupta, 2009, p. 108)

This book began with the story of Bina; thus, it is appropriate to end with her as well. In the summer of 2005, I attended Bina's graduation from high school in Cincinnati. Surrounded by her friends and adopted families—which included the Bengali family who supported her throughout her journey in the United States, her American host family, the doctors at Shriner's Hospital and Children's Hospital, Jharna, and her coworkers and fellow graduates—Bina, in her typical vibrant fashion, thanked everyone for standing by her in all her years in the United States. Many tears were shed at this gathering as guests at the party gave speeches remembering various parts of Bina's journey in the United States. Though it was a different kind of a party than the one five years prior at the Yale Club, nonetheless the admiration and respect everyone had for this young woman was palpable. It was a honor once again to witness one of Bina's achievements, and I have no doubt there will be many more. And so the story continues.

In another location, in Dhaka, Nasreen Huq, lead activist of the anti-acid campaign, initiated Ponchom Shur (The Fifth Note), a singing group of acid-violence survivor women. Led by their instructor, vocalist Ms. Alpona, these young women would meet every Saturday afternoon in Huq's apartment in Dhanmondi Residential Area. With the cool breeze wafting into the living room through the open verandah overlooking the Dhanmondi Lake, and over mugs of tea, and plates of *mishti* (sweets) and *shingara* (flour pastry stuffed with potatoes and peas), I spent many afternoons filled with laughter, stories, and songs with this group in the early to mid-2000s. The support and healing power these women found in one another can be hardly described in words. Even though Huq no longer worked with Naripokkho, or with ASF, and was then country director of Action Aid—a British donor agency—she remained in solidarity with the acid campaign through her inspiring relationship to this group.

The last time I met Huq before her tragic and untimely death in April 2006, was in the summer of 2005 in her home.[1] She and I had been communicating over e-mail about drafts of my writings on the anti-acid campaign. It was at this meeting that she expressed both appreciation and indignation over some aspects of the analysis, namely the depiction of the internal disagreements in Naripokkho with regard to Bina's story. She thought I was being unfair to the organization and as a "researcher based in the North" could not possibly understand their position. I was once again reminded of my shifting "insider/outsider" relationship to the campaign over its multiyear and multisited trajectories. Having integrated Huq's comments into previous drafts, as I write the conclusion to this book, I must allude, once again, to the discussion on the politics of transnational praxis detailed in the Introduction to this book. That is, even as I see this project as an intellectual and political collaboration with Naripokkho activists, as the privileged feminist researcher located in the Northern academy, I am nevertheless far removed from the day-to-day feminist mobilizing done by the organization's members. The circulation and reception of this book, therefore, will have differential meanings and impacts for people with different relationships to this project.

This point is cogently made by Piya Chatterjee (2009) as she writes about the incongruences of her own locations in the U.S. academy, and among women organizers at a tea plantation in North Bengal:

Epistemological divides are geopolitical divides, and some bridges between "activisms" and "scholarship" span the incommensurable. It is through these impossibilities, then, that I counterintuitively attempt to build an "imagined bridge." In so doing, I make no claims about chasms crossed: incommensurabilities made commensurable; the strange, familiar. Rather, through careful ethnographic reflexivities on my own positionalities and knowledge claims, and through the careful tracking of difference and power, I seek to build the possibilities of both understanding and solidarity. These require, in the deepest ways, leaps of faith, hope, and tenacious optimism. (p. 132)

In this book, I posit that transnational and intranational politics are valuable to help us understand the multiple and competing narratives framing the anti–acid violence campaign in Bangladesh. By specifically emphasizing the range of actors involved, including international, national, and local organizations, I suggest that it is important to begin to examine the ways in which homogenizing discourses of women's movements do not accurately analyze relationships among women, and that even feminist collaborations can take on decidedly hierarchical characteristics. I look at the growth of a campaign launched by a small number of women within a women's advocacy group in Dhaka, Bangladesh, who forged key alliances with national and international actors. By doing so, I examine how the progression of the campaign simultaneously led to the reshaping of the group's own feminist beliefs and practices that were the cornerstone of its collaborations with key institutions such as the state, international aid agencies, and the media. Moreover, I have shown that the dynamics of local activist networks are also related to the class politics of their leaders' conflicting interests, in seeking state and international support, in meeting the needs of their clients, and also in enforcing their middle-class development agendas on working-class women (Poster and Salime, 2002). Thus, it is the relationship of all these factors that creates tensions for participants of local networks.

Like many women's NGOs around the world, Naripokkho is headed primarily by western-educated, professional, urban elite organizers. They employ and manage a staff of mostly middle-class, highly educated local women who have a different socio-economic background from the leaders. Both of these groups, in turn, are of higher social and economic status than the clients or women who avail the services of such organizations. These complex class differences generate tensions between leaders, members, staff, and "clients" as has been shown in studies of women's NGOs around the world (Ford-Smith, 1997). These tensions are a result of issues such as class, geographic location, education, language, and modes and levels of movement engagement. Fragmentation within a campaign on the basis of social class interests and the concomitant distrust among and between communities of women further complicate intragroup dynamics.

The chapters in this book interweave multiple narratives of gender violence organizing aimed to tell a complex story of transnational feminist praxis. As I was completing this project, I was happy to find that other scholars are also looking closely at the contradictions of NGO feminism, in other locations. For example, in her book, *Playing with Fire*, Richa Nagar (2006) has beautifully demonstrated the exigencies of donor-driven colonialist discourses of empowerment furthered through the NGOization of women's movement in Uttar Pradesh, India. Her analysis demonstrates how middle-class urban-based women's networks are complicit in the continuing margin-alization and silencing of poorer women living in rural communities in third world countries. This book builds on that genre of work and additionally shows the exigencies of the dynamic of local and transnational organizing. The multiple levels of power operating in diverse contexts sometimes create opportunities and at other times circumscribe women's organizing within nor-mative conventions. Marnia Lazreg calls this eclipsing of grassroots women's organizing within the discourse of global feminism a "containment through inclusion" that hinges on searching and revealing more and more aspects of third world women's lives to fit into the logic of global feminism (Lazreg, 2002, pp. 130–33). As a result, divisions among feminists on different sides of the global divide become difficult to discern.

Since global feminism gained momentum and prominence in the 1980s and 1990s, it has been a key player in global human rights advocacy operating through international aid organizations and political and legal mechanisms of the United Nations. However, the workings of global feminism through these channels obscures the geopolitics of empire (Chatterjee, 2009, p. 134). U.N. conferences on women have been criticized for their reliance on a western liberal framework whereby the "local," "regional," or both contradicts the "universal," and "woman" is in conflict with the "human" (Rajan, 2004, p. 119). I would further suggest that the "Other" woman is in conflict with the "woman" of the western liberal framework, making "Other" women twice removed from an international human rights regime. For instance, even though global feminist platforms enabled the mobilization of gender violence organiz-ing in Bangladesh, the anti-acid campaign being one such example, they did not allow for a complex intersectional understanding of gender. This tension unfolded when Bina Akhter was transformed from the good victim/survivor/activist to a self-serving agent. Her particular agency was incommensurate with conventional understandings of survivors of human rights abuse. When Healing the Children withdrew support for Bina and Jharna's treatment, not only did the eighteen young women suffer the gravest consequence, but also Naripokkho's credibility as a Southern feminist organization was tarnished. This organization also revealed its own privileged location within the local context by chosing to pull away from active involvement in the campaign.

Scholars like Inderpal Grewal (1998) have critiqued the universalizing rhetoric of human rights and pointed to the "silences that are embedded within it." She posits three predominant conceptualizations that have come to explain human rights violation: First, human rights literature relies on a framework of a modernized first world that should go in and rescue, civilize, and liberate those facing yet another crisis in the third world, always imagined as a "region of aberrant violence." Second, human rights discourse presumes women only as individual, autonomous beings, rather than as members of families or other group identities, who in turn can be extricated/rescued from those collectivities. Third, this paradigm presumes that women can be identified as a singular unit. In other words, the collective rights of women in this paradigm, "assumes women live their lives solely as women, a universalizing move that ignores the fact that women are not all gendered in the same ways" (Grewal, 1998, pp. 505–507). Such colonial frameworks are replicated within women's groups in the global South where even one espousing a woman-centered strategy like Naripokkho was ultimately uncomfortable with Bina's "disobedience" to those who had "helped" her. Bina, on the other hand, was not only an activist "empowered" through the feminist spaces of Naripokkho but also a member of her family and community, whose interests seemed to be at odds with the feminism of Naripokkho. Women in Bina's family in particular faced class and security issues on a daily basis that were markedly different from those of the members of the feminist community. Moreover, the feminism of Bina and the alternative ways she crafted her own narrative of victimization, empowerment, and choice could not be given voice within the larger script of global feminism. Rather, this script made her a pariah of the movement, focusing much of the attention on individual action and hardly any on structural inequalities within feminist transnational politics.

I hope that this study reveals how activists in Bangladesh have been successful in using the platform of global feminism and naming certain types of violence against women as human rights abuses and using such as an avenue to garner resources from international aid agencies. They have also used international law (UN CEDAW) to put pressure on the government to enact policy changes on the ground. Most of these abuses are what Rajeswari Sunder Rajan (2004) has called the *spectacular* kind, like acid throwing, rather than more "mundane" forms of violence, such as domestic violence, poverty, or exploitative labor conditions. Moreover, the "interventions" funded and formulated have been almost entirely in the policy, legal, and medical arenas and minimally in the social/economic arenas. This is an example of the danger of uniform norms which disregard complexities of situations on the ground and prioritize certain issues over others.

Meghna Guhathakurta (2004) has argued that violence against women should be considered essentially related to the more general problems of women's oppression. Instead of conceptually isolating the two phenomena, she encourages policy makers to consider oppression as the wider term, and gendered violence to indicate the actual exercising of that oppression. I would like to point to three related consequences of such globalization of feminism that looks at gendered violence as an "issue," separate from women's oppression:

1. *Development aid serving as human rights intervention gains direct access to the lives of vulnerable women.* This is particularly the case in the discourse and practice of neoliberal development, which provide victims of violence with individual opportunities of "uplift" just as they capitalize on women's so-called docility and obedience, which make them safer and malleable clients. Women survivors of violence are integrated into the ever-expanding tentacles of global capitalist development, but little is done to disrupt wider economic and political inequalities or to transform unequal social structures of gender, imperialism, or class. We have seen in the processes of founding and designing ASF and its programs how victims of acid violence were channeled into welfarist rehabilitation projects. Additionally, Bina Akhter's story of "arrival" to America follows the same logic.

2. *Women's NGOs in developing countries do important work at the community level but are made accountable to their funders, rather than members.* Structurally, NGOs are positioned such that they transmit powerful values of western-dependent development and global feminism. As part of civil society, they

have enforced the shift from viewing women as beneficiaries to participants in development. Yet the subject status that is seemingly bestowed on these "Other" woman participants, however, is vitiated by the assumption of a self constituted by the conceptual schemes and structure of global feminism. This is what Marnia Lazreg (2002) calls "the cul-de-sac" of feminist theorizing, where other women are intelligible primarily through the script of global feminism, "a confessional mode to give marginalized women a voice, a romantic feminist act of creationism" (pp. 136–41). Stories such as the heroic victim-survivor-activist narrative used by both Naripokho and global feminist media transform women's lives into discourse, conceptualize their speech as a sign of "empowerment," and are often interchangeable across geographic location. These stories—abundantly available on websites of NGOs, including ASF—come to be seen as tangible "proof" of women's "empowerment." which Northern-based funders demand by way of producing "measurable" outcomes of development projects.

3. *Participating in transnationalized policy advocacy entailed by global feminist interventions requires connecting with diverse actors at the local, national, and transnational levels and framing feminist issues in ways that are acceptable to them.* Mallika Dutt (1998) characterizes policy advocacy as a powerful yet limited form of feminist activism because its impact is minimal at the level of cultural change. While gender has become currency in the global feminist arena, issues of inclusion and representation are highly contestable. Politics of global feminism complicate the ability of "grassroots/local" advocates to influence the scope of "intervention," which is determined by the more powerful "savior" entity.

Another related point is raised by Lazreg (2002), who sees the professionalization of gender and development—and I extend that argument to global feminism—as an alliance of academic and professional women working for INGOs doing development/human rights work in third world countries, facilitated by the U.N. Decade for Women and the types of global or U.N. feminism enabled by it. These two groups (academics and NGO workers), she says, are mutually sustained by one another in the growing field of gender consultancy, training, and advocacy. Lazreg argues that, "the discourse of gender training may have resulted in empowering individual trainers, possibly at the expense of the women they intend to help" (p. 132). The acquisition of specialized knowledge obtained through various undergraduate and graduate degrees in western institutions of higher education becomes the only measure of competency for these policy advocates and gender trainers, who are the gatekeepers of development and feminism in the name of "women's interests." This point is made here less as a critique of individual feminists who are in leadership positions of women's NGOs and who do invaluable work in creating avenues to support women in need, but more to draw attention to the dependent links of the structure of transnationalism, whereby accountability only travels upward. Clearly, the loss of support for the acid violence victims as a consequence of Bina and Jharna's "defection" points to this vertical traffic of accountability.

The limits of such organizational structures on feminist practice need to be analyzed. Women's NGOs are perpetuating the patron-clientelist relationships with their poor women constituencies, furthering NGO-driven neoliberal agendas, yet disrupting the patriarchal state, as well as power structures of the international development apparatus and local elite. Without minimizing the tremendously important work of feminists, we nevertheless need to be critical of the structures within which they operate with dependent links to governments, donors, and other international organizations.

As Lamia Karim (2004) said, referring to the Bangladeshi context, such institutional structures enable feminist alliances and transnational networks yet impede autonomous feminist practices and movements. Citing the case of Naripokkho, one of its senior members, Firdous Azim (2001), states, "We have constantly been relegated to the margins, but as a marginal voice, we were strong and were successful in making ourselves heard" on multiple fronts including local, national, and transnational contexts (p. 391). She continues, "We also have to guard our autonomy as a women's group very strongly, because there is always an effort to see us as part of some other political alliance or movement. Forming alliances or joining them, while jealously guarding the autonomy of our standpoints, is a real challenge" (Azim, F., 2001, p. 391). This brings home the point that the myriad hierarchies in transnational organizing and the complicated relationships women as activists have with their differentially located "partners" make "feminist autonomy" perhaps a contradiction in terms.

One cannot be overly optimistic about the victories of the women's movement, because its hierarchical dynamics negatively impact marginalized people disproportionately. It should be noted that although NGOs may not always be agents of radical change, they are to some extent weakening the power of the established rural patriarchy through the integration of women into their programs. NGOs link rural women to globalization (as consumers and producers in the capitalist market), and they rupture some local-level power systems that exercise social and economic control over women. Certainly, NGOs serving the poor are also constantly innovating in difficult circumstances with limited resources. Yet, in the final analysis, development NGOs and donor organizations have barely engaged in anticolonial and anticlassist interrogations and continue to operate with the assumption that development and empowerment are about integrating poor women into the global economy, thereby reducing emphasis on issues of dignity and social justice.

Of course, Bangladesh's diverse NGO sector, feminist ones included, should not be understood as completely dependent on development aid or bound by imposed policy agendas. While retaining their externally determined resource bases (although several larger NGOs are now generating more than half of their own income through their own economic activities), some NGOs have been gaining more room to maneuver in recent years. For example, feminist NGOs are working at the grassroots level setting up *shalish* (the village adjudication bodies) parallel to the ones run by rural elite men. Nonetheless, the patron-client relationship between development professionals and workers, and grassroots activists and NGO members continues to limit the scope for collective social and structural transformation.

Finally, I would like to address the question of a rigorous feminist solidarity. Critiques such as the one offered in this book should assist in shifting the discourse of global feminism to a more democratic and accountable one. First, what I have been calling "global feminism" must move beyond narrowly conceptualized agendas based on sexual rights and gender equality, to call for meaningful change in development policy that would address the structural oppression within which violence against women has to be conceptualized. This means renewing feminist understanding of gendered violence as a manifestation of women's oppression, and applying an intersectional lens to understand the different ways diverse women experience and respond to oppression. Second, we must move beyond the rescue narratives of "savior" and "victim," that pit third world states, cultures, and men as the sole "oppressors," and instead ask questions about global inequalities, and power relations. Third, we must continue to exercise persistent and rigorous self-critique and reflection to strive for more ethical relations and alliances across various borders.

I agree with Anne Marie Goetz (2001), who has pointed to the need for women's solidarity networks in the development arena. These networks would enable women to build a support systems for one another, connect with other women's associations, and imagine more democratic development practices. Some NGOs have already taken steps toward this, such as BRAC, which in the early 1990s set up a Women's Advisory Committee (WAC) to learn about female staff members' needs and concerns on the job (Goetz, 2001). This committee, however, operated in a top-down system where the Dhaka-based women staff controlled the agenda and reported to upper management while not informing the grassroots staff of meeting outcomes. Many women working in locations outside of Dhaka complained that instead of engaging in an organizational critique, WAC members found these grassroots' groups concerns unimportant, and they were asked to change their situations on their own. Further, male staff vehemently opposed the idea of women's networks on the grounds, arguing that it would be a "time-wasting perk" that would detract women from work and encourage personal rather than professional concerns. Thus, women workers and members of NGOs are faced with "double patriarchy" of the home and the NGO. The level of objection voiced by men leads Goetz to conclude that there are anxieties about such solidarity networks for women because they actually could alleviate women's isolation and lack of power (pp. 269–70).

The purpose of networks such as the WAC should be to allow for more horizontal linkages and accountability between mixed groups of women, not to replicate the vertical power relationships seen in the chain of dependency comprising development initiatives. In the quotation that I used to introduce this conclusion, Carty and Das Gupta (2009) talk about the need for more lateral linkages for feminists based in the North. The same is required of feminists in the global South, and for feminists anywhere for that matter, as they negotiate various hierarchies in their variegated locales. As Carty and Das Gupta note further, "In order not to reproduce the severe limits of white, middle-class versions of U.S. feminism in transnational feminism that has self-consciously chosen another path, we must tackle the question of class—and nationality-based privilege not through crippling guilt but through addressing those structures of inequality that have differential yet connected impacts on those with whom we yearn to build solidarity, whether they are located in the North or the South" (2009, p. 108).

A truly transnational feminism would reclaim the domains of development and human rights through a focus on cross-border, laterally negotiated struggles with global implications. In other words, it must be accountable to women's struggles of survival and fulfillment in their incommensurable manifestations, as opposed to fitting them into the "always already" normative registers of patriarchy or imperialism. The documentation and juxtaposition of contesting narratives of gender violence in this study urge a more complex understanding of doing feminist work and its often unintended consequences and implications. I hope this critique inspires and strengthens our commitment to feminist struggles and solidarity.

Notes

Prologue

1. Unless specifically requested by an interlocutor, I have not used pseudonyms for the various movement participants and organizations quoted and represented in this book. The reason for this decision in part is related to the fact that the anti–acid violence campaign has been a highly publicized and high-profile one in Bangladesh and beyond. Most of these participating actors and organizations have been featured many times in various media over the years, including scholarly and popular publications, and are thus easily identifiable through these reports. During the course of my research, however, some participants specifically asked that their names be used in the book. When, however, specific individuals asked that their names be changed, their requests have been honored and noted.

2. Throughout this book I have deliberately not capitalized the words *western*, *first world*, and *third world*. I do this so as not to perpetuate the hegemonic meanings associated with these terms. However, because the terms global *North* and *South*, arguably, do not reflect the same analytical and political history, I have chosen to capitalize them.

3. Emma Brooker's article about acid violence appeared in *Marie Claire* magazine in 1998. See: Brooker, Emma (1998), "Scarred by Hate," *Marie Claire* magazine.

4. I should note here, the first time I covered Naripokkho's work with acid survivors as a journalist in 1996, the activists did not want names of individuals or the organization to be published because they did not feel secure enough. The next time I wrote about their work seven months later in 1997, the survivors and Naripokkho members explicitly wanted to be named. The reason was the tremendous mobilizing that had occurred in those months, and the strength these women had garnered from one another. The solidarity among the survivors and Naripokkho activists encouraged these young women to speak out in public. This was an extraordinary act of courage and vision as acid attacks against women and girls are often intended to end their public lives. Therefore visibilization of the survivors was a strategic part of the anti–acid violence campaign.

5. In this book terms such as *local, national,* and *global* are used in the manner in which Saskia Sassen (2000) has explained. These are meant to be understood as

191

discrete, but not mutually exclusive, spatialities for analytic purposes although they exist in dynamic, overlapping, and interactive relationships (p. 215). See Sassen, S. (2000), "Spatialities and Temporalities of the Global: Elements for a Theorization," *Public Culture*, 12(1), 215–32.

Introduction

1. For a detailed discussion of the NGOization of women's social movements, please see Alvarez, S, 1999. "Advocating Feminism: The Latin American Feminist NGO 'Boom,'" *International Feminist Journal of Politics*, 1(2), 181–209. Please also see, Alvarez, S., 2009, "Beyond NGO-ization?: Reflections from Latin America," *Development* 52(2), 175–84.

2. For more information about the unequal relationships between NGOs and local clients in Bangladesh see my previous article: Chowdhury, E. (2007), "Negotiating State and NGO Politics in Bangladesh: Women Mobilize Against Acid Violence," *Violence Against Women: An International and Interdisciplinary Journal*, 13(3), 857–73; and Shehabuddin, Elora (1999), "Contesting the Illicit: Gender and the Politics of Fatwas in Bangladesh," *Signs: Journal of Women in Culture and Society*, 24(4), 1011–44.

Chapter One

1. For the most part, I have used the terms *gender violence* and *gendered violence* interchangeably in this book. In this instance, I purposely use the term *gendered violence* to emphasize that acid attacks against women are both gendered and violent. That is, the violence has very specific functions: to destroy a woman's appearance, to undermine her societal value, to restrict her mobility, to punish her for daring to defy or challenge male authority. It serves to oppress women. While there are male victims of acid attacks, and increasingly so, the intent and consequences of the violence differ by gender.

2. I am indebted to Cynthia Enloe for this conceptualization. She suggests that rather than thinking of women's labor as always already cheap, we should pay attention to the gendered processes that actively devalue women, cheapening their work.

3. Feminist scholar Deniz Kandiyoti (1988) defines patriarchal bargains as the strategies women employ to deal with patriarchy, which may vary aross time and culture. The terms of the bargaining influence the particular ways in which women are able to resist oppression, actively or passively. Importantly, patriarchal bargains offer up possibilities of struggle, renegotiations, and transformations in relations between genders. This is an important concept, which aids in imagining patriarchy not as a monolithic structure of total domination, and illuminates ways in which women are

able to exert agency within oppressive structures. For details see, Kandiyoti, Deniz (1988), "Bargaining with Patriarchy," *Gender & Society*, 2, 274–90.

4. For a more detailed description of these implications, see Kabeer, Naila, (2000). *The Power to Choose: Bangladeshi Women and Labor Market Decisions in London and Dhaka*, London: Verso; Rozario, Santi (1998), "Disjunctions and Continuities: Dowry and the Position of Single Women in Bangladesh, in C. Risseeuw & K. Ganesh (Eds.), *Negotiation and Social Space: A Gendered Analysis of Changing Kin and Security Networks in South Asia and Sub-Saharan Africa* (pp. 259–75), London: Sage Publications; and Feldman, S. (1998), "(Re)presenting Islam: Manipulating Gender, Shifting State Practices, and Class Frustrations in Bangladesh," in A. Basu & P. Jeffery (Eds.), *Appropriating Gender: Women's Activism and Politicized Religion in South Asia* (pp. 33–52), New York: Routledge.

5. In Islamic legal context *fatwa* means clarification of an ambiguous point or opinion of a jurist. In recent decades impoverished women in Bangladesh have been the targets of *fatwas*—edicts punishing women for transgressing patriarchal codes of behavior—by elite men of their communities. In addition, NGO offices and schools offering development and literacy programs for rural women have been targets. Cases include stoning and whipping of women, and setting fire to NGO offices and schools. See Shehabuddin, Elora (1999), "Contesting the Illicit: Gender and the Politics of Fatwas in Bangladesh," *Signs: Journal of Women in Culture and Society*, 24(4), 1011–44.

6. Uma Narayan (1997) has demonstrated "dowry murder" phenomenon in India as an "expedient" and not "exotic" form of violence against women, wherein the fire that kills the victim also effectively destroys all evidence. Moreover, most middle-class households have handy kerosene stoves and extra cans of fuel. See Narayan, U. (1997), *Dislocating Cultures: Identities, Traditions, and Third World Feminism*, New York: Routledge.

7. It was during these years that I studied the campaign activities, first as a journalist, second as a consultant with UNICEF-Bangladesh, and third as an independent researcher.

8. The medicalization of the anti–acid violence campaign by international actors is addressed in more detail later in the chapter.

9. Although a Burns Center at GK did not eventually materialize, following Naripokkho's workshop on acid violence the government of Bangladesh undertook a project to build a fifty-bed Burns Center on the premises of the state-sponsored Dhaka Medical College Hospital.

10. I have deliberately chosen not to name this minister, as his comments were in the context of a private workshop rather than a public or political forum.

11. The term *mastaan* has multiple meanings. Here it refers to local crime lords often protected by politicians.

12. See bibliography for full references.

13. The 1992 United Nations Conference on Environment and Development (UNCED, also known as the Rio Earth Summit); the 1993 Vienna World Conference on Human Rights; the 1994 International Conference on Population and Development in Cairo; the 1995 World Social Summit in Copenhagen; the Fourth World Conference on Women in Beijing; and the 1996 Conference on Human Settlement (Habitat II) in Istanbul.

14. See www.emdr.com for a description of EMDR, the history of EMDR, populations treated with EMDR, and a list of references.

15. I have withheld the names of the UNICEF staff at their requests.

16. The idea of "third world horror" is explained further in chapter 3.

Chapter Two

1. In Bangladesh, acid attacks resulting in severe injuries are punishable by death.

2. Bangladesh is divided into six administrative divisions, which are further categorized into sixty-four districts. Each district consist of several subdistricts or *thana* (police stations) made up of multiple unions and then villages.

3. The topic of competition between women's NGOs over resources is discussed further in chapter 5.

4. A *shalish* is a system of informal justice in Bangladesh. It is not legally binding, but a traditional system that plays an important role, particularly in rural Bangladesh, in providing justice to the poor. It is usually run by the village elite, who can misuse their power in administering justice. In recent decades, various NGOs have been working to organize people in the villages to make the *shalish* process more equitable for all.

Chapter Three

1. Ms. Khan is an alias, the interviewee requested that her name not be used in this book.

Chapter Four

1. The 2006 World Development Indicators suggest that 29 percent of households in Bangladesh own a television set.

2. In Bengali, *ukeel* means lawyer, and *apa* means older sister. Addressing the character by her profession implies respect as well as her higher social status than the community who enlists her help.

Chapter Five

1. A term widely used to describe South Asians as a racialized community in the west.

2. In the context of Bangladesh, secular at the nation's founding and as defined by "father of the nation," Sheikh Mujibur Rahman implied coexistence and tolerance of plural religious beliefs and practices as opposed to a strict separation of religion from state. Subsequent regimes, however, as a result of complex global and regional social, economic, and political forces dropped secularism from the Constitution and declared Islam as the state religion. Increasingly, however, and particularly in relation to current global politics, it is important to keep in mind for any discussion on Islam versus secularism the ways in which the latter has been deployed in the service of imperialism by idealizing a linear narrative of progress and development in opposition to the term *religious/Islamic*. Gil Anidjar quotes Talal Asad, "the 'religious' and the 'secular' are not essentially fixed categories," but gain in prominence and hegemony by the culture—more specifically, "Western Christendom" (Gil Anidjar, "On Secularism," pp. 57–58). Further, Ashis Nandy has argued that the birth of secularism as an ideology in modernity makes it deeply intolerant because modernity undermines faith in favor of secular values of rationality and development, which is achieved by abandoning or devaluing "traditional" belief systems. A belief in secular development, constructed as the opposite of traditional belief systems, overlooks the accommodating ways faith systems coexisted historically.

3. The term *Bengali* has an ethno-linguistic or cultural connotation, whereas *Bangladeshi* has a more nationalistic connotation. While Bengali nationalism emphasizes a more plural culture, recognizing the syncretic Hindu and Muslim traditions of the region, it too can assume hegemonic characteristics.

4. The leadership of women-focused NGOs is provided by women while most of those that are not women-focused are led by men with women serving at mid- and lower levels.

5. The state of Bangladesh has ratified CEDAW with reservations to Article 2, which has to do with the implementation of *Sharia* law in personal/family matters.

6. In this book, I use the term *Islamist/Islamism* to refer to the political actors and organizations who are acting to establish an Islamic state in Bangladesh based on their interpretation(s) of *Shari'a* (Islamic law). For a discussion of the AL, BNP, and Islamist political party, Jamaat-e-Islami positions regarding women as reflected in their election manifestos (2008), please see, Nazneen, S. et al., 2010, "National Discourses on Women's Empowerment in Bangladesh: Enabling or Constraining Women's Choices?" *Development*, 53(2), 239–46.

7. It should be noted that the report was published before the outcome of the latest election in 2008.

8. The ethnic nationalities of the CHT are collectively known as Jumma people.

9. 1952, 1969, 1971, and 1990 are all significant dates in the struggle for autonomy and democracy in pre- and postindependent Bangladesh. Known as the Language Martyrs' Day, on 21 February 1952, then–East Pakistanis revolted against West Pakistan's declaration that Urdu would be the official language of both wings of Pakistan. This was a controversial declaration, as Bengali was the predominant language of East Pakistan. In 1969, mass uprising broke out in East Pakistan in protest of West Pakistan's martial law regime and the killing of students. In 1971, Bangladesh became an independent nation after a nine-month-long Liberation War fought in East Pakistan. In 1990, the democratic parties in Bangladesh cooperated to end fifteen years of military rule. A democratic government came into power through the election process.

Conclusion

1. Huq was killed in a tragic accident in April 24, 2006, at age 48. The controversy over the circumstances of her death can be found at: http://www.guardian.co.uk/world/2006/sep/03/bangladesh. (Doward, J. and M. Haider, "The Mystery Death, a Town in Uproar, and a $1bn U.K. Mines Deal," the *Guardian;* retrieved May 24, 2010 from http://www.guardian.co.uk/world/2006/sep/03/bangladesh.)

For more information on her activist work against opencast mining in Bangladesh, and politics of international development, see Chowdhury, E. (2009), "Challenges for the Women's Movement in Bangladesh: Engaging Religion, State, and NGO Politics," in F. Khan, A. Ahmad, and M. Quddus (Eds.), *Recreating the Commons? NGOs in Bangladesh* (pp. 207–246), Dhaka: University Press Limited. *Ponchom Shur* continues to meet in Huq's apartment, and her mother's house, on alternate Saturdays.

Bibliography

ABC News, 20/20 wins amnesty international media award: Connie Chung's report on women in Bangladesh honored. ABC News. Retrieved September 7, 2002 from http://abcnews.go.com/onair/2020/2020_000330_amnestyaward_feature.html.

Abu-Lughod, L. (2002). Do Muslim women really need saving? *American Anthropologist*, 102(3), 783–90.

Abu-Lughod, L. (2005). On- and off-camera in Egyptian soap operas: Women, television, and the public sphere. In F. Nouraie-Simone (Ed.), *On Shifting Ground: Muslim Women in the Global Era* (pp. 17–34). The Feminist Press, New York.

Acid Survivors Foundation. Introduction. Retrieved September 10, 2002 from http://www.acidsurvivors.org/html/intro.htm.

Acid Survivor's Foundation (2003). *Hope for acid victim Promila Shabdakor*, a case study. Dhaka: Rehabilitation Unit, Acid Survivor's Foundation.

Ain O Salish Kendro (2001). Annual report. Retrieved December 21, 2004 from http://www.askbd.org/web/?page_id=447.

Ain O Salish Kendro (2003). Annual report. Retrieved December 21, 2004 from http://www.askbd.org/web/?page_id=447.

Akhtar, N. (1997). Personal communication. April 27.

Akhter, B. (1997). Personal communication. February 21.

Akhter, B. (1997). Personal communication. April 27.

Akhter, B. (1998). Personal communication. July 10.

Akhter, B. (2004). Personal communication. December 27–28.

Akhter, H., and S. Nahar. (2003). *A study on acid violence in Mymensingh*. Dhaka: Women for Women Report.

Alcoff, L. and Gray, L. (1993). Survivor discourse: Transgression or recuperation? *Signs*, 18(2): 260–90.

Alexander, J. (2005). *Pedagogies of crossing: Meditations on feminism, sexual politics, memory, and the sacred*. Durham, NC: Duke University Press.

Alexander, J., and Mohanty, C. (1997). Introduction. In J. Alexander and C. Mohanty (Eds.), *Feminist genealogies, colonial legacies, democratic futures* (pp. xiii–xlii). New York: Routledge.

All they need is social commitment to peaceful life (July 23, 1999). *Daily Star*.

Alvares, C. (1997). Science. In Sachs W. (Ed.), *The development dictionary* (pp. 219–232). London: Zed Books.

Alvarez, S. (1999). Advocating feminism: The Latin American feminist NGO "boom." *International Feminist Journal of Politics*, 1(2), 181–209.

Alvarez, S. (Autumn 2000). Translating the global: Effects of transnational organizing on local feminist discourses and practices in Latin America. *Meridians*, 1(1), 29–67.

Alvarez, S. (2009). Beyond NGO-ization?: Reflections from Latin America. *Development*, 52(2), 175–184.

Amin, S. N. (1994). The New Woman in literature and the novels of Nojibur Rahman and Rokeya Sakhawat Hossein. In F. Azim and N. Zaman (Eds.), *Infinite variety: Women in society and literature* (pp. 119–41). Dhaka: University Press Limited.

Amir, T. (n.d.). *Violence against women and children as tools of systematic political persecution*. Dhaka: Unpublished conference paper.

Anidjar, G. (2006). Secularism. *Critical Inquiry*, 33(1), 52–77.

Anonymous a (1998). Personal communication. June 25.

Anonymous b (1998). Personal communication. June 25.

Anonymous c (1998). Personal communication. June 25.

Anonymous d (1998). Personal communication. June 25.

Anonymous e (1998). E-mail communication. August 6.

Anonymous f (1998). E-mail communication. August 6.

Anonymous g (1998). E-mail communication. June 23.

Anonymous h (1998). E-mail communication. July 23.

ASF Staff (2003). Personal communication. April 6.

Azim, F. (2001). Formulating an agenda for the women's movement: A review of Naripokkho, *Inter-Asia Cultural Studies*, 2(3), 389–394.

Azim, S. (1997). Personal communication. April 27.

Azim, S. (1998). Personal communication. June 15.

Azim, S. (2001). *Naripokkho's pilot study on violence against women in Bangladesh*. Dhaka: Naripokkho.

Barry, K. (1990). The new historical syntheses: Women's biography. *Journal of Women's History*, 1, 75–105.

Basu, A. (2000). Globalization of the local/localization of the global: Mapping transnational women's movements. *Meridians*, 1(1), 68–84.

BBC News. (1999, July 22). *Joyous homecoming for acid attack victims* (Television broadcast).

Behar, R. (1993). *Translated woman: Crossing the border with Esperanza's story*. Boston: Beacon Press.

Bergeron, S. (2006). *Fragments of development: Nation, gender, and the space of modernity*. Ann Arbor: University of Michigan Press.

Bhavnani, K., Foran, J., and Kurian, P. (Eds.). (2003). *Feminist futures: Re-imagining women, culture and development*. London: Zed Books.

Bloom, L. R. (1995). *Under the sign of hope: Feminist methodology and narrative interpretation*. New York: State University of New York Press.

Bonfield, T. (Sunday August 15, 1999). Women burned in acid attacks to get care here. *Cincinnati Enquirer*.

Bose, S., and Jalal, A. (1998). *Modern South Asia: History, culture, political economy*. London: Routledge.

Brooker, E. (1998). Scarred by hate. *Marie Claire*.

Carty, L., and Das Gupta, M. (2009). Solidarity work in transnational feminism: The question of class and location. In J. Sudbury and M. Ozakawa-Rey (Eds.), *Activist scholarship: Antiracism, feminism, and social change* (pp. 95–110). Boulder: Paradigm Publishers.

Chang, D. Y. (June 21, 1999). One woman's lesson on true beauty. *Honolulu Star-Bulletin*.

Chatterjee, P. (1989). Nationalist resolution of the woman's question. In K. Sangari and S. Vaid (Eds.), *Recasting Women* (pp. 233–53). New Delhi: Kali for Women.

Chatterjee, P. (2009). Transforming pedagogies: Imagining internationalist/feminist/antiracist literacies. In J. Sudbury and M. Ozakawa-Rey (Eds.), *Activist scholarship: Antiracism, feminism, and social change* (pp. 131–148). Boulder, CO: Paradigm Publishers.

Chowdhury, B. (1997). *Burning passions: A study of acid violence in Bangladesh*. Dhaka: Naripokkho.

Chowdhury, B. (2003). Personal communication. March 7.

Chowdhury, B. (2003). Personal communication. March 9.

Chowdhury, E. (2005). Feminist negotiations: Contesting narratives of the campaign against acid violence in Bangladesh. *Meridians: Feminism, Race, Transnationalism*, 6(1), 162–93.

Chowdhury, E. (2007). Negotiating state and NGO politics in Bangladesh: Women mobilize against acid violence. *Violence Against Women: An International and Interdisciplinary Journal*, 13(3), 857–73.

Chowdhury, E. (2009). Challenges for the women's movement in Bangladesh: Engaging religion, state, and NGO politics. In F. Khan, A. Ahmad and M. Quddus (Eds.), *Recreating the commons? NGOs in Bangladesh* (pp. 207–46). Dhaka: University Press Limited.

Chowdhury, N. (2001). The politics of implementing women's rights in Bangladesh. In J. H. Bayes and N. Tohidi (Eds.), *Globalization, gender, and religion: The politics of women's rights in Catholic and Muslim contexts* (pp. 203–30). NY: Palgrave.

Conte, A. (1999). Shriners to treat acid-attack victims. *Cincinnati Post*. Retrieved August 3, 2005 from http://www.cincypost.com/news/1999/acid102999.html.

Convenor. (2003). Personal communication. April.

de Lauretis, T. (Ed). (1986). *Feminist studies, critical Studies*. Bloomington: Indiana University Press.

de Lauretis, T. (1987). *Technologies of gender: Essays on theory, film, and fiction*. Bloomington: Indiana University Press.

Del Franco, N. (1999). Changing gender relations and new forms of violence: Acid throwing against women in Bangladesh and the NGO response. *A master's Thesis*. IDS, University of Sussex.

Do, M. and Kincaid, L. D. (2006). Impact of an entertainment-education television drama on health knowledge and behavior in Bangladesh: An application of propensity score matching. *The Journal of Health Communication* 11(3), 301–25.

Dutt, M. (1998). Reclaiming human rights culture: Feminism of difference and alliance. In E. Shohat (Ed.), *Talking visions: Multicultural feminism in a transnational age* (pp. 225–46). Cambridge, MA: MIT Press.

Eclipse (1994). (Motion picture.) Dhaka, Bangladesh: Ain O Salish Kendro.

EMDR. Retrieved October 10, 2003 from http://www.emdr.com.

Escobar, A. (1995). *Encountering development: The making and unmaking of the third world*. Princeton, NJ: Princeton University Press.

Falvo, C. (1997). *Violence against women—for UNICEF Health Unit. A report*. Dhaka: UNICEF.

Feldman, S. (2001). Exploring theories of patriarchy: A perspective from contemporary Bangladesh. *Signs: Journal of Women in Culture and Society*, 26(4), 1097–1121.

Ferguson, J. (1994). *The anti-politics machine: "Development," depoliticization, and bureaucratic power in Lesotho*. Minneapolis: University of Minnesota Press.

Ford-Smith, H. (1997). Ring ding in a tight corner: Sistren, collective democracy, and the organization of cultural production. In J. Alexander, and C. Mohanty (Eds.), *Feminist genealogies colonial legacies, democratic futures* (pp. 213–58). New York: Routledge.

Friedman, E. (Autumn 1999). The effects of "transnationalism reversed" in Venezuela: Assessing the impact of UN global conferences on the women's movement. *International Feminist Journal of Politics*, 1, 357–81.

Goetz, A. M. (2001). *Women development workers: Implementing rural credit programmes in Bangladesh*. New Delhi: Sage Publications.

Gregory, S. (2006). Transnational storytelling: Human rights, WITNESS, and video advocacy. *American Anthropologist*, 108(1), 195–204.

Grewal, I. (1998). On the new global feminism and the family of nations: Dilemmas of transnational feminist practice. In Shohat, E. (Ed.), *Talking visions: multicultural feminism in a transnational age* (pp. 501–32), Cambridge, MA: MIT Press.

Guhathakurta, M. (1985). Gender violence in Bangladesh: The role of the state. *Journal of Social Studies*, 30, 77–90.

Guhathakurta, M. (1994). The aid discourse and the politics of gender: A perspective from Bangladesh. *Journal of Social Studies*, 65, 101–114.

Guhathakurta, M. (2004). Women negotiating change: The structure and transformation of gendered violence in Bangladesh. *Cultural Dynamics*, 16(2/3),
193–211.

Gupta, A. (1998). *Postcolonial developments: Agriculture in the making of modern India.*
Durham, NC: Duke University Press.

Halim, S. (2003). Strategies and tools to empower women in Bangladesh. Unpublished
conference paper. Dhaka University, Bangladesh.

Halim, S. (2008a). *Gender needs assessment MDG-3 situational analysis report.* Submitted to the General Economic Division and UNDP, Dhaka, Bangladesh.
June 22.

Halim, S. (2008b). Personal communication. October 6.

Halim, S., and Haq, A. (2004). Globalization, gender and labor market: Some evidence from RMG sector. Faculty working paper, Department of Sociology,
Dhaka University, Bangladesh.

Hesford W. (Winter 2004). Documenting violations: Rhetorical witnessing and the
spectacle of distant suffering. *Biography*, 27(1), 104–44.

Howe, C. (2008). Spectacles of sexuality: Televisionary activism in Nicaragua. *Cultural
Anthropology*, 23(1), 48–84.

Huq, M. (2003). Personal communication. April 14.

Huq, N. (1996). Personal communication. October 10.

Huq, N. (1998). Personal communication. July 10.

Huq, N. (2003). Personal communication. April 5.

Huq, N. (2003). Personal communication. April 11.

Huq, N. (2003). Personal communication. April 12.

Islam, K. (July 2, 2004). Campaigning against crime. *Star Weekend Magazine*, 4(2).
Retrieved from http://www.thedailystar.net/magazine/2004/07/01/endeavour.
htm.

John, M. E. (1996). *Discrepant dislocations: Feminism, theory, and postcolonial histories.*
Berkeley: University of California.

Kabeer, N. (1994). *Reversed realities: Gender hierarchies in development thought.* London: Verso.

Kabeer, N. (2000). *The power to choose: Bangladeshi women and labour market decisions
in London and Dhaka.* London: Verso.

Kabeer, N. (2005). Gender equality and women's empowerment: A critical analysis
of the third Millennium Development Goal. *Gender and Development*, 13
(1), 13–24.

Kandiyoti, D. (1988). Bargaining with patriarchy. *Gender & Society*, 2, 274–90.

Kaplan, E. A. (2004). Global feminisms and the state of feminist film theory. *Signs:
Journal of Women in Culture and Society*, 30(1), 1236–48.

Karim, L. (2004). Democratizing Bangladesh: State, NGOs, and militant Islam.
Cultural Dynamics, 16(2/3), 291–318.

Karim, L. (2008). Demystifying micro-credit: The Grameen Bank, NGOs, and
neoliberalism in Bangladesh. *Cultural Dynamics*, 20(1), 5–29.

Kelly, L. (2005). Inside outsiders: Mainstreaming violence against women into human rights discourse and practice. *International Feminist Journal of Politics*, 7(4), 471–95.

Khan (2003). Personal communication. April 14.

Khan, M. (March 10, 2005). *Ayna*: Reflecting a woman's woes. *New Age*. Retrieved January 19, 2009 from http://www.newagebd.com/2005/mar/10/time.html.

Khan, S. (2008). Afghan women: The limits of colonial rescue. In R. L. Riley, C. T. Mohanty, and M. B. Pratt (Eds.), *Feminism and war: Confronting U.S. imperialism* (pp. 161–78). New York: Zed Books.

Khuku, B. (2003). Personal communication. April 15.

Landry, D., and Maclean, G. (1996). *The Spivak reader: Selected works of Gayatri Chakravorty Spivak*. New York: Routledge.

Lal, J. (1996). Situating locations: The politics of self, identity, and "other" in living and writing the text. In Wolf, D. (Ed.), *Feminist dilemmas in fieldwork* (pp. 185–214). Boulder, CO: Westview Press.

Lawless, E. (2001). *Women escaping violence: Empowering through narrative*. Columbia, MO: University of Missouri.

Lazreg, M. (1994). *The eloquence of silence: Algerian women in question*. London: Routledge.

Lazreg, M. (2002). Development: Feminist theory's cul-de-sac. In K. Saunders (Ed.), *Feminist post-development thought: Rethinking modernity, post-colonialism, and representation* (pp. 123–45). London: Zed Press.

Leve, L. (2007). Secularism is a human right!: Double-binds of Buddhism, democracy, and identity in Nepal. In M. Goodale and S. E. Merry (Eds.), *The practice of human rights: Tracking law between the global and the local* (pp. 78–114), Cambridge, UK: Cambridge University Press.

Lind, A., and Share, J. (2003). Queering development: Institutionalized heterosexuality in development theory, practice and politics in Latin America. In Bhavnani, K., et al. (Eds.), *Feminist futures: Re-imagining women, culture and development* (pp. 55–73). London: Zed Press.

Lyons, L., and Franklin, C. (2004). "On the cusp of the personal and the impersonal": An interview with Gayatri Chakravorty Spivak. *Biography*, 4(1), 203–21.

Mahmood, S. (2005). Feminist theory, agency and the liberatory subject. In F. Nouraie-Simone (Ed.), *On shifting ground* (pp. 111–52). New York: Feminist Press.

Mankekar, P. (1999). *Screening culture, viewing politics: An ethnography of television, womanhood, and nation in postcolonial India*. Durham, NC: Duke University Press.

Mani, L. (1990). *Multiple mediations: Feminist scholarship in the age of multinational reception*. Feminist Review, 35, 24–41.

Matin, N. et al. (2000). Violence against women and the legal system: A Bangladesh study. Dhaka: Ain O Salish Kendro Publication.

McFadden, P. (2005). African women em-body-ing feminism. *FITO: Fringe Feminist Forum*. Retrieved August 3, 2005 from http://www.fito.co.za.

McLagan, M. (2006). Introduction: Making human rights claims public. *American Anthropologist*, 108(1), 190–93.

Merry, S. E. (2006). *Human rights and gender violence: Translating international law into local justice*. Chicago: University of Chicago Press.

Mitra, A., and Delinder, J. V. (2007). Elite women's roles in empowering oppressed women: Volunteer work in NGOs in Kolkata, India. In K. Misra and J. H. Lowry (Eds.), *Recent Studies on Indian Women* (pp. 355–82), New Delhi: Rawat.

Moallem, M. (1999). Transnationalism, feminism and fundamentalism. In C. Kaplan, N. Alarcon, and M. Moallem (Eds.), *Between woman and nation: Nationalisms, transnational feminisms, and the state* (pp. 320–48). Durham, NC: Duke University Press.

Mohanty, C. (2003). *Feminism without borders: Decolonizing theory, practicing solidarity*. Durham, NC: Duke University Press.

Mutua, M. (2001, winter). Savages, victims, and saviors: The metaphor of human rights. *Harvard International Law Journal*, 42, 201–46.

Nagar, R., and Writers S. (2006). *Playing with fire: Feminist thought and activism through seven lives in India*. Minneapolis: University of Minnesota Press.

Nahar, N. (1998). Personal communication. July 10.

Nahar, K. (2003). Personal communication. April 11.

Nandy, A. (2002). *Time warps: Silent and evasive pasts in Indian politics and religions*. New Brunswick, NJ: Rutgers University Press.

Naples, N. (2002). Changing the terms. In N. A. Naples and M. Desai, (Eds.), *Women's activism and globalization: Linking local struggles and transnational politics* (pp. 3–14). New York: Routledge.

Narayan, U. (1997). *Dislocating cultures: Identities, traditions, and third world feminism*. New York: Routledge.

Naripokkho (1998). *A brief on the issues for women's development in Bangladesh*. Dhaka: Naripokkho.

Naripokkho. Retrieved September 10, 2002 from www.naripokkho.org.

Naripokkho Workshop. (1997). April 24–27. Dhaka, Bangladesh.

Nazneen, A. (March 19, 2003). How do you define a good girl? *Prothom Alo* (Dhaka).

Nazneen, S., and Sultan, M. (2009). Struggling for survival and autonomy: Impact of NGO-ization on women's organizations in Bangladesh. *Development*, 52, 193–99.

Nazneen, S., Sultan, M., and Hossain, N. (2010). National discourses on women's empowerment in Bangladesh: Enabling or constraining women's choices? *Development*, 53(2), 239–46.

Nelson, P. (2002). Agendas, accountability, and legitimacy among transnational networks lobbying the World Bank. In Khagram, S., Riker, J., and Sikking, K. (Eds.), *Restructuring world politics: Transnational social movements, networks, and norms* (pp. 131–54). Minneapolis: University of Minnesota Press.

Nnaemeka, O. (2003). Nego-feminism: Theorizing, practicing, and pruning Africa's way. *Signs: Journal of Women in Culture and Society,* 29(2), 357–86.

Odhikar (August 2007). *Acid violence and rape—Ending impunity.* Action AID Bangladesh and Odhikar.

Oprah.com (2000). Jane Fonda on sanctioned violence against women. Retrieved September 10, 2002 from http://www.oprah.com/tows_2000/tows_past_20000929_g.jhtml.

Perez, R. (2002). Practicing theory through women's bodies: Public violence and women's strategies of power and place. In Saunders, K. (Ed.), *Feminist post-development thought: Rethinking modernity, post-colonialism and representation* (pp. 263–80). London: Zed Books.

Philipose, E. (2008). Decolonizing the racial grammar of international law. In R. L. Riley, C. T. Mohanty and M. B. Pratt (Eds.), *Feminism and war: Confronting U.S. imperialism* (pp. 103–16). New York: Zed Books.

Pereira, F. (2002). *The fractured scales: The search for a uniform personal code.* Dhaka: University Press Limited.

Potter, J., Wetherell, M., Gill, R., and Edwards, D. (1990). Discourse: Noun, verb or social practice? *Philosophical Psychology,* 3(2), 205–17.

Poster, W., and Salime, Z. (2002). The limits of microcredit: Transnational feminism and USAID activities in the United States and Morocco. In N. Naples and M. Desai (Eds.), *Women's activism and globalization: Linking local struggles and transnational politics* (pp. 189–219). New York: Routledge.

Prasad, S. (1999). Medicolegal response to violence against women in India. *Violence Against Women,* 5(5), 478–506.

Pratt, G. et al. (2010). Seeing beyond the state: Toward transnational feminist organizing. In A. L. Swarr and R. Nagar (Eds.), *Critical transnational feminist praxis* (pp. 65–86). Albany: State University of New York Press.

Queen Elizabeth honours director of Acid Survivors Foundation in Bangladesh (2002). *Daily Star.* Retrieved June 10, 2002 from http://www.dailystarnews.com/200206/18/n2061808.htm.

Rahman, T. (April 9, 2003). An afternoon at acid burnt Rumana's household. *Prothom Alo* (Dhaka).

Rajan, R. S. (1993). *Real and imagined women: Gender, culture and postcolonialism.* London: Routledge.

Rajan, R. S. (2004). *Women's human rights in the third world.* Paper presented at Columbia University Forum, New York.

Ray, R. (1999). *Fields of protest: Women's movements in India.* Minneapolis: University of Minnesota Press.

Razack, S. H. (2008). *Casting out: The eviction of Muslims from western law and politics.* Buffalo: University of Toronto Press.

Riaz, A. (2004). *God willing: The politics of Islamism in Bangladesh.* Lanham: Rowman and Littlefield Publishers.

Riker, J. (2002). NGOs, transnational networks, international donor agencies, and the prospects for democratic governance in Indonesia. In Khagram, S. et al. (Eds.), *Restructuring world politics* (pp. 181–205). Minneapolis: University of Minnesota Press.

Rozario, S. (1998). Disjunctions and continuities: Dowry and the position of single women in Bangladesh. In Risseeuw, C., and Ganesh, K. (Eds.), *Negotiation and social space: A gendered analysis of changing kin and security networks in South Asia and Sub-Saharan Africa* (pp. 259–75). London: Sage Publications.

Rozario, S. (2004). *Building solidarity against patriarchy.* Report for CARE Bangladesh.

Sangari, K. (May 1, 1993). Consent, agency and rhetorics of incitement. *Economic and Political Weekly*, 867–82.

Sarwar, K. (Director) (2006). *Ayna* (motion picture, DVD). Dhaka, Bangladesh: Maachranga Productions.

Sassen, S. (2000). Spatialities and temporalities of the global: Elements for a theorization. *Public Culture*, 12(1), 215–32.

Saunders, K. (Ed.). (2002). *Feminist post-development thought: Rethinking modernity, post-colonialism and representation.* London: Zed Press.

Schaffer, K., and Smith, S. (2004). *Human rights and narrated lives: The ethics of recognition.* New York: Palgrave Macmillan.

Schild, V. (2002). Engendering the new social citizenship in Chile: NGOs and social provisioning under neo-liberalism. In Molyneux, M. and Razavi, S. (Eds.), *Gender Justice, Development, and Rights* (pp. 170–203). London: Oxford University Press.

Sharpe, J. (Winter 2003). A conversation with Gayatri Chakravorty Spivak: Politics and the imagination. *Signs*, 28, 609–627.

Shehabuddin, E. (1999). Contesting the illicit: Gender and the politics of fatwas in Bangladesh. *Signs: Journal of Women in Culture and Society*, 24(4), 1011–44.

Siddiqi, D. (1991). Discipline and protect: Women factory workers in Bangladesh. *Grassroots*, 2, 42–49.

Siddiqi, D. (1998). Taslima Nasreen and others: The contest over gender in Bangladesh. In H. L Bodman and N. Tohidi (Eds.), *Women in Muslim societies: Diversity within unity* (pp. 205–27). Boulder: Lynne Rienner Publishers.

Siddiqi, D. (2006). In the name of Islam? Gender, politics and women's rights in Bangladesh. *Harvard Asia Quarterly*. Retrieved August 9, 2006 from http:// ww.asiaquarterly.com/index2.

Sperling, V. (1999). *Organizing women in contemporary Russia: Engendering transition.* Cambridge: Cambridge University Press.

Spivak, G. C. (1989). The new historicism: Political commitment and the postmodern critic. In Vesser, H. Aram (Ed.), *The new historicism* (pp. 277–92). New York: Routledge.

Spivak, G. C. (1994). Can the subaltern speak? In P. Williams and L. Chrisman (Eds.), *Colonial discourse and post colonial theory: A reader* (pp. 66–11). New York: Columbia University Press.

Spivak, G. C. (1999). A critique of postcolonial reason: Toward a history of the vanishing present. Cambridge: Harvard University Press.

Spry, T. (1995). In the absence of word and body: Hegemonic implications of "victim" and "survivor" in women's narratives of sexual violence. *Women and Language*, XVIII(2), 27–32.

Stienstra, D. (2000). Dancing resistance from Rio to Beijing: Transnational women's organizing and United Nation's conferences. In Marchand, M. and Runyan, A. (Eds.), *Gender and global restructuring: Sightings, sites and resistances* (pp. 209–24). New York: Routledge.

Stiles, K. (2002). *Civil society by design: Donors, NGOs, and the intermestic development circle in Bangladesh*. London: Praeger.

Stone-Mediatore, S. (2003). *Reading across borders: Storytelling and the knowledges of resistance*. New York: Palgrave Macmillan.

Swarr, A. L., and Nagar, R. (Eds.). (2010). *Critical transnational feminist praxis*. Albany: State University of New York Press.

Torchin, L. (2006). Ravished Armenia: Visual media, humanitarian advocacy, and the formation of witnessing publics. *American Anthropologist*, 108(1), 214–219.

Townsend, J.G., and Townsend, A.R. (June 2004). "Accountability, motivation and practice: NGOS North and South." *Social and Cultural Geography*, 5(2), 217–284.

Two laws on the anvil to fight acid attacks: These will make the grim battle easier (February 6, 2002). *Daily Star*.

Trihn, T. M. (1989). *Woman native other: Writing postcoloniality and feminism*. Bloomington: Indiana University Press.

UNICEF Bangladesh (2000). *Countering acid violence and supporting survivors in Bangladesh*. Dhaka: UNICEF.

Visweswaran, K. (1994). *Fictions of feminist ethnography*. Minneapolis: University of Minnesota Press.

Welch, L. (June 19, 1999). Uppity Women. *Ms. Magazine Online*. Retrieved from http://www.msmagazine.com/jun99/uppitywomen-jun.asp.

Whitcraft, T. (Producer), and Chung, C., and Ford, J. (Correspondent). (November 1, 1999). Faces of hope. ABC News *20/20* (television broadcast). New York: American Broadcasting Company.

Whitcraft, T. (2002). Personal communication. November 23.

The White House Office of the Press Secretary (July 30, 2009). President Obama names Medal of Honor recipients. *The White House*. Retrieved May 24, 2009 from http://www.whitehouse.gov/the_press_office/president-obama-names-medal-of-freedom-recipients/.

World Development Indicators. (2006). International Bank for Reconstruction and Development.

Wu, E. (April 11–17, 2002). Splash of death: Victims of acid attacks find new life in the West. *CityBeat*, 8(22).

Index

ABC Network (television), xiii, xiv, xviii, 94, 101, 102, 104

Abu-Lughod, L., 17, 133

Accountability: collaboration and, 14; to feminist communities, 7; in nongovernmental organizations, 3, 5; in transnational feminist exchanges, 13

Acid Control Board and Special Tribunal, 73

Acid Control Law 2002, 51, 73

Acid Crime Prevention Law 2002, 51, 73

Acid Survivors Foundation (ASF), xv, 102; assumes role of consolidation service provider, 28; awareness-raising by, 58; becomes leader of anti-acid violence campaign, 50–57; collaboration with influential NGOs, 58; consolidation of, 8, 50–57; departure of goals from initial Naripokkho-based agenda, 167; development of legal, research and prevention units in, 51; donor-determined agenda in, 121; establishment of, 28; founding, xix, 42; funding for, xix, 42, 76; involvement of survivors in program planning, 56; lack of survivor participation in decision-making, 58; leadership chosen without local input, 52, 53; lobbying for laws to crimininalize attacks and sale of acid, 63; loss of Naripokkho's involvement, 115; noteworthy developments in, 58; objectives of, 54; pressure on government from, 29; Prevention Unit, 58, 59; recruitment of Naripokkho staff by, 56, 110; Referral, Legal, and Medical Unit, 56, 68; rehabilitation model of, 54, 55; research by, 58; as "savior" organization, 55, 102; service provision by, 57; shift in campaign from woman-centered to skill building, 121; survivors as "passive" clients in, 77; view of survivors as recipients of services in need of reintegration into society, 58; welfarist campaign in, 77; western donors, 51

ActionAid (NGO), 43, 44, 45, 47, 48, 63, 118, 180

Activism and women activists: alliances with development and human rights organizations, 1; complicated relationships of women in, 186; contexts for operation by, 19; diverse forms of, 1; erasure of agency of in fight against violence, xix; local, 1, 23; negotiations with institutions transnationally by, 10; provision of opportunities to elites by NGOs, 76; suppression of grassroots, 57; transnational feminist, 6; unacknowledged privilege among, 125

Advocacy: campaigns, 27; cross-border, 6; human rights, 20, 131, 133; interaction with diverse actors in, 185; mobilization of transnational collaborations and, 6; policy, 133, 185; shaping by hegemonic powers,